SIGNPOST BIOGRAPHY

John Wanamaker

SIGNPOST BIOGRAPHY

John Wanamaker

Philadelphia Merchant

HERBERT ERSHKOWITZ

COMBINED PUBLISHING
Pennsylvania

PUBLISHER'S NOTE

The headquarters of Combined Publishing are located midway between Valley Forge and the Germantown battlefield, on the outskirts of Philadelphia. From its beginnings, our company has been steeped in the oldest traditions of American history and publishing. Our historic surroundings help maintain our focus on history and our books strive to uphold the standards of style, quality and durability first established by the earliest bookmakers of Germantown and Philadelphia so many years ago. Our famous monk-and-console logo reflects our commitment to the modern and yet historic enterprise of publishing.

We call ourselves Combined Publishing because we have always felt that our goals could only be achieved through a "combined" effort by authors, publishers and readers. We have always tried to maintain maximum communication between these three key players in the reading experience.

We are always interested in hearing from prospective authors about new books in our field. We also like to hear from our readers and invite you to contact us at our offices in Pennsylvania with any questions, comments or suggestions, or if you have difficulty finding our books at a local bookseller.

For information, address:

Combined Publishing
P.O. Box 307
Conshohocken, PA 19428
E-mail: combined@dca.net
Web: www.combinedpublishing.com
Orders: 1-800-418-6065

Copyright © 1999 Herbert Ershkowitz

All illustrations are used with the permission and courtesy of The Historical Society of Pennsylvania, Philadelphia.
Library of Congress Cataloging-in-Publication Data available

ISBN 1-58097-004-4

Printed in the United States of America.

CONTENTS

ACKNOWLEDGMENTS

ANY COMPLETED MANUSCRIPT has had the input of many persons and it is usually impossible to thank everyone who has helped. I wish to thank Rod Olson and Margaret Marsh of the Department of History at Temple University, Charlene Miers of Villanova University, Alan Kraut of American University, and Jon Wakelyn of Kent State University who read the work. I benefited from their suggestions. Linda Stanley and the staff at the Historical Society of Pennsylvania spent many hours helping me with my research for which I am greatly in their debt. I would like to express my appreciation to William Zulker, who knows more about John Wanamaker than anyone in the world, for sharing his knowledge with me and for aiding me in my work. Grateful acknowledgment is also made to the Temple University Faculty Committee on Research and Study Leave, which granted me a study leave to make this book possible. I would also like to thank my wife Sheila Cosminsky, and my daughter Anna and son Jeff, to whom this book is dedicated.

Permission has been granted by the Historical Society of Pennsylvania for pictures used in this book. I thank Pam Webster of HSP for the work she did in preparing these illustrations for publication.

Preface to the Series

BIOGRAPHY IS THE SOUL OF HISTORY–the stories of individual lives that give meaning and life to the past, and allow the reader to share vicariously in the drama of other times and places. It is the classic form of historical narrative, for it is through the lives of individual men and women that we can best come to comprehend the complexities of other ages. At the same time, good biography does not reduce the past to "Great Men"—and occasionally women. Rather, it appreciates the limits we all face in defining our lives, whether imposed by social forces beyond our control, the framework in which we interpret reality and opportunity, or our own limited experience and knowledge. Biography reflects the human condition: our actions, our decisions, our thinking have consequences. Biography also reflects and illuminates the world in which its subjects lived, an expression of another time and place.

Signpost Biographies are designed to bring the past alive through the stories of individuals whose lives have helped make their world, and whose lives provide the modern reader with an opportunity to be part of that world. Biographies in the series reflect the best in contemporary historical scholarship while never forgetting that the essence of history is storytelling, and that good history is also good literature. The subjects of Signpost Biographies are men and women whose lives were inherently interesting, often spanning a broad range of endeavors, and whose stories provide insight into their world. They include men and women from different cultures and social positions, those who protested their age as well as those who guided it. Among our authors are both professional historians and compelling writers with a love of historical scholarship.

Michael E. Burke
Editor, Signpost Biographies

Introduction

Many of us who grew up near urban centers during the middle of the twentieth century had a love affair with the department store. Our parents' trips to the central business districts with children in hand were great events, similar to a visit to Disneyland today. The seasonal calendar marked in other cultures by harvest festivals, by spring rituals, and by winter celebrations was marked for this urban child by department store visits. These included a spring pre-Easter clothing trip, a late-summer school shopping trip, that reminded the child that only a few weeks remained in the vacation, and the department store's Thanksgiving Day parade, which more than anything, ushered in the holiday season and winter. Most memorable of all for the child was the Christmas season and the visit to the toy floors of the major department stores. Decorated with gaudy lights and displays, thronged with thousands of visitors, and graced by the ever-present Santa Claus, the department store was the centerpiece of the season. The religious festivals, the family gatherings, and even the Christmas Day opening of packages, were almost obscured by the visit to Bamberger's, to Macy's, to Filene's, to Hudson's, or to countless other wonderlands. For Philadelphians, it was a visit to Wanamaker's that created some of the most memorable moments of urban life.

Of the merchants who opened department stores in the late nineteenth century, John Wanamaker was the most innovative and the best known retailer on the East Coast, rivaled only by Marshall Field of Chicago. In 1899, with two large stores in Philadelphia and New York, he had 15,000 workers and sold $15 million of merchandise per year—more than any other retailer in the world. He was worth $25 million and drew $1 million from his business each year. By the time of his death in 1922, Wanamaker's customers had spent almost one billion dollars with him.

Why did Wanamaker stand out among the dozens of retailers who opened department stores in the late nineteenth century? He brought to his retailing the imagination of a circus master like P.T. Barnum or the medicine men who turned village commons into magical shows that attracted young and old. Wanamaker provided entertainment and a vast array of merchandise. Wanamaker's was never dull; it was a constant circus in which the visitor had all his senses treated with delights. The merchandise displayed on the counters was the piece de resistance. Silks from China, prints from Japan, woolens from Scotland, lace from Ireland, toys from Germany, and the latest fashions, hats, and perfumes from Paris were brought as if by magic from all the corners of the world and displayed before Wanamaker's customers. Wanamaker advertised, "Surely there is romance in merchandise to those who have eyes to see. A tour through Wanamaker's is a tour 'round the world.'"

Wanamaker brought the magic of the future to his visitors. There were moving stairs to upper level floors, electric lights when the rest of the city was dark, moving–pictures before the nickelodeon, automobiles, airplanes, and wireless telegrams were displayed almost before the inventor had time to announce the new discovery.

He took the marvels of his store and advertised it throughout the Philadelphia metropolitan area and beyond. Wanamaker was acknowledged to be in the forefront of retailing advertising in the country. One of the first businessmen to print full page ads in the newspaper, Wanamaker not only bolstered his own retailing operations, but at the same time played a major role in the development of the metropolitan newspaper.

Although a master of the art of retailing, Wanamaker's greatest success came as a promoter, booster and developer of Philadelphia.

From the moment he walked to the city from his rural home several blocks south of the city line, Wanamaker had a love affair with the city.

Wanamaker's acted as an anchor for the center of Philadelphia. With its many activities, the store acted as a magnet, holding the urban population together by providing entertainment, civic ceremonies, and pageants. Individuals, particularly women, would be drawn into the metropolis, would mingle with other consumers, and would taste the myriad delights the city had to offer. In a November 21, 1995, interview with a reporter from *The Wall Street Journal* the mayor of Nashville said that to prosper as a city "it's important that it present itself with wonderful parks, a great symphony, and major-league sports." For an early twentieth–century city, the important attraction was a downtown shopping area anchored by department stores.

But John Wanamaker had an even greater impact on urban life in the early twentieth century. His store and its ancillary businesses provided over 8,000 jobs in Philadelphia and another 7,000 jobs in New York City. He also ran a 3,000 member church, which besides providing religion, ran educational activities, operated a savings bank, had a library, and ran an employment service. Wanamaker's other contributions to Philadelphia included Y.M.C.A's, a temporary housing shelter for men down on their luck, the construction of a hospital, the building of a museum, and involvement in a number of infrastructure businesses. His overall contribution to the city's life earned him accolades as Philadelphia's "First Citizen." To know his life story is also to know the biography of the city of Philadelphia.

Now Philadelphia, like other great urban centers, has fallen upon hard times. Many of the great urban department stores have disappeared. The name John Wanamaker vanished when his remaining stores became part of the May department store chain in 1995. Thus, this may be an appropriate time to consider the interconnection between the rise of the great nineteenth-century cities and the department stores that helped give these cities so much vitality. A biography of Wanamaker is a good place to begin this analysis.

CHAPTER ONE

Beginnings

1838-1861

*I*n his old age, John Wanamaker recalled that as an adolescent, "I took an enormous sheet of brown paper and wrote down on it all the different things I thought I should like to be." His list included minister, architect, merchant, journalist, and doctor. Deeply committed to his religious beliefs, Wanamaker considered becoming a minister, something his mother wished him to do. He had great regard for the ministry and felt a pull in that direction. In 1860 at age 22, he wrote in his diary, "Oh that I might be more like Christ." Even in later years when he had chosen a business career, ministers and associates suggested to Wanamaker that he should be a minister instead. Two friends urged him to make the move because "God has endowed you with a wonderful gift for reaching the masses."[1]

John Wanamaker's difficult choice between a mercantile and a ministerial life followed him throughout his life. Although he became a merchant and not a minister, connections between religion and business became the foundation for his long career. From evangelical Protestantism, he learned techniques of self promotion. In his business, he became a master showman and salesman, turning his stores into consumer revival meetings. Christian holidays—Christmas, Easter, and St. Valentine's Day—became consumer festivals. Because of his religious affiliation, Wanamaker gained a reputation for honesty which in turn supported his merchandising efforts. Just as religion permeated his livelihood, his business skills enhanced his religious life. While building the largest department store in the United States, Wanamaker engaged in a myriad of religious activities: building churches, leading Sunday schools and missionary societies, and giving sermons. He attracted worshipers to his churches much as he brought consumers to his stores—creating masterpieces of the showman's art. Far from separating the sacred from the commercial, as the Catholic church had sought to do in the Middle Ages, Wanamaker brought them together in Protestant churches in nineteenth-century Philadelphia.[2]

Just as religion and business intertwine in John Wanamaker's life, so does his life story with the history of Philadelphia between 1838 and 1922. In his youth, except for one year, Wanamaker lived south of Philadelphia in an area that in 1854 became consolidated with the city. Even though he joined other rich urbanites in building a home in the suburbs in his middle and later years, he always maintained a residence in Philadelphia. Most of his business, personal, and religious connections were in Philadelphia. His wealth was a product of Philadelphia, and to Philadelphia a portion of it returned. As a rich man, Wanamaker generally made his charitable contributions in the city that had always been his home.

Like many successful men in the nineteenth century, Wanamaker's rise to prominence was tied to a rapid increase in the population and wealth of the city. Recognizing this, he dedicated his life to uniting various elements of the city into one community. Throughout the United States in the period between the Civil War and the Great Depression, community builders in the nation's great metropolises forged a golden era of American cities. Marshall Field in Chicago, Edward Filene in Boston, the Straus brothers in New York, and other founders of department stores in smaller cities played important roles in the creation and development of the urban milieu. But few community builders dominated their areas to the extent that Wanamaker dominated Philadelphia. Recognizing his efforts, Philadelphians patronized his stores and proclaimed him the first citizen of Philadelphia.[3]

John Wanamaker, the future department store giant of Philadelphia, was born on July 11, 1838 (although sometimes he gave his birthday as July 11, 1837) on Buck Road south of Philadelphia. The area, known as the Neck because it lay between the Schuylkill and Delaware rivers, consisted largely of vacant lots, brickyards and farms. It was the backyard for the bustling nineteenth-century city, less populated than the city, but still urban. In later life, Wanamaker called himself a "country boy" because he lived on a small farm owned by his mother's family, but this was an exaggeration. As a boy in the 1840s, he lived just a few blocks below South Street, the southernmost avenue in Philadelphia.[4]

Wanamaker was born without wealth. As a child, his father worked for John's grandfather, who operated a nearby brick-making plant. Such humble origins were common among the founders of department stores in the nineteenth century. Unlike many of the industrial and commercial elite born to upper middle class urban parents, most department store founders began as peddlers or the owners of small shops. A number of them were immigrants or the children of immigrants or came from outside of the mainstream of American life. Many were Jews. Others, like Wanamaker, were Protestants from Calvinistic backgrounds.[5]

By Wanamaker's lifetime, wealth was no longer a prerequisite for success. In a major change in post-Revolutionary America, an individual without wealth and prominence could achieve social mobility. Although he became a wealthy man, Wanamaker later expressed disdain for wealth and family connection, saying that they would have hindered his creativity. "Had we inherited a business or been able to command the assistance of rich friends we might have had easier times," he said, "but never could have had the schooling that cut the backlog of this business."[6]

The region that Wanamaker called home throughout his life had been home to his ancestors for generations. The Wanamaker name was German. John Wanamaker's paternal ancestors left the Palatinate at the time of the religious persecution between 1730 and 1740. They settled in New Jersey in Kingwood Township on the Delaware River, in the German Valley section of Hunterdon County. Wanamaker's great-grandfather Henry, who died about 1831, owned a home there.[7]

The family left New Jersey briefly, from 1811 to 1819, when Wanamaker's grandfather, John S. Wanamaker, tried his luck at frontier farming near Dayton, Ohio. There, Wanamaker's father, Nelson, was born. The agricultural depression after the War of 1812 hurt the family financially, prompting John S. Wanamaker and his children to return to the Philadelphia area, where he bought a brickyard. He seems to have been moderately successful, even serving as president of the eighth district school board. Deeply religious, he belonged to the Western Methodist Church. His sole surviving letter to John and Margaret Furey, family friends, was addressed, "dear Brother and Sister in Christ." John S. Wanamaker's relative success in Philadelphia soured when the economically turbulent 1840s seriously impacted the building trade, hurting his business. In 1849, although he was 62 years old, he decided to move west again. This time he settled on a 250-acre farm near his sister in Kosciusko County, Indiana.[8]

John S. left behind his eldest son, Nelson, who had helped him operate the brick works. By the time his father left for Indiana, Nelson Wanamaker, who married Elizabeth Deshong Kochersperger in 1836, had five children of his own, including his 11-year-old eldest son, John. The other children—William, Elizabeth, Mary, and Samuel—were each separated by two years. Nelson found he could not operate the works himself and followed his father to Indiana. After a year in rural isolation, Elizabeth forced him to return to Philadelphia. Like other women in similar circumstances, Elizabeth suffered from these moves. She was upset living in a log cabin and longed to return to the "luxuries" of Philadelphia. John also expressed his regret at his separation from his "dear teacher" and his schoolmates. John wrote later about his experiences in Indiana, "I was planted when a boy & did not grow. After six months of a winter trapping squirrels, gunning and tramping through the woods in the midst of which our log cabin was placed we left & came back to Phila."[9]

When he returned east, Nelson bought back his share in the brickyard, but the business failed. He moved to Chambersburg, Pennsylvania, in 1855, leaving John, then 17, in Philadelphia. In addition to the moves in and out of Pennsylvania, John had experienced the loss of John S. Wanamaker, his grandfather, who died in Indiana in 1851. The boy inherited his religion as well as his adventurous spirit from his grandfather, who was a lay preacher in the Methodist Church and delighted in attending prayer meetings. "Standing at the grave,"

John Wanamaker wrote of his grandfather's funeral fifty years later, "I prayed that I might become as good a man as he was."[10]

John Wanamaker identified with his grandfather more than he did with his father, Nelson Wanamaker. His grandfather was a pioneer. In contrast, Nelson, who died in Chambersburg in 1861 at age 50, lived in his father's shadow and may have suffered from alcoholism. Because of the pain Nelson Wanamaker caused his family, John Wanamaker seldom spoke about his father or indicated any great attachment to him. After Nelson's death, John Wanamaker took over the role of breadwinner and helped his younger siblings. As he matured, he turned to strong men who acted as surrogate fathers and role models.

Wanamaker formed a strong attachment to his mother, Elizabeth, who was born on February 13, 1818, and died June 27, 1881, at age 63. Her grandparents were Huguenots who migrated from Holland, settling in Darby, Pennsylvania, in the late eighteenth century. At the time of his birth, Wanamaker's mother was only 20 years of age. During the next decade she had four other children while her father-in-law and husband were suffering economic hardships and probably a turbulent family life. She resisted leaving her family and friends to live in Indiana and then moving again to Chambersburg. According to Wanamaker, she maintained a strong bearing, was a religious inspiration, and created a safe and comfortable environment for her children despite his father's moves from place to place. When she returned to Philadelphia from Chambersburg after her husband's death, her son John bought her a brick house.[11]

Wanamaker later described his mother in a stereotypical Victorian manner. He wrote sentimentally of his mother cleansing his hand, hurt while chopping wood. "Can't you see her now ... bareheaded and smiling, waiving a goodby to you with her dear hand as you trotted off to school every morning!" Wanamaker contrasted his mother's care to his father's frequent absences from home for work: "Her smile was like a bit of Heaven, and it never faded out of her face to her dying day." Wanamaker credited his mother with shaping his character and giving him the fiber to accomplish what he had done. Like her father-in-law, Elizabeth was a pious church-goer.[12]

In adulthood, Wanamaker extended his deep psychological attachment to his mother to his relationship with other women. With his wife Mary and his two daughters, he was strongly attached and paternalistic. With women who worked for him, shopped in his stores, or attended his church, he maintained a large correspondence, frequently giving financial, religious, and family advice. In these letters he was warm and affectionate, but not sexually threatening. His letters conveyed the same sentimentality he often expressed toward his mother, whom he often mentioned. His image of a woman's place within the family, based upon his view of his mother, played a prominent role in the development of his department store. Women were the primary customers in Wanamaker's stores and were treated with special courtesy. Most of the consumer goods in the store were either clothes or household goods aimed at enhancing a middle class household.

Other members of Wanamaker's family also played an important role in his life. As the oldest of six brothers and sisters, he acted as the leader of his clan and dominated the lives of each member of his family. William H. Wanamaker, the next oldest, joined his brother in his business, eventually taking over one of Wanamaker's stores. Samuel Wanamaker also worked for his brother. Wanamaker's sister Mary ran some of his charities. Only Wanamaker's third brother, Francis Marion, and his youngest sister, Louise Wanamaker Fry, were not involved in his businesses.[13]

Wanamaker's relationship with his parents and family tell us a great deal about him, but we have no precise records of his personality. From contemporary observations, however, a profile of both appearance and personality emerges. Wanamaker was 5 foot 8 or 10 inches tall (according to two different passports) and in his prime in the 1880s, he weighed 175 to 185 pounds. Later in life, he tended to become heavy. He had light brown hair, which turned gray after 50. He had a fairly large nose and a strong mouth and chin.[14]

In 1897, when Wanamaker was 59 years old, a reporter described him as having a strong straight figure and looking closer to 40 than 60, with cheeks that were ruddy and often flushed with blood. In 1900, another commentator described him as "striking in appearance, strong rather than handsome." He always wore a black suit and a black necktie under a "turn-down collar." Up to his death he displayed great energy, still stood straight, and had a sunny disposition with a whimsical smile.[15]

Although he had been a sickly child who suffered from a respiratory disease that almost took his life when he was 20, Wanamaker remained free of other major illnesses until his 60s and was quite vigorous until his final illness at age 84. Because of his respiratory problem, in 1863 he was given a medical exemption from serving in the Civil War.[16]

His high energy level, his ambition, optimism, honesty, and imagination, impressed his colleagues and rivals. At work and in other activities, Wanamaker displayed an unusual restlessness and energy. He amazed one observer when, at age 71, he could arrive at his New York store at 7 a.m. and work through to 1:30 the next morning without serious effect. His energy seemed to diminish only when he took his annual extended leave from business. In his later years, to conserve energy, Wanamaker spent part of the time in isolation to gain complete relaxation. He would go to the spa at Carlsbad, Germany, in winter, when he was the only guest.[17]

Wanamaker's restlessness showed when he moved around his store, talking to customers and employees. He could also be impatient, quickly dismissing someone when he was ready to go on. Such restlessness partially explains Wanamaker's ambition. Even when he was still an adolescent, acquaintances picked him out for his ambition. At every step of his subsequent career, he pushed himself to increase his wealth and power. In 1860, in his diary there are references to the passage of time, how fast it goes, and that one may never return.[18]

Wanamaker had a reputation for honesty both in Philadelphia and nationally. Because of his strong ties to religion, he became known as a pious merchant. Nathan Straus, his retail rival, asserted that Wanamaker was "100 percent honest." Joseph Appel, who was associated with Wanamaker for the last 25 years of his life, maintained that Wanamaker had a great honesty and that his business methods were based on squareness and fairness. Wanamaker became known as "Honest John." Although the nickname originated with his rivals as a term of derision, it worked to his advantage with consumers who were looking for a retailer they could trust.[19]

Perhaps because people felt Wanamaker was being honest with them, they tended to trust him and feel secure in his presence. Playing upon these feelings, which were fortified by his warm and hospitable personality, Wanamaker easily made friends, keeping many of his friendships from childhood into old age.[20]

Wanamaker had a broad vision of the future of retailing which led to great creativity in his stores. According to one commentator, "He was the pioneer advertising merchant who made business articulate and thus established mutual confidence between buyer and seller." As Herbert Gibbons, his first biographer, observed, "...[I]n religious and store meetings, in gatherings of friends, in his own element, J.W. was magnetic on the platform." He had an ability to inspire colleagues with his ideas. Some of this imagination came from an almost childlike quality which allowed him to throw himself into a project with great energy while rejecting more sophisticated advice. Displaying great showmanship and a flair for advertising, the merchant's methods resembled those used by the nineteenth-century showman P.T. Barnum. Wanamaker constantly created circuses to advance his business.[21]

Throughout his career, Wanamaker exhibited an unbounded optimism, which sometimes got him into trouble. When he opened his department store during the 1870s, he bought too much merchandise, leading to a near default. During later economic depressions, against the advice of others, he opened his New York store and rebuilt his Philadelphia store, with disastrous results. In 1921, during another recession, Wanamaker took a typically optimistic view. "There will be plenty of work for all if we show our faith, not by relaxing our efforts," he said. Buoyed by such optimism, he dared to do what he felt was right, often scaring his associates. But Wanamaker also believed that daring must be restrained by a view of the whole picture. He wrote:"The merchant must be big enough, broad enough, far-seeing enough to survey the whole field and then stand as a bulwark amid the confusions, heresies and fears of his times."[22]

Wanamaker had several significant personality liabilities. Although he could listen when he had to do so, especially when it came to the business, he would often talk without hearing what others said. According to Herbert Gibbons, Wanamaker could be "cold and lacking in magnetism on the stump." This was a quality which hurt him in his ambitions for a political career. Although a great merchandiser, Wanamaker was often financially naive, which got him into trouble at several stages of his career and almost led to his bankruptcy.[23]

With his many religious ties, Wanamaker often appeared sanctimonious. In one of the most scathing attacks on the retailer, William Bullitt, the aristocrat and diplomat, created a character based on Wanamaker in his novel about Philadelphia, *It's Not Done*. The character, Roediger, runs Sunday schools while at the same time ruthlessly driving honest businessmen out of business and creating a fortune by dishonest means. Wanamaker's rivals in business or politics shared Bullitt's view, particularly if Wanamaker had targeted them.[24]

Wanamaker also had a rather narrow view of non-Protestant groups. He was a leader of the Sunday School Movement, which often attempted to convert Catholic children. However, he did hire Catholics in his store, he contributed to Catholic charities, and he had a warm relationship with several bishops of Philadelphia. Although he had a friendly relationship with a number of prominent Jews, in his private correspondence Wanamaker used the term Jew in a pejorative way and spoke of a Jewish conspiracy. In 1915 while visiting the Congress Hotel in Saratoga, Wanamaker wrote, "The Jews are in the majority at the Springs & of the commoner sort. You know I do not mind the heat but this beats me out." He hired few Jews in his Philadelphia store, but when he opened his store in New York, he publicly announced his intentions to make such hires. Because Jews perceived him as hostile, they avoided shopping in his stores.[25]

Although Wanamaker and his siblings grew up in a household that was middle class, it was not secure. Like others of their social group, the Wanamakers often struggled to maintain their place in society. Elizabeth Wanamaker never had much money for luxuries, and the family had to save every possible penny to meet expenses. With little in the way of economic resources, the family could not afford to give their children much of an education. Wanamaker attended the Landreth Public School, next to a brickyard a few hundred yards from his home, for a short time before leaving for Indiana with his family. After returning to Philadelphia, he had one more year of education, graduating at age 14. He had no other formal schooling, although he claimed he always continued to learn. His schooling was like that of many middle–class children in the years before the Civil War.[26]

Despite his limited formal schooling, Wanamaker received an alternative education that profoundly affected his thinking and life. On

January 17, 1848, when he was not quite ten years old, he became a student in a Sunday school run by the Trinity Lutheran Church. The school had been established by John Neff, a bookkeeper in a hardware store, who came to Philadelphia from rural Pennsylvania and founded five churches and two missions, including the Sunday School which met at the Landreth Public School. At the first session of the Sunday school which Wanamaker and his brothers attended, their grandfather gave the opening address. Strongly influenced by Neff, Wanamaker retained a strong interest in the Sunday School Movement throughout his life. He later reminisced, "I regard the Sunday School as the principal educator of my life. Through the Holy Scriptures, the Bible, I found knowledge not to be obtained elsewhere, which established and developed fixed principles."[27]

As Wanamaker grew up in an increasingly urban environment of change and conflict, his "fixed principles" were important guides for finding a steady path through increasingly confusing times. Philadelphia grew rapidly in the nineteenth century, from only 81,009 people in 1800 to 408,952 in 1850. The population numbered 570,000 by the time of the Civil War and 1,293,697 by the end of the century. The city was the second largest in the Republic, next to New York, a ranking it had retained since 1830.

Most of the city's new population came from the rural areas of the middle states, particularly western New Jersey and the nearest Pennsylvania counties of Bucks, Montgomery, Chester, and Delaware. However, 27 percent of Philadelphia's population was born outside of the United States, primarily in Germany and Ireland. The sudden increase in size and the arrival of so many immigrants between 1830 and 1880 shattered the old community, which had been largely homogeneous and under the control of a small elite. Each of the immigrant groups settled in a semi-segregated area and developed local institutions. Communication between these groups was tenuous.[28]

Especially, in the 1840s, the city became an arena for conflict between whites and African-Americans, and Catholics and Protestants. Religious conflict erupted in two major riots in Philadelphia in 1844 which left scores of people dead. Blacks worked in the Wanamaker family brick works, and occasional attacks were made upon them. The worst violence occurred in September 1848 when a group of coal heavers from the docks came to assault them. The brick workers protected them; in fact, John's grandfather, who was an abolitionist, kept several of them in his house for protection. This violence was one of the reasons the family patriarch gave for moving to Indiana. Wanamaker never forgot this incident. He was an advocate for African-Americans until his death.[29]

By the time he reached adolescence, Wanamaker had begun a lifelong fascination with the city of Philadelphia. He first walked by himself to the city on Long Lane when he was eight years old. Greatly affected by this adventure, he later asserted that the hike was the start of a love affair. The growing city was a Mecca for the young seeking jobs and financial success. The new population had to be housed, clothed, and fed, which created many opportunities for employment. As a thriving industrial and commercial center, the city also offered jobs in textile manufacturing, locomotive building, heavy industry, banking, and importing. An expanding middle class working in mercantile, commercial, and managerial occupations demanded a wide range of consumer goods such as expensive clothing, pianos, and furniture. Like other ambitious young men, Wanamaker found this urban environment enticing.

Wanamaker brought the dynamism of an outsider to a city controlled largely by the old colonial families. Wanamaker's brash approach to urban life often challenged this establishment, creating resentment. In this respect, he was a little like Benjamin Franklin, who came from Boston and changed the way the Quakers ran the city, helping to give it a lead over its rivals which lasted until the nineteenth century. In propagating his ideas, Wanamaker often behaved like a missionary, contending not only that his opponents were wrong, but also that they were corrupt or evil. Nevertheless, Wanamaker followed a path that was often necessary to meet Philadelphia's changing social and economic conditions.

During his first visits to the city, Wanamaker was fascinated, but he felt embarrassed by his lack of sophistication. He remembered walking through the city to play or work and feeling that city residents were staring at his country clothing. He compared himself to Benjamin Franklin, who arrived in Philadelphia poor and alone. Although he often commented on these slights, Wanamaker felt that his success in the "city has never shaded down my sense of indebtedness to my country home, to my country father and especially to my country mother." He once felt tricked by a storekeeper who sold him a piece of jewelry as a gift for his mother, but who would not take it back when it turned out not to be what Wanamaker thought it was. It was his sense of being something less than a middle–class urban boy that inspired his ambition to excel at being a merchant, the most urban of occupations.[30]

Wanamaker was drawn to Philadelphia not only by the opportunity it offered him to make a living, but also by its religious activities. John Neff, the founder of his Sunday school, got him his first job in the city in 1851, when he was 13 years old. As an errand boy for a bookstore in the Philadelphia business district, Wanamaker earned $1.50 per week.[31] Living with his parents near the brickyards, he used his meager wages to help support the family. To get to work, he walked several miles along dirt roads into the city. In 1852, when the Wanamaker family moved to town, Wanamaker left the bookstore, first to work in a law office and then in the retail clothing store of Barclay and Lippincott, where he earned $2.50 a week.

Wanamaker next went to work in a journeyman position at $6 per week for Joseph M. Bennett who owned Tower Hall Clothing Store, the largest men's clothier in Philadelphia. A distant relative and a friend of Wanamaker's father, Bennett taught him the business and treated him like a son. Believing Wanamaker was the most ambitious boy he had ever seen, Bennett gave him control of buying for the men's furnishing department. But in 1858, Wanamaker had a quarrel with Bennett and quit, saying that someday "I'll lay over you." Wanamaker's break with Bennett, which seemed so out of character, was similar to identity crises suffered by other adolescents at this period of their lives. In attacking Bennett, Wanamaker was rebelling against a surrogate father.[31]

At the time Wanamaker left Tower Hall, he developed respiratory problems which threatened his life. In 1857, at the urging of his physician who wanted him to leave the city, he went to Minnesota for about a year. Wanamaker wrote a friend, "Since my absence from home I have wandered over three thousand five hundred miles of our country. Seen much to call forth admiration—much to regret." The experience was both educational and helpful to his health, and he returned to Philadelphia at the end of the year.[33]

By the time he had left for Minnesota, Wanamaker had decided upon a mercantile career. Many aspiring middle-class men hoped to open stores. Unless they were rich or had good contacts, these small scale entrepreneurs often failed. As historian Stuart Blumin has shown, these stores often lasted a year or two, then threw the owner into bankruptcy and into an unskilled position. Still, for an adolescent, a low-paying or even a nonpaying position in a store provided the apprenticeship training for going out on his own. For Wanamaker, whose ambition was to rise above the failures of his father and grandfather, a life as a merchant offered the best opportunity to escape the ranks of the lower middle class. A merchant's life also appealed to the risk-taking side of his personality. The years he spent at Tower Hall proved to be his major apprenticeship as he learned the basics of buying and selling men's clothing. In contrast to Wanamaker's training in men's dry goods, most founders of department stores began by selling cloth and sewing materials to women.[34]

Despite Wanamaker's rejection of the ministry as a profession, evangelical Christianity shaped all aspects of his life. Wanamaker's grandfather, father, and mother were all Methodists. John's first memory of a religious service came from the Old West Methodist Episcopal Church in Philadelphia. Through his teacher John Neff, Wanamaker was drawn to some of Philadelphia's prominent evangelical preachers. One of his friends took him to hear the Rev. Albert Barnes, the controversial Presbyterian "New Light" minister. He was impressed by Barnes and in later life would often discuss his sermons.[35]

The greatest influence on Wanamaker's religious ideas was John Chambers, the minister of an independent Presbyterian church. Wanamaker first heard Chambers preach in 1851. He became a regular member of Chambers' church after he moved with his parents into Philadelphia. This church, at the corner of Broad and George Streets, became the center of almost constant religious revival. Chambers was interested in reaching the young, and he would bring children off the street to receive instruction. Wanamaker was one of those children. Thomas P. Dill, who worked with Wanamaker, introduced him to Chambers. Years later, Wanamaker described Chambers "as a man of commanding personality, full of spirituality and great force of character, and he made an impression on my young life, which has not grown less with the years."[36]

Chambers had come to Philadelphia from Baltimore in 1824 to take charge of the Ninth Presbyterian Church, a small congregation of seventy people. A controversy broke out because, contrary to church dogma, Chambers believed that the Bible was "all-sufficient as a rule of faith and practice." When he refused to accept anything other than the Bible and rejected the Westminster Confession, the basic beliefs of Presbyterianism, he was dismissed from the pulpit. In response, his congregation declared itself independent of Presbyterian synod control.[37]

Under Chambers' leadership, the congregation grew and built a new church. By January 1860, it was one of the largest religious organizations in the city, with 1200 members. To attract new followers, Chambers employed a variety of advertising techniques. Regular revival meetings included visits by well-known evangelists who brought out large crowds. Much of the activity of the church tried to convert young people through a large Sunday school, a youth temperance group, and a missionary society. Chambers tried to reach the young with revivals, writing in 1854 "that infidelity is making sad havoc among our young men." That year, Chambers helped plan a youth revival. Wanamaker became very active in these activities. During the revival of 1857, he worked among the volunteer firemen, mainly younger men, holding meetings in the fire companies.[38]

As the Civil War approached, Chambers took a pro-Southern position and defended the unpopular Fugitive Slave Law. Although Wanamaker became a strong advocate of the North in the Civil War and a proponent of African-American rights, he defended Chambers and embraced many doctrines that linked Christianity with early nineteenth-century principles of citizenship. Influenced by Chambers, Wanamaker became a strong partisan of the belief that the Bible was the guide toward "the practical duties of life, without the performance of which we cannot be good citizens." Although Chambers' pro-Southern views became anathema once the war broke out and led to a rapid decline in his church's membership, Wanamaker remained friendly with him, acknowledging his indebtedness to the minister not only in religion but also in his style of advertising and merchandising.[39]

At one of Chambers' evening prayer sessions, Wanamaker had his conversion experience. After the service, alone with the minister, Wanamaker told him he had discovered God that night. During the service, Wanamaker realized his connection to Christ. Wanamaker often described his conversion. To one correspondent he wrote, "I united with the church when I was eighteen years of age, upon conviction of the truth of the Scriptures, relying wholly upon the promises of God."[40]

For Wanamaker, membership in one of the largest and most active churches in Philadelphia not only provided the religious life he felt he needed, but it also gave him opportunities to meet influential people who would advance his career. He became a teacher in the Sunday school, then was elected president of the teacher's association. Another young Sunday school teacher, Nathan Brown, the son of a wealthy grocer, became Wanamaker's partner in setting up his first store. Wanamaker also married Nathan's sister Mary.[41]

Chambers' missionary program assumed a large role in Wanamaker's life. In February 1858, when Wanamaker was not yet 20, he started a Sunday school not far from his birthplace. Seventeen boys attended, but some of them were members of local gangs and carried clubs. Wanamaker canceled that meeting, but the following week he rented a room for $7 per month at 2135 South Street. The seats were pieces of wood on bricks. He attracted some students. "We had a beautiful afternoon," he later recalled. "I was the leader of the singing." By 1860, Wanamaker's Bethany Sunday School had 234 students, 17 teachers, and a permanent building largely because of his campaign. Many of these boys and girls also joined Chambers' church with their parents. These parishioners would later join the Bethany Church, an outgrowth of the Bethany Sunday School.[42]

Another outgrowth of Wanamaker's attachment to Chambers was his association with the Young Men's Christian Association, which he joined in 1854. Members of Chambers' church conducted many of the activities of the first Y.M.C.A. in Philadelphia. For example, the city's first Y was founded by George H. Stuart, a wealthy dry goods merchant and president of the Merchants' National Bank, as well a friend of the Chambers' and a prominent Christian activist. Evangelical Christians like Stuart supported the Y movement, which they imported from England, as a means of bringing their message to young men.[43]

In January 1858, when Wanamaker was only 20, Stuart offered him a position as the Y's paid secretary, with a handsome salary of $1,000 per year, almost twice what he had made working for Bennett and much more than the $400 the average minister made. Stuart made the appointment despite Wanamaker's youth and the opposition of board members who preferred an older, more experienced man. For Wanamaker, the position provided not only a source of income, which he largely saved, but also exposure to a larger world. He became known to members of the Christian benevolence community in Philadelphia. In 1860 he attended a Y.M.C.A. meeting in New Orleans where he met many Christian lay leaders. Retaining an interest in the Y.M.C.A. until his death, Wanamaker donated money to building campaigns both in the United States and abroad. He also served in many state, national, and international Y.M.C.A. offices.[44]

At the beginning of 1860, the Bethany school and the Y.M.C.A. occupied most of Wanamaker's time. His Sunday activities included getting children to Sunday school and getting businessmen to close their shops on Sunday. Wanamaker spent much time traveling around the city, speaking at various churches to raise money for the Y.

Two years after he arrived back in the city from his recuperation trip to the west, on September 27, 1860, John Wanamaker married Mary Erringer Brown. Mary was born in Philadelphia on November 23, 1839, a very quiet woman whose life centered on her family and a small body of friends. "She is one of the most retiring and modest women in the world," a reporter described her later in life. The reporter found it hard to write about her outside her family life, her charities, and her church work. Like her husband, she was quite religious, taking an active part in the activities of the Bethany Sunday School. For Wanamaker, the marriage completed his transition to the solid middle class. In the early years of his business, Wanamaker's father-in-law provided capital when times became tough and gave him important contacts necessary for success.[45]

John Wanamaker expressed a great deal of affection for his wife in a very Victorian way, writing once, "Blessing on you for never losing the way yourself & for always helping me along the rising path." When he arrived home at night, he would usually go to her sitting room first. On his sixty-fourth birthday, in 1902, John wrote to Mary, who was in Europe at the time, "You do not know how deeply I feel today all your ... intensive goodness to me all these trying years." In 1903 he summed up his view of the family, writing, "I may seem at times too much occupied to care for my home things but I do. I am always working at re-setting life in jewels but the dear family forms the jewel & my part would be but an empty frame of dull metal if it stood alone."[46]

John and Mary had six children: one, Horace, died at birth in 1864 and another, Hattie, died at five years of age, an event that seemed to haunt John into his old age. The Wanamakers' eldest son, Thomas Brown, was born in 1861, the first year of their marriage, while their second son, Lewis Rodman, was born in 1863. Both sons entered the business, with Rodman becoming second in command to Wanamaker and inheriting the bulk of the estate after the death of his brother in 1908. A daughter, Mary Brown, was born in 1871 and married a prominent Philadelphia stock broker, while her sister Elizabeth, born in 1876, married the owner of the *Philadelphia Telegraph*. Both sisters were active in their father's religious activities and Mary (Minnie) was also politically active, serving in 1920 as the first woman on the Republican State Committee.[47]

Soon after his marriage, Wanamaker prepared for the next step in his career. Using money he saved and the contacts he made while at the Y.M.C.A., on April 8, 1861, Wanamaker opened the Oak Hall men's clothing store in partnership with Nathan Brown. Located on Market Street, the major shopping center in Philadelphia, Wanamaker & Brown was a small store, next to older and established firms. Wanamaker had ended his apprenticeship.

The connections between religion and business that Wanamaker forged during his early life remained the basis for his long career. In his personal life, Wanamaker adhered rigidly to practices that supported his religious beliefs. He did not attend the theater, gamble, drink alcohol, or use tobacco. Wanamaker was always working on people—including his employees—to sign the pledge to give up alcohol. He led the Sabbath Association, which strove to prohibit all activities on Sunday. Privately, Wanamaker often gave religious advice, writing one friend, "Will you let me sit down by your side and whisper in your ear some reasons why you should this *moment* accept of and rejoice in an offered Savior."[48]

In his first store as well as the later store that made his reputation, the Grand Depot, Wanamaker's business methods derived from his evangelical beliefs. His stores, like a large camp meeting, had an openness that attracted individuals to come, look around, listen, and make a decision. Before the Grand Depot opened for business in 1876, it was used for a camp meeting for Dwight Moody, the most famous late nineteenth-century evangelist. Nineteenth-century Evangelicals made their greatest appeal to women, drawing thousands to their churches, often without their husbands. Wanamaker's department stores similarly attracted a largely female audience, often shopping with other women in the absence of males.

Evangelicalism also largely reversed the traditional puritanical view of holidays. Under the Puritans, the many feast days celebrated in England were abolished for only the observance of the Sabbath. Days off were considered opportunities for the devil to interfere. Evangelicals fostered large gatherings of congregants who often spent a number of days at a camp meeting. Dwight Moody, for example, held large urban rallies that lasted six to eight weeks, attracting thousands of persons who took a day or more to attend. As part of this attack on Puritanism, Evangelicals turned many of the ancient festivals including St. Valentine's Day, Christmas, and Easter into open celebrations. As a business leader during the fifty years when these religious holidays increased in importance, Wanamaker led the movement for their commercialization. These feast days became a central part of his stores' activities and produced a substantial portion of its revenue.[49]

John Wanamaker was also a representative of mid-nineteenth century capitalism. He was a bridge between the anti-materialism of the early republic and the emphasis on consumerism and materialism in the twentieth century. Like many late nineteenth-century evangelicals, he had no great fear of either production or consumption. He feared the curse of national poverty more. His major concern was that in the midst of the enjoyment of such wealth, Christ might be forgotten.

Wanamaker believed that by making religion so central, the dangers of affluence would be easily overcome.

By 1860, for a majority of the population, evangelicalism had replaced the republicanism of the early part of the century as the dominant philosophy. Republicanism, like Puritanism, from which it had grown, put its emphasis on simplicity and virtue as opposed to the corrupt opulence of the European monarchies. Evangelicals, although not rejecting virtue or even simplicity, were more open about the possibility of a progressive material development of society and were less concerned that people were consuming goods. Wanamaker believed that business and religion were allies. "The temptations of business are great," he said, employing the evangelical language of sin and damnation, "and unless a merchant has more than a creed or the ordinary ground-work of honesty and faithfulness he may be caught by the sudden wind of plausible opportunity and tumble over the precipice and be ruined."[50]

Becoming the best-known Christian lay activist of his generation, Wanamaker was often cited in turn-of-the-century sermons. The Rev. Francis E. Clark, president of the World Christian Endeavor Union, wrote, "I think that such a career as yours is a great stimulus to all young men, & shows them, as securely anything else can do that strict integrity, purity of life & religious principles do count in business life as any where else, & that these qualities also make success worth having."[51]

Religious ties helped him start his business, while his business skills advanced his goals in the Bethany Sunday School. The reputation which Wanamaker developed at Bethany helped him through some of his toughest times as his moral standing helped him secure favorable credit ratings. For Wanamaker, religion and business ties complemented each other, allowing him to build wealth in this world and the next.

CHAPTER TWO

A Philadelphia Merchant

1861-1877

When John Wanamaker opened his men's shop in April 1861 with his partner Nathan Brown, he was participating in a revolution in urban retailing that was every bit as impressive as the changes in production that were occurring in industry during the same period. Railroads, canals, and roads made it easy to transport goods. Through the increase in the number of banks, capital became readily available. Retailers built larger stores constructed of new and technically improved materials, and they sold new lines of consumer goods. The chief innovators of the new retailing were a group of young shopkeepers, most of whom entered the dry goods business in the 1850s and 1860s and created department stores a decade or two later.

Wanamaker's background and upbringing were similar to many of his successful retailing contemporaries like Marshall Field, Potter Palmer, and Samuel Carson in Chicago, and Eban Jordan in Boston. Like them, he came from the lower middle class and was barely out of his teens when he opened his first store. The retailers had similar adolescent experiences, learning about business through apprentice-ships and then borrowing or saving $3,000 to $5,000 to go into partnership with someone else who brought a little capital and similar expertise.[1]

In many ways, Wanamaker followed the same path at almost the same time as Marshall Field, who was born on a farm in Massachusetts. After working five years for someone during his teens, Field moved to Chicago to become a traveling salesman, then entered a junior partnership with Potter Palmer. In the 1860s and 1870s, Field created one of the largest and most innovative dry goods stores in the Middle West. His partner was a Quaker who left school and went to work for a shopkeeper in upstate New York. After several years Palmer borrowed money from his family and opened a successful dry goods store in Chicago. Field eventually bought out the business from Palmer, who went into the real estate and hotel business. A similar relationship developed in Boston in 1841 when Eban Jordan opened a dry goods store and later, in 1851, went into partnership with Benjamin Marsh with a capitalization of $5,000. Samuel Carson and James Pirie were two Scotch-Irish immigrants who opened a business in rural Illinois before moving to Chicago's Lake Street.

Several German Jewish immigrants, obviously from a different background, also participated in this retailing revolution, usually starting as peddlers. E.J. Lehmann from Mecklenburg, Germany, founded the Fair, a dry goods store in Chicago near Field's emporium. William Filene in the 1860s founded a chain of women's and children's shops in Massachusetts. His sons, led by Edward, moved to Boston and opened a department store. Adam Gimbel worked as a Midwestern peddler in the 1850s and 1860s before opening a dry goods store in Indiana. He later moved to Milwaukee and his sons opened stores in Philadelphia and New York. Simon Lazarus opened a men's shop in Columbus, Ohio, in 1850, adopting the motto, "It fits or you don't pay." He began with $3,000 and expanded during the Civil War, selling ready-made clothing, but he gradually added women's clothing and other household goods.[2]

All of these successful retailers were showmen and great promoters of themselves. They also borrowed ideas from each other. Wanamaker tended to draw a greater amount of publicity to himself and was perhaps the greatest merchandiser of his generation.[3]

The retailing world which Wanamaker entered in 1861 was a mosaic of the old and the new. Impacted by the market revolution, merchants opened up shops everywhere. There were fancy shops, bargain shops, and merchandise peddled house to house. Most stores were still small, dirty, and crowded, usually occupying an 18- by 24-foot space on the first floor of a three- or four-story building. Merchants also peddled goods on the street from stalls and counters. As one writer described the myriad of goods on Catharine Street, a shopping thoroughfare in New York City, in the 1840s:

> Such a conglomeration of merchandise of every sort and description cannot be found jumbled together in the same space any where else in this great metropolis. And the crowd that is continually passing, jostling, dodging, and buffeting, is fully answerable to the vast mass of wares and goods crammed into every building, and oozing out of every window, crevice, loophole, and door in postures of inducement and temptation, irresistible, one would think, to the seekers after bargains that perpetually haunt this quarter.[4]

Business practices also varied greatly. Urban merchants had a reputation for dealing dishonestly with customers. One former retailer described the business as "the most abject calling that a free man was ever induced to follow. Without recompense or absolution, it denies the power of conscience, perverts all notions of justice, depraves the mind, ruins the disposition, corrodes the heart." The great nineteenth-century showman P.T. Barnum claimed he gained his talent for deceit as a young man working as a shop clerk, practicing chicanery on unsuspecting customers. But in truth, there were as many honest shopkeepers as there were merchants who shortchanged customers by selling inferior goods or selling a smaller amount of cloth than a customer ordered.[5]

Whether the merchant was honest or unscrupulous, owning a small store was a hard way to make a living. With little capital, shopkeepers bought goods on credit from jobbers or other middle men who had purchased the goods from manufacturers or importers. Because shopkeepers often sold on credit while bearing high fixed costs, as many as 25 percent of all establishments failed each year.

By 1861, established stores selling all kinds of domestic and imported goods for women and men attracted an affluent clientele in each major city. In New York in 1818, Henry Sands Brooks opened a men's clothing store. Taken over by his sons in the 1840s, Brooks Brothers became the most famous men's stores in the country. In Philadelphia,

Jacob Reed's men's shop opened in 1824 and remained an institution until the late twentieth century. Several jewelry firms—J.W. Caldwell and Bailey, Banks, and Biddle in Philadelphia, and Tiffany in New York—dominated the carriage trade. The Chickering Company of Philadelphia, which had the largest piano showroom in the United States, sold 25,000 pianos between 1823 and 1859.

A few retailers in New York City had expanded beyond the specialty shop, adding merchandise different from their original lines. The major innovators were in dry goods. These merchants originally sold cloth by the yard. Dealing largely with women, some dry goods merchants expanded into ribbons, hats, shoes, soap, and perfume.

Wanamaker and other businessmen of the Civil War era modeled their establishments after the largest dry goods retailer in the United States, Alexander T. Stewart of New York City. An immigrant from Ireland with about $5,000 in inherited money, Stewart opened a small dry goods shop in the 1820s on Broadway in downtown New York City. By 1862 he had two large stores in New York. He also maintained agencies in Boston, Philadelphia, and several foreign countries, a mail-order business, and an extensive wholesale operation. Stewart's Astor Place store cost $250,000 to build in 1862, had 2,000 employees, and was the largest store in the country. It had a cast-iron structure allowing the builder to dispense with the traditional masonry base to support the structure as each floor supported itself.[6]

Stewart appealed to women by making his stores easy to shop in. He introduced counter stools to allow customers to sit while examining and purchasing cloth, dress goods, tailored and ready-made clothes, hats, and home furnishings. Women also thronged the store because it was possible to remain there browsing for hours without being harassed by salespeople. Stewart also won his customers' trust by treating everyone equally, charging one price to everyone, and charging cash.[7]

Among Stewart's competitors in New York was Rowland Macy, who started selling fancy goods at Sixth Avenue and West Fourteenth Street and added hats and millinery before the Civil War. By the 1860s, he had moved beyond dry goods and sold silks and perfumes to a largely affluent clientele.[8]

Although Stewart and Macy were leading an expansion in American retailing, their enterprises were still surpassed by a number of stores in Europe, particularly in London and Paris. Bon Marché in Paris was the first true department store, carrying by 1879 a full line of merchandise for women, men, children, and the home. The store offered employee benefits that included pensions and housing for women and younger men. The department stores of Paris were marketplaces of ideas for Wanamaker, who after becoming a successful merchant often traveled abroad. "Paris is the best store keeping city in the world and there's lots to learn every day out of those great stores," he wrote. "I often feel that we let slip so much that is good after we get home by not putting into practice what we always learn."[9]

Philadelphia had nothing like A.T. Stewart's, so its elite shopped in New York City. But by 1859, Philadelphia had developed a downtown shopping district containing approximately 3,200 business establishments. Within this area, which extended from Second Street to Ninth Street and from Arch Street to Chestnut Street, each thoroughfare developed a specialty. Eighth Street had millinery stores, while Market Street was lined with clothiers.

Chestnut Street's shopping area, which specialized in bookstores, ran from Second to Tenth Streets. On a fashionable middle-class thoroughfare lined with buildings three to six stories tall, the stores also sold everything from perfumes, jewelry, medicines, including such universal cures as Swain's "Celebrated Panacea," to dry goods and men's clothing. The Sharpless Brothers Dry Goods Establishment, located at Chestnut and Eighth Streets in a 50-by-165-foot, four-story building, was the largest store in the city. It sold men's and boys' wear, women's dress goods, silks, gloves, dry goods, and domestic goods. Scattered among the shops were residences, hotels, and a number of publication offices, including the *Public Ledger*, the *Dollar Newspaper*, and *Godey's Lady Book*. Facing the street were also some of the most revered institutions in Philadelphia, including the Bank of the United States and the Old State House in which the Declaration of Independence had been signed.[10]

Although some of the Philadelphia stores achieved a degree of stability, many of the shops still resembled the shops on Catherine Street in New York. Retailing grew out of the old stalls found earlier in the century on Market or Second Streets. Stores had boys outside hawking goods and negotiating prices. It was in this retail environment that John Wanamaker started his first store, a move that would change retailing in Philadelphia. With his partner Nathan Brown, Wanamaker opened the Oak Hall men's shop on April 8, 1861, on the southeast corner of Sixth and Market Streets, the center of retail activity in the 1850s and 1860s. In calling the store the Oak Hall Clothing Bazaar, Wanamaker imitated a name created by George Simmons of Boston, the proprietor of a successful Boston men's shop. Simmons was one of the first retailers to use newspapers to advertise his elegant store, and he initiated promotion methods—free gifts, no bargaining, and elaborate delivery carts—that were imitated around the country. By borrowing from Simmons, Wanamaker was doing what he did best throughout his career: taking a retailing idea from another city, introducing it to Philadelphia, and improving upon it.[11]

Wanamaker's original store was 30 by 80 feet and was on the first floor of a building on Market Street. To start the business, the two partners had capital of $4,000. Initially, Wanamaker and his partner hired two salesmen-cutters and an errand boy to assist them.

The Civil War began only 96 hours after Oak Hall opened. George H. Stuart warned Wanamaker that he was making a mistake, that the war "would cause grass to grow in the streets of Philadelphia." The Civil War did take a toll on the city's business. In 1862, 137 men's clothing stores existed in Philadelphia, but by 1865 only 99 remained. By contrast, during the post-war years, a great expansion occurred so that by 1869, the city had 270 clothiers.[12]

At the start of their operations, Wanamaker and Brown nearly failed. The Wanamaker and Brown cash book from the first year of operation provides a candid picture of the operations of a small store in the nineteenth century. Starting with a cash balance of $3,462 on April 5, 1861, after paying for the initial expenses, the two young partners watched their resources gradually decline. Burdened with wages of about $20 per day, rent of $70 per month, and material and advertising expenses, they saw their cash reserve fall to $264 by the end of March 1862. At this point, Nathan's father, Thomas Brown, intervened in the operation to bring in needed cash and credit. Thomas Brown, whose net worth was over $100,000, joined the concern in August 1862 as a special partner, contributing $6,000 in capital and lifting the credit rating of the new store.[13]

With the help of Brown, the partners survived 1862 and began to enjoy steady growth. The first year of the business produced revenue of $24,367. In 1862, Wanamaker took in $93,794. By 1863, his gross receipts reached $200,000. In 1864, Wanamaker paid his income tax on wages of $27,230, a princely sum compared to average wages for a skilled laborer of $1,500 annually. The store was worth approximately $50,000 and Wanamaker even had enough capital to speculate in oil. By the end of 1865, Oak Hall was the largest men's store in Philadelphia.[14]

What allowed Wanamaker's business to survive during the Civil War, a time in which even established firms failed? The most important factors were powerful friends and in-laws. George Stuart, one of the most influential businessmen in the city, was Wanamaker's surrogate father. On his recommendation, Wanamaker obtained cloth on credit in New York City from William Libbey, a partner of A.T. Stewart. This relationship with the Stewart firm became very important for the early years of the Wanamaker enterprise. The New York wholesaler became his chief supplier and often held back in demanding payment when Wanamaker was unable to redeem his notes.[15]

Members of the Philadelphia establishment who knew Wanamaker from Chambers' church or the Y.M.C.A. also supported him. Wanamaker's religious background also helped his standing with the R.G. Dun Company, whose credit-rating reports could make or break a young merchant. The company was founded by an evangelist lay leader and often tied religiosity to credit worthiness. Dun's reporter gave Wanamaker and Brown a strong credit rating because the Philadelphia business community considered them honest. This helped Wanamaker and Brown secure contracts for uniforms from the United States Customs Service, Union Army regiments, Girard College, and the fire and police departments. Wanamaker & Brown also profited from sales of custom-made uniforms for officers in the Union Army.[16]

Advertising played a key role in Wanamaker's success, shaking up the staid merchants in the city. From the first, he recognized the need to distinguish his store from the other shops doing business in central Philadelphia. Wanamaker gained an understanding of the value of advertising during his training at Joseph Bennett's Tower Hall, and he learned from George Simmons' Oak Hall in Boston, which had the most sensational advertising in the country. However, Wanamaker developed his own flamboyant style, some of it coming to him naturally and some of it learned from Chambers. He began advertising during a period in which advertisers competed with each other by trying to be more extravagant than their opponents. Like P.T. Barnum, they were putting on a good show.[17]

Three weeks after opening Oak Hall, Wanamaker placed a small ad in the *Public Ledger* promoting a complete line of ready-made suits for three dollars. After Wanamaker's first big sale, tailoring suits for the Philadelphia Customs House, he took the $38 profit to buy advertising in the *Philadelphia Inquirer*. In some of his advertisements, he mimicked Bennett by turning to doggerel, urging his customers to make,

> A thorough, strict investigation
> Of coming styles, and meditation,
> To put to your consideration
> At very small remuneration [18]

Wanamaker adopted newspapers as his primary means of advertising. Although he lacked formal education, Wanamaker wrote his own advertisements in a clear, literate, and folksy style of writing. He was an advertising innovator: the first advertiser to buy a full page and the first in Philadelphia to deal directly with the newspaper, rather than through an agent. He believed it was important to advertise during both boom and bust periods. "You want to get the people in to see what you have to sell, and you must advertise to do that," he wrote. "When the times are good they will come of their own accord." Although the pioneer in Philadelphia in the use of newspapers, Wanamaker never advertised on Sundays, a policy the store's management followed until Sunday, March 16, 1947.[19]

In his first years, Wanamaker used whatever means he could find to advertise. He distributed small magazines, booklets, and leaflets around Philadelphia. He installed clocks with the initials W & B around railroad stations and in other public places. He bought advertising space on the top of every page in the annual city directory. Messages read, "THE POPULAR CLOTHING HOUSE OF PHILADELPHIA, WANAMAKER & BROWN, Sixth and Market." Although advertising pages were a normal feature of the directory, it was a departure for a firm to buy space on every page. Wanamaker also built thirteen large billboards, each more than 100 feet long.[20]

Contemporaries recognized Wanamaker's pioneering efforts in store advertising. He was honored later with numerous awards by newspaper and advertising associations who realized how much of their growth resulted from retail advertising which he helped initiate. By purchasing hundreds of thousands of dollars worth of advertising yearly from newspapers, Wanamaker not only helped launch a revolution in retailing, but one in journalism as well. The urban newspaper which became such an important part of American life in the late nineteenth century was supported economically by the large retailers. Years later, a New York newspaper satirized Wanamaker's reputation as an advertiser in a bit of doggerel of its own:

> My name is John; I run a great big store.
> And I make money; which is not surprising,
> When you reflect that each year I do more
> of advertising.[21]

Wanamaker's innovations in business were not limited to advertising. Other practices that he introduced in Philadelphia included going directly to importers for cloth, cutting out the jobbers. They were so upset by his purchasing practices that they tried to pressure his suppliers to cut him off. Wanamaker paid cash to employees upon completion of a job; he also cut work hours. During the Civil War, he continued to sell all-wool suits, rather than resorting to "shoddy," which contained a mixture of new and recycled materials.[22]

By 1865 Wanamaker had adopted the one-price system and took merchandise back with a full refund of the money. Wanamaker advertised that everyone paid the same price for clothing, whether a stranger who wanted one pair of pants or an old customer who spent $1,000 annually. The other part of his appeal was the return guarantee for ten days, with no questions asked. The purchase price was to be refunded in full. Although Wanamaker claimed to have invented both practices, other retail outlets used them for many years. Wanamaker gave them greater prominence in his advertising.[23]

The one-price system and the return guarantee reached out to customers who mistrusted all merchants. These strategies, with Wanamaker's reputation as a religious man, attracted consumers who otherwise feared going into a store. For many newcomers, the city seemed a cold and dangerous place. But Wanamaker's advertisements captured the essence of small-town life, with its small groups, close personal relationships, and family ties. He tried to create the village in the city.

One key to Wanamaker's efforts to recapture the small town was his emphasis on the trust that linked the seller to the buyer. This kind of trust was often present in a small-town commercial transaction, but was missing in a large city. In one advertisement Wanamaker wrote: "This Store is not here for nothing. It is a watch tower, observing the lights along the shore and trimming its own light hour by hour, that none may lose their way nor regret that they followed its clear shining along the paths of its daily work." As in so many of his other advertisements, Wanamaker drew upon a religious image—the watch tower.[24]

Wanamaker's folksy advertisements further built this trust by associating him with the old country store owner who knew the craftsman and guaranteed his work. In one newspaper notice, Wanamaker publicized, "Silk-and-Wool Lansdownes. Made in old Philadelphia, not far from the Wanamaker store. We always knew William F. Reade, and were the first to introduce and to stand for the first Lansdownes that he made."[25]

Any understanding of Wanamaker's success as a retailer must allow for his empathy with customers and their needs. Imitating a minister's relationship to his flock, he wrote thousands of letters to individual consumers, answering their complaints, mollifying them, gathering information about the operations of his store, and correcting errors by salespeople. His replies were always polite, usually accepting the return of unwanted goods. In one letter he told a customer to return the coat he bought for a refund because it turned out to be the wrong size. "The salesman must have made a mistake or misunderstood the lady as we have so many goods it would make no difference what size you took." Wanamaker offered to handle the return personally.[26]

In his advertising and all his other public relations, Wanamaker constantly sought to keep consumers' confidence. He wrote, "Public sentiment is an autocrat whose stamp goes and cannot be questioned, when it sets itself for or against certain things in cities and communities." As a retailer, all Wanamaker had was his reputation; he could not afford to pursue a public-be-damned attitude like many industrialists of the era. Writing many years later to a friend, Wanamaker summed up his philosophy of maintaining public confidence in his integrity. "This has been called the age of the Trust: it is also an age of distrust. The merchant must be big enough—broad enough—far seeing enough to survey the whole field and then stand as a bulwark amid the confusions, heresies and fear of his time."[27]

In the years immediately after the Civil War, Wanamaker & Brown grew still further, doing a retail trade and a jobber's business as well. In 1867 Wanamaker and Brown, worth $120,000, expanded their store by buying the building next door. Although expansion into the second building, which cost $60,000, resulted in a financial loss for the year and reduced the firm's credit rating, the new facilities soon paid off, producing a profit the next year.[28]

At the same time Wanamaker created one of the most profitable businesses in Philadelphia, he continued to devote himself to the religious causes. He never seemed to be able to confine his energy to one or even two enterprises at a time. This excess energy allowed him to commit himself to a vision of an urban civic culture in which citizens participated in building the city. Wanamaker wrote, "Let us be citizens first and foremost, and not merely bankers, lawyers, merchants, and manufacturers: and we need not hesitate to tackle large city enterprises."[29]

Although on September 18, 1863, the Provost Marshall certified him as unfit for army service because of his lung illness, Wanamaker ardently supported the Lincoln Administration and Republican policies. As a rising young businessmen active in Christian causes, he participated in many wartime organizations. He was the secretary of a national Christian Commission that sent agents to the battlefield to preach and to bring supplies to the troops. Stuart was secretary of the commission and thus brought his protégé along to expose him to other individuals involved in national Christian activities. Joining other shopkeepers in Philadelphia, Wanamaker supported the 1864 Sanitary Fair by donating a day's receipts to the fair.[30]

His activism within the Christian community became a second career that blended with his mercantile career for the rest of his life. Wanamaker threw himself into Christian work, with his great energy and ambition, intent on creating the largest and most successful enterprise in Philadelphia. In his two parallel worlds, he often used techniques borrowed from the church in his stores, and he used advertising methods borrowed from retailing to advance the church. When he began a building in one world, he often started a building in the other world. His reputation as an important Christian layman helped attract customers who believed that so devout an individual would not cheat them. Many of Philadelphia's Protestant ministers shopped in Wanamaker's, where they received a 10 percent discount. It's not unlikely that the middle class churchgoers of the city followed their religious leaders into the store. In addition, many of Wanamaker's employees were graduates of Sunday schools from around the city.

Wanamaker's most important religious ties were with the Bethany Sunday School. John Chambers described Bethany's location at the southern edge of the city as "an expanse of vacant lots occupied here and there with squatters' cabins, goose pastures, and roaming cows, the streets not yet being cut through." Wanamaker in 1865 decided to convert the Sunday school, which had 900 students, into a church, obtaining a charter for it. Incorporated by the Presbyterians, Bethany moved into a large building at Twentieth and Bainbridge Streets in 1868. Contributing $5,000 to the building fund, Wanamaker hired the Rev. Samuel T. Lowrie, the pastor of a church in Moyamensing, to take over the new ministry. By 1870, the Sunday school part of the building had more than 3,000 seats, while the auditorium adjoining the Sunday school held 2,300 persons, making it the largest church in the city. Active in all aspects of church life, Wanamaker taught Sunday school, supervised the school, and answered much of the correspondence of the church.[31]

Of all the activities at Bethany, Wanamaker felt closest to its Sunday School. "I do not know of anything that offers better returns for the time and for the money spent [than Sunday School]," Wanamaker wrote. Besides saving souls, the Sunday School often bought fuel and food for the students' parents. Wanamaker worried that cold and hunger would deter parents from sending their children to the school.[32]

By the late 1870s, Bethany was the largest religious center in Philadelphia and was among the earliest institutional churches in the country. Such churches, which became common in the late nineteenth century, provided a full range of secular services as well as religious services to the urban poor. Through its outreach program, Bethany provided job counseling, education, health services, and personal counseling. Wanamaker often gave money himself or dispensed money from others to "lend a helping hand" in this area of the city. Under Wanamaker's leadership, Bethany became the city's most active congregation, running a soup kitchen, a society that provided clothes for the needy, a young people's church, and the largest Sunday school in Philadelphia. Wanamaker also organized the Penny Savings Bank at Bethany. The Penny Bank, which became one of the most important savings and loan societies in Philadelphia, fit Wanamaker's philosophy of self-help. It provided a safe place to invest small savings, and it loaned money to persons buying homes.[33]

Although many individuals held lay offices at Bethany, Wanamaker dominated its boards and controlled its finances, new construction, new activities, and choice of pastors. He took a lively interest in the parishioners and, when asked, often intervened in personal and marital problems. When necessary, Wanamaker provided medical care for the poorer members of the church. Sending one "of our nice little Bethany girls to a dentist," he wrote, "She is supporting herself and her people are poor. I found her yesterday suffering with a three-weeks toothache."[34]

Beyond Bethany, Wanamaker became a prominent national lay person. He served on the boards of the Pennsylvania and the United States Sunday School Association, and he was president of the board of directors of the Pennsylvania Sabbath Association which tried to ban all Sunday entertainments. His own strict adherence to the Sabbath ideal meant keeping his store closed on Sundays. "It is a cause for profound thanksgiving to God," he wrote in 1884, "that since our State and our City are a Christian Commonwealth, founded on the Christian religion as its basal rock, we have a statutory law which saves the Lord's Day." A dedicated temperance advocate, Wanamaker belonged to Christian organizations trying to eliminate alcohol in Pennsylvania. When an effort was launched to allow the sale of alcohol on Sunday, Wanamaker attacked it, arguing that liquor led to the destruction of society. "It means anarchy, demoralization, and wholesale debauchery," he said.[35]

Although Wanamaker tried to divide his life into retail and church spheres, there was a great deal of overlap. Many of Bethany's parishioners were also Wanamaker's customers, while many of his younger employees attended Sunday school at Bethany. Some of his closest associates in business became involved in Bethany's affairs.

In November 1868 Nathan Brown died, leaving Wanamaker in exclusive charge of the operations, although he continued to use the Wanamaker and Brown name for many years. When the Brown estate was settled, Brown's share of the store was worth about $175,000. Although Brown's death created problems for Wanamaker, such as the need to raise money to pay the estate its share of the business, the partnership had been extremely profitable. Shortly before his brother-in-law's death, Wanamaker was worth $250,000, owned his own home, and had an inventory worth over $100,000. To release himself from some of the burdens of operation, Wanamaker took on John R. Houghton as second-in-command. Houghton, a master tailor, had worked for Wanamaker from the start of the business.[36]

On April 5, 1869, Wanamaker opened a second store at 818 and 820 Chestnut Street, with his brother Sam Wanamaker as a partner. Next to the Continental Hotel, the four-story men's outlet was the most fashionable on the street, decorated with medieval stained-glass show windows. The store had six departments, including a ladies' coat department and a made-to-measure department. The women's department, in this first attempt, failed.[37]

In the year after Brown's death, Oak Hall took in $1,144,000 in sales while the Chestnut Street store reached $400,000 in revenues. The large cash flow allowed Wanamaker to pay for his inventory in cash between thirty and ninety days after he received the merchandise, allowing him a five-percent discount. He made most of his purchases in New York City where he had a line of credit at A.T. Stewart for $100,000.[38]

By 1871, the stores achieved a $2,085,528 annual business and were taking in $15,000 to $20,000 per day. Employing forty-three salesmen, seventy cutters, and twenty clerks, Wanamaker was the largest men's retailer in the country. He sent buyers to Europe, particularly to Scotland, to bring back imported woolens. In May 1871, he made his first personal buying trip to Europe, where he also picked up merchandising ideas. In 1871, despite some concern in the Philadelphia financial community that Wanamaker had overextended himself, the Mercantile Agency upgraded his credit rating, reporting, "J.W.'s progress has been remarkable. He is an ambitious man & a man of great energy & it is believed that he will make a fiscal success, unless some great revulsion should suddenly reduce values & paralyze business."[39]

Such a paralysis began in 1873, with the failure of the Philadelphia financier Jay Cooke. The depression left Wanamaker short of cash. Having bought sewing machines from A.T. Stewart, Wanamaker failed to meet his six-month notes, taking two years to pay them back. As at several other times in his career, William Libbey, Stewart's partner, saved Wanamaker from default by allowing him extra time to raise money. Although Cooke's failure taught Wanamaker the dangers of a quick financial panic and made him even more cautious of credit, he did not escape from such credit crunches in the future.[40]

Despite the bad economic times, Wanamaker by 1875 was worth about $1 million and was looking for new worlds to conquer. The W & B original store occupied all of Sixth Street from Market to Minor Streets, with a large frontage on Market. Taking in several million dollars each year, the store employed more than 1,000 clerks and offered a variety of merchandise that appealed to shoppers from the lower middle class to the very wealthy.[41]

In his advertising, the merchant publicized what he called the Wanamaker "system of retailing." Emphasizing a contract with consumers, all merchandise carried a warranty that it was exactly as represented and a label indicating quality. To prevent salespersons from pressuring customers, Wanamaker ended commissions, a move that also gave him control over wages.[42]

Although Wanamaker contended that he was the first retailer to adopt these principles, each had been around for some years, having been introduced by A.T. Stewart in New York City and Bon Marché in Paris. Even in Philadelphia, Strawbridge & Clothier, a rival men's clothing business that would soon convert into a department store, had adopted many of these principles. Although Wanamaker's "system" was not new, the publicity he gave to it encouraged large retailers to standardize their customer relations. He also tended to justify his actions in moral rather than strictly economic terms, as did most of his rivals, turning his one-price idea into a moral crusade against bargaining in stores in which the consumer paid dearly. By giving his advertising a moral tone, Wanamaker persuaded many people that he was a safe and honest alternative to other ways of buying goods. On the other hand, many of his critics in Philadelphia attacked his approach as sanctimonious. Besides convincing customers of a retailer's honesty, posted prices and clear labeling made it possible for a large store employing hundreds or even thousands of sales clerks to control them. Salespeople were paid a salary for exhibiting merchandise whose quality and price were clearly labeled, excluding haggling over price.[43]

Wanamaker's policies were not always as clear as his advertising suggested. When he first opened his store, he gave discounts to his best customers. When he began to advertise one price, he continued to give discounts to ministers, newspaper editors, local distributors who bought goods from Wanamaker and resold them, seamstresses who bought sewing supplies, and employees of the store. Wanamaker also maintained credit sales. Credit accounts were due within thirty days. Half of all sales were on credit and many accounts were not promptly paid, leaving Wanamaker with hundreds of thousands of dollars uncollected. In times of tight money, this debt often drove the store to the edge of disaster.[44]

By 1876, Wanamaker was seeking to broaden his horizons. Although his innovations in men's wear had made him wealthy, his trips to Europe had given him an idea for a large store selling a wide variety of general merchandise, a modern department store where shoppers would buy everything including dry goods, ready to wear clothing for both men and women, home furnishings, and toys. But 1876 was momentous for Wanamaker in other ways. He played an important role in the centennial celebration of American independence, which was held in

Philadelphia's Fairmount Park. And shortly before he opened his new store, the Grand Depot, Wanamaker sponsored a three-month-long revival by Dwight Moody, the evangelical Protestant leader.

Moody and his singing companion, Ira D. Sankey, came to Philadelphia as Wanamaker's guests. A successful mission to Great Britain in 1873 had made Moody a major promoter of urban revival in the United States. Preaching in a black business suit, Moody made his appeal to the rising urban middle class. His sermons, emphasizing the free market, hostility to immigrants and the poor, and anti-union sentiments, appealed to the new business elite and drew strong support from such merchants as Marshall Field and John Farwell of Chicago. Probably no one in the late nineteenth century did more to encourage the growth of a conservative postmillennialist Christianity than Moody. The postmillennialists believed in individual salvation and felt it was not necessary to reform society before Christ's return. Moody preached that poverty was the result of laziness and sin. God used poverty to bring the sinner to his knees but would bring prosperity to the believer.[45]

Moody and Wanamaker had much in common. Moody had an earlier career in business and he was involved with the Christian Commission during the Civil War, the Young Men's Christian Association, and the Sunday School Movement. Wanamaker first met Moody at a Y.M.C.A. meeting in Albany in 1866 and was enormously impressed. Because of his original contacts with John Chambers, Wanamaker felt a strong affinity toward evangelical ministers because of their oratorical style and their emphasis on individual responsibility for salvation. He liked their mass appeal and their ability to use the media to bring out large crowds, something he also did in retailing. In his social beliefs, Wanamaker was less conservative than Moody. Like most Evangelicals, Wanamaker believed in individual salvation. He was a strong supporter of self-help and contributed to projects which allowed persons to gain an education, put aside money in a savings account, or get off alcohol. But he was reluctant to support charities which gave out doles and he refused to give out money himself to help needy persons. This put Wanamaker in opposition to Moody's social Darwinist position that the poor could never be saved and should be kept in their place. But Wanamaker never accepted the Social Gospel movement which held that changing the environment of the poor through a redistribution of wealth would lead to their betterment. Although Wanamaker had objections to Moody's philosophy, he loved his showmanship and his ability to reach out to people, bringing them into the churches.[46]

For the Moody revival and for his Grand Depot store, Wanamaker began negotiating in 1875 to buy the Pennsylvania Railroad's freight depot on Market Street and Juniper next to Center Square, where Philadelphia's new city hall was under construction. For Wanamaker, the site touching on the new center of the downtown area was a perfect spot for a store.

The great 1875 revival meeting began Sunday, November 21, and lasted until January 21, 1876, held primarily at the former freight depot. The platform held 1,000 people while 8,904 individuals sat on the floor. In all, 1.1 million people attended the revival, traveling into the city on special street cars and trains. At meeting time, a huge crowd surged around the building, kept under control by a chief usher and 300 assistants, who talked by speaking tubes. Many of these ushers were salespeople at the Wanamaker stores. Wanamaker joined Stuart every evening on the platform and helped raise the expenses for the meetings—about $40,000. He also put Moody up at his house.[47]

Although the revival was the most successful in Philadelphia's history, Moody's visit created much controversy. Moody was an eloquent speaker, but he was largely unschooled and spoke with poor grammar. This stirred up a good deal of criticism in the newspapers. His message caused some concern among persons trying to deal with the increased number of poor in Philadelphia. His attack on Jews as killers of Christ led to demands for an apology from that community. Because of Wanamaker's close association with Moody, this incident probably contributed to his image in Philadelphia as anti-Jewish.[48]

Memories of the revival followed Wanamaker throughout his life as he maintained a friendship with Moody and his family. In November 1876, Wanamaker wrote Moody how close he felt to him on the anniversary of the Moody revival. Wanamaker tried to put together a second Moody revival twenty-five years later to celebrate the end of the century, even hiring a building for the purpose and raising the necessary money, but Moody's death in 1899 ended any possibility of such a revival. Wanamaker was a major benefactor of all of Moody's educational enterprises, contributing to the founding of Moody's Northfield School for Girls and his adjoining Mount Hermon School for Boys.[49]

For Wanamaker, the Moody revival, like many of his other religious enterprises, had important business consequences. When he acquired the Grand Depot, it was an abandoned freight yard on the outskirts of the Philadelphia central district. For the hundreds of thousands of persons who came to the two or three religious services held every day, the Depot became part of their mental maps, familiar and friendly. When Wanamaker's Grand Depot opened a few weeks after the revival, it was not out of the way from the main shopping center, but easily accessible.

Moody's 1875-76 revival ended just a few months before the beginning of the great fair celebrating the hundredth anniversary of American independence. The centennial fair was another milestone in Wanamaker's life. Although not yet 40, he enjoyed a high degree of exposure in both Philadelphia and the nation, becoming one of the city's best-known leaders. His participation in the centennial celebration played as large a role in his future as did the Moody revival. He was chairman of the Subcommittee on Revenue and the Press under the Board of Finance, which built the fair buildings and raised money for the exhibition. Wanamaker managed the stock subscription and arranged plans for the construction of the buildings.[50]

Although the Panic of 1873 complicated financing, the centennial secured public funding from the federal government, the state of Pennsylvania, and the city of Philadelphia. To get $75,000 from the city council, Wanamaker collected thousands of petitions. Private donations supplemented public funding. Wanamaker became a major stockholder, owning $17,500 worth of securities. One of his major accomplishments on the finance committee was to persuade the board to keep the fair closed on Sundays.[51]

On the whole, the centennial fair was an artistic success. Seven million people viewed a grand display of merchandise sent from around the world and enjoyed the latest technological advances from American and foreign inventors. The exhibitions spurred American inventions as Alexander Bell and other inventors displayed their wares. American businessmen soon copied new European technologies such as the bicycle, creating new industries. The fair also gave new direction to the decorative arts, stirring interest with the demonstration of Japanese arts.[52]

The centennial was an important step in the development of modern retailing. Thousands of items manufactured in the United States and abroad were displayed at the exposition, many of them for the first time. Development of the department store dates from about the time of the fair, and there may have been more than a casual relationship between the two. Wanamaker believed that the exhibition of so many items both old and new in a comparatively opulent setting was the inspiration for the department store. Certainly, over the next ten years Wanamaker drew heavily from the 1876 event in creating the idea for his department store.[53]

When Wanamaker purchased the Pennsylvania Railroad depot, he had a limited view of what he wanted to create in Philadelphia. When the new Wanamaker's opened in April 1876, it was still largely a men's shop like the original Oak Hall. But the centennial fair displays focused Wanamaker's ideas on the possibilities of a grand emporium. Wanamaker's in the late 1870s imitated the fair in that it contained a large inventory of both foreign and domestic items, artfully displayed, and, like the fair, showed off the latest technologies for consumer purchase. The centennial also heightened Wanamaker's sense of the value of civic celebrations for the development of community consciousness. For Philadelphia, the fair was the most successful staged event in its history. Wanamaker attempted to duplicate its success on a smaller scale in his department store by holding pageants, musical events, and patriotic festivals. He thus hoped to duplicate for urban dwellers the same sense of being part of a great event that the centennial had given them.[54]

The Pennsylvania Railroad Board sold its freight depot property, which occupied the block from Thirteenth Street to Juniper and from Market Street to Kelly's Alley, to Wanamaker on November 11, 1875, for $550,000. When the transfer of land took place on November 15, Wanamaker put up $150,000 in cash. For the remainder of the sale price, he gave the railroad eight notes worth $50,000 each and paying six percent, which Wanamaker paid over the next five years.[55]

The store opened on March 12, almost simultaneously with the Centennial Exhibition. Moody and Sankey had left the building on January 10, and the building renovation was completed by April 10. At first Wanamaker considered consolidating the other two stores, but decided against it. Opening with only hats, men's clothing, and furnishings, the new store added shoes and children's clothes a few weeks later.[56]

For individuals visiting the Centennial Exposition, the Grand Depot was as attractive as the fair buildings. Wanamaker advertised that the store celebrated "freedom from the shackles of the old, burdensome customs of business." It became an instant hit. Drawn to the store by souvenir maps of the city pinpointing Wanamaker's new enterprise, visitors discovered the largest men's and children's clothing store in the United States that also sold cloth for women's clothing. All the merchandise was displayed amid a circus-like atmosphere of free shows. Wanamaker provided tired shoppers with waiting rooms offering newspapers and magazines.[57]

After the fair closed in the fall, Wanamaker prepared for the Christmas season selling men's suits and accessories. Early in 1877, he closed the Grand Depot for a complete reconstruction, reopening in March advertising the Grand Depot as "A New Type of Store." In a note of irony, Alexander T. Stewart died on April 10, 1876, a few days after Wanamaker opened the Grand Depot. Henry Hilton and William Libbey purchased the business from the estate and renamed it the A.T. Stewart & Co.[58]

By 1877 Wanamaker had come a long way from the inexperienced shopkeeper who opened a small men's wear store at the beginning of the Civil War. Like merchants in the major American cities, Wanamaker was about to embark on an experiment in retailing that would change the face of consumerism in the country. The department store was not only a "new type of store;" it was a museum, a circus, and one of the ceremonial centers of the city. Wanamaker was particularly important in promoting the idea, as the 1911 Economists medal for notable achievement stated, "that a great retail store is a public as much as it is a private institution."[59]

CHAPTER THREE

Grand Depot

1877-1888

One year after Wanamaker opened the Grand Depot, he began a great expansion, transforming his men's clothing operation into an outlet selling a variety of merchandise for women, men, children, and the home. The Grand Depot allowed him to test his dream of "a new type of store" which he believed would begin a consumer-oriented era in retailing. The store would be a collection of small specialty shops under one roof, selling high quality merchandise at fair prices. Wanamaker had big dreams, and they carried a high price.

By opening a large retail store for the sale of many types of goods arranged by departments, Wanamaker was participating in one of the most sweeping changes in retailing in American history. Hundreds of department stores around the country would become the primary marketplace for most urban shoppers and, through catalogs, for many rural shoppers as well. Becoming an arbitrator of middle class buying habits, department stores managed and directed the consumer culture that so distinguishes modern American culture. These stores also provided employment for millions of urban residents as clerks, buyers, and managers.

For Philadelphia, by now a city of more than 800,000 people, the Grand Depot provided a new attraction. The store helped to create a new city center and a feeling of community. Wanamaker wrote in an advertisement:

> We labor to increase the importance of the city, to add to its employments, and increase the conveniences of shopping to the 817,000 of her residents, and the 800,000 more whose homes are in the outlying towns and villages, to whom Philadelphia ought to be an attractive resort. The floating population that made our streets so lively and our stores so busy during 1876 may become permanent by due enterprise and joint action of Philadelphia business men.[1]

Wanamaker envisioned a central Philadelphia community that would hold together the city's various sections, each with its own institutions and peculiarities. Wanamaker's efforts in promoting Philadelphia were summed up by his longtime partner Robert S. Ogden, who wrote, "Business is ... not an end in itself, therein it is a means toward an end: a means for building up all virtues ... making the life of the city a unity—stronger, more patriotic, nobler."[2]

Abhorring the chaos left by the disappearance of an older stability, Wanamaker sought to create a new Philadelphia held together by jobs, a common shopping district, and civic ceremonies. He believed his generation could duplicate the community spirit created in earlier periods by Benjamin Franklin, Robert Morris, and Stephen Girard. Praising one merchant for his contributions, Wanamaker in a speech expressed his own aspirations: "Always a Philadelphian you have watched her interests with jealous fidelity, and have ever been among the foremost a friend, advocate, and promoter of every enterprise for the advancement of her welfare."[3]

One thing Wanamaker did by moving into the Grand Depot and successfully promoting his new store was to shift the center of the downtown business district from the Independence Hall area adjoining Sixth and Chestnut Streets to Twelfth and Market. Before the 1870s, the area next to Independence Hall was the judicial, business, and governmental center of Philadelphia as well as its main retail area. With the building of Wanamaker's adjoining the new City Hall, other businesses and retail stores also moved westward. The completion of the Reading Railroad terminal, a block from the store, and the location of the Pennsylvania Railroad a short distance away, guaranteed the centrality of Wanamaker's. In taking over and enlarging the Grand Depot, Wanamaker displaced a number of small retailers and some industrial spaces, including the United States Mint. For the next hundred years, the store's immediate vicinity contained the highest priced real estate in Philadelphia. A similar transformation took place in other large metropolises and in many smaller cities as the large department stores became the new urban commons.[4]

When Wanamaker opened his Grand Depot, it was still a men's shop, but he re-created it in 1877 as a department store on the European model. He added women's shoes first, followed by other women's clothing, both custom and ready-made. He added dry goods and notions next, followed by a hosiery department, a China store, and a special shop for little children's clothes. Soon afterward, he created furniture, carpet, and wholesale departments.[5]

At the rebirth of the Grand Depot, Wanamaker advertised it as the "Stewart's" of the Quaker City. "The ladies will come from far and near," said the ad, "in never-ending streams to purchase their dry goods and wearing apparel of every description—for the house will supply all articles of a lady's wardrobe, from a paper of pins to a camel's hair shawl." In converting from a men's store to one that was primarily a middle class women's emporium, Wanamaker was offering his merchandise to the main urban consumers. The "two spheres" idea popular with many persons during the late nineteenth century required that women act as homemakers, raising the children and providing a comfortable living environment for their husbands who went to work. But such an arrangement gave the wife a greater control over the household budget. Even feminists, who opposed segregating women out of the workforce, saw that control over spending gave wives greater independence. Elizabeth Cady Stanton, a leader of the suffrage movement, urged women to do the buying in their homes as a means of working toward equality. As historian Mary Ryan has pointed out, shopping areas on safe commercial streets became one of the few places where respectable middle class women could congregate. Wanamaker was unique among department store founders as he started with a men's shop while many of his competitors had gotten their first experiences in dry goods working with women.[6]

As part of the remodeling of the Grand Depot, Wanamaker re-arranged counters so that it would be easier to find goods. He displayed his merchandise on counters arranged in five large concentric circles, broken by three long aisles. With the aisles intersecting in the center like the spokes of a wheel, each circle was divided into six counters. At the center, a large round table provided information and handled transactions. Signs above the counters divided the store into major sections such as "Linen Sheeting," "Ladies Furnishing," and "Soap." Each department, controlled by a buyer who directed both purchasing and sales, was identified by a letter from A to Z (there was no Q). When Wanamaker ran out of letters, he numbered new departments, starting with 26. The store was quite festive in its displays, but it still had the look of the freight depot. Massive steel beams crisscrossed the ceiling. Huge gas lights hanging from these beams cast an odd illumination over the displays.[7]

Because Wanamaker added new space by acquiring adjacent buildings, the store took shape without a real plan. Starting with a series of specialty shops, each run by an expert, Wanamaker tried to attract concessionaires to rent space. This was only partially successful. He persuaded a hatter and a jeweler to join him. Nathan Straus, who later as the owner of Macy's became one of Wanamaker's rivals, opened a glassware department. By 1883, Straus owned $60,000 worth of merchandise in the store.[8]

Wanamaker advertised his emporium as the "NEW KIND OF STORE." Several businesses were combined under one roof, with each section running as if it were in a separate building. Wanamaker advertised that unlike a department store, "A village of temporary shops has grown up instead; shops on shops; shops on top of them; only some of the walls out between, so that people and things can move about."[9]

Wanamaker spent much of his time between 1877 and 1881 adding to the store. He purchased several buildings on Chestnut Street, the other major shopping street, and built a bridge across Kelly Street, which separated the rear of the Grand Depot from his new acquisitions. A basement, a balcony, and a second floor with an elevator gave Wanamaker additional space. Pneumatic tubes, which he introduced to America and which soon became a common feature of American retailing, transported cash and sales slips across this selling area, allowing Wanamaker to reduce his reliance on cashboys. Because cashboys were the lowest-paid individuals in the store, making three dollars a week, Wanamaker probably did not save much money with the pneumatic tubes, but they were more efficient and eliminated a source of theft. He often introduced new technology into the Grand Depot just to give it a modern look.[10]

Despite Wanamaker's protestations, by 1879 the Grand Depot was a true department store with forty-nine departments and ten miscellaneous counters, including one for Japanese goods. Wanamaker advertised the store as the "Big Everybody's House." James Forney, editor of the *North American*, agreed with him, calling the store a continuing Centennial Exhibition. "There is the same width of display extending about as far as the eye can reach, the riches of the world brought together from all lands, and representing all departments of art and industry, tastefully arranged to be shown with advantage." One impartial observer wrote, "His store presents a great scene of activity and is beyond question the most gigantic retail thoroughfare on the continent."[11]

The Grand Depot was an exciting show palace, almost a wonderland for the thousands of tourists who made the store a major stop on a visit to Philadelphia and for city and suburban residents who came shopping with their children. For the Christmas season, the store blazed with ornate decorations, attracting 40,000 people in a single day in 1878. For urban residents who lived in dingy quarters, the brightly lighted, opulent Grand Depot was a haven from the harshness of winter. The centerpiece of the Grand Depot was its Christmas Headquarters, where customers could buy gifts and ship them anywhere they wanted, including overseas. Wanamaker advertised the headquarters "as an entire innovation in the mercantile world—another example of the Wanamaker method of being the first to introduce a better way to do things."[12]

Religion had an important influence on the ceremonial nature of the Grand Depot and on its profitability. In Philadelphia, Wanamaker played a dominant influence in transforming the two major Christian holidays, Christmas and Easter, and two minor festivals, St. Valentine's Day and Halloween, into consumer affairs. Although these festivals had already changed from church-oriented to more secular holidays a generation before Wanamaker opened his first store, he was able to make the next step by turning these holidays into major sales events. Wanamaker combined the sacred with the secular, decorating the store with the religious symbols of the holidays such as mangers, angels, and crosses. To many customers, the almost hallowed nature of the store made this centerpiece of the market place seem almost like a church. Wanamaker was able to bring about a union of his two great loves and make quite a large profit. The Christmas bazaar, lasting about one month, provided the store with about forty percent of its annual revenues while Easter, with its emphasis on the sale of clothes, made another important contribution to the store's revenues.[14]

The most attractive part of the store was its vast array of domestic and imported merchandise of all prices. Wanamaker had some of the goods manufactured specially for him and sold under his label. Wanamaker felt that if he supplied the latest fashions for the women of Philadelphia, they would not have to look to New York for guidance. At his store, women could purchase designer dresses, French perfume, and shoes, hats, and jewelry made in Europe.[14]

Wanamaker envisioned the store as a center of culture as well as merchandising. He set aside days to celebrate special events and made the store available for grand public gatherings. He began a Children's Day on November 20, 1880. Wanamaker advertised the store as an educational event for children: "We believe in an institution with ideals, such as this, can be made a mighty force for education."[15]

The sheer size of Wanamaker's store radically changed the ways in which many people purchased merchandise in Philadelphia. Wanamaker and other large stores replaced many small purveyors of retail goods. Wanamaker launched a full-scale attack on small shops and peddlers, charging that their sales methods were dishonest and advising consumers to compare his business practices with those "common among the lowest grade of tradesmen." Buying directly from manufacturers, large retailers also pushed jobbers to the wall.[16]

Wanamaker's methods were similar to John D. Rockefeller's tactics in eliminating inefficient petroleum refiners on his way to creating the Standard Oil monopoly. Like Rockefeller's tactics, Wanamaker's actions had dire consequences for many small businesses in the city of Philadelphia. Many young persons opened small stores as a means of escaping poverty. This was a hard way to survive economically and usually mandated enlisting all members of the family, including young children, to work long hours, seven days a week. Wanamaker forced many of these small retailers out of business by selling everything from cloth to books to home furnishings more cheaply and with a return guarantee. He justified his ruthlessness as growing out of the natural evolution of business. In a 1900 speech to the American Academy of Social Sciences, Wanamaker said, "It must be remembered that society is not constituted for the benefit of any one particular class of population.... Without sentiment or prejudice the interests of all must be justly weighed and the greatest good for the greatest number must be gained."[17]

In his attack on small retailers, Wanamaker took the highest moral ground. He charged that they deceived their customers by falsely advertising the quality of their goods, and he said that their prices were too high. In a 1909 speech, Wanamaker argued that the "paramount purpose of the Founder of this business was from the first to stop the ... fakirlike practices of the mercantile world." He was correct in his belief that department stores improved retailing. Consumers got a better deal from Wanamaker. By eliminating the middle man, Wanamaker was able to cut prices and give his customers a reasonably priced, quality product. The manufacturer also benefitted because they were able to sell new products efficiently through department stores. As Wanamaker saw it, "We have been ... related to the manufacturers of the United States and the old world, to whom we give ideas as well as knowledge of what is wanted."[18]

Wanamaker's overall impact on small retailing in Philadelphia is somewhat hard to assess. During his lifetime, Philadelphia's population continued to expand rapidly. As a result, there were more small business establishments in 1920 than there were in 1875. But there were fewer stores for each 100,000 people than previously. Writing an editorial in 1898, Wanamaker observed: "Instead of hurting the business of the city, as many predicted, the large stores grew larger, and the small stores greatly increased its numbers." However, the consequences for many small retailers and peddlers who could not compete with Wanamaker were similar to the artisan's fate earlier in the century. The shopkeeper driven out of trade had either to join the industrial proletariat or become a wage worker in a department store, an option taken by many.[19]

Wanamaker's efforts to change retailing met strong opposition from these small shopkeepers. They naturally found support from persons in Philadelphia who either had sympathy for small owners or whom Wanamaker threatened. To counter Wanamaker, a number of retailers got together and threatened to pull their business from jobbers who sold to Wanamaker. Several newspapers also came to the defense of the small retailers. *Philadelphia Day* denounced Wanamaker, writing: "There has been a greedy, grasping and godless spirit at work in the mind of somebody, prompting him to break down other businesses and absorb almost every branch of mercantile business in his own establishment." The editor compared Wanamaker to Alexander Stewart as "one of the meanest men and merchants that ever lived." In creating the first department store in the United States, Stewart had set the pattern for retailing dominated by a few large retailers who eliminated many smaller stores and consequently had a reputation for ruthlessness.[20]

Many people in Philadelphia not only disliked Wanamaker's methods, but also felt the enterprise was too big and too far from the city's traditional business center to succeed. One businessman wrote: "The consensus of opinion was that the purchase would prove a ruinous one. The idea seemed chimerical in the extreme—to start a clothing store so far from the general current of retail traffic." For a time, it looked as if the naysayers were correct. Economically, the late 1870s were difficult times. The country had yet to recover from the long 1873 depression which led to many financial failures and high unemployment. It was a bad time to begin a new business.[21]

Wanamaker's startup expenses were high. He spent $500,000 on the building and land. His total yearly expenses for the store were $500,000, including advertising, mortgage payments, personnel, and heating. Just to break even, Wanamaker needed a $5 million inventory generating a 10 percent profit, a magnificent sum for the era. The representative of the largest national credit-rating organization worried that Wanamaker was "putting too many eggs in one basket." But he added, "The Philadelphians are rather dazed at this wonderful departure from the staid old ways they were brought up with."[22]

Wanamaker's competitors in the dry goods business treated their new rival with a mixture of awe and fear. The opening of the Grand Depot led to a price war in the city. Determined to meet him head-on, several of his rivals, including Sam Strawbridge of Strawbridge & Clothier and the Sharpless Store, attempted to drive Wanamaker out of business by cutting prices to cost. To overcome this assault, in the spring of 1877, Wanamaker made the most of the acclaim won by his spectacular new site and launched a heavy advertising campaign. Buying large amounts of merchandise in New York City at discount prices, he garnered $40,000 in receipts during his first two days. He took in $1 million in three months of operation at all his stores.[23]

In the summer of 1877, however, Wanamaker's finances began to come apart. His situation in 1877 and 1878 illustrates the narrow margins in which retailers operated. Wanamaker overstocked his new store. Although he managed to make a $100,000 payment on his mortgage in May 1877, he fell behind in his payments to his New York jobbers for merchandise he bought to open the Depot. Some of his creditors refused to sell him any more merchandise for the fall after the Mercantile Agency warned creditors about his credit worthiness.[24]

During the summer of 1877, Wanamaker began writing to his New York distributors to explain why he had not paid his bills on time. Appealing to the bias of the business community, he blamed his lack of resources on labor troubles in Philadelphia rather than on overbuying, which was the real reason for his distress. Although he remained optimistic, his letters contained notes of panic. In one letter he suggested to a creditor that the check would be in the mail next week. He had to refuse to accept drafts on his account that he had signed earlier to secure goods. Wanamaker wrote one major creditor: "This strain has been a bitter lesson that I think will do me good."[25]

Rumors of his imminent failure forced Wanamaker to pay high prices to secure merchandise for the fall, but he also hit back at the stories in both the New York and Philadelphia newspapers, which carried what he called the "malicious efforts to 'knock me down.'" As in the past, William Libbey from Alexander Stewart Company protected Wanamaker. In November and December 1877, Wanamaker tried to pay off some of his past-due debts. In cases where he felt he was being hounded for this money, he paid the debts with something less than graciousness. Wanamaker also got into a fight with an agent from the Mercantile Credit Agency, accusing him of spying and handing out inaccurate information about him, an indication that his finances were getting to him. Wanamaker charged that young businessmen "suffered from the unjust & malicious insensitiveness of an agency manipulated often by inimical parties." Rumors that the Alexander Stewart Company had a special lien upon his property particularly incensed him.[26]

After the 1877 Christmas season, Wanamaker made a desperate effort to save himself by cutting his staff. He fired buyers and managers whom he blamed for overstocking. To get rid of part of his surplus stock, he opened branches in Louisville, Baltimore, Richmond, and Pittsburgh. He also held a sale to dispose of merchandise, selling the goods below cost. At this point the Mercantile Agency believed that Wanamaker's efforts would fail because he had lost the confidence of his suppliers. "This is a matter for regret as he is a man of great enterprise & has done a vast amount of good for this city," the agency commented.[27]

Wanamaker lost about $250,000 in 1877, and his sales did not generate enough money in early 1878 to bail him out. Although by his own estimate, Wanamaker still had unencumbered assets of $1,221,798, there was a potential that the whole business might evaporate quickly. While trying to consolidate his bills, Wanamaker constantly received dunning letters. He apologized for his predicament, indicating that on some days he had just enough receipts to pay his wages. Even William Libbey became anxious about the large sums Wanamaker owed. Wanamaker did allow his buyers to shop for the spring at jobbers who would still do business with him.[28]

To make purchases from anxious creditors, Wanamaker reluctantly gave pre-dated notes for his purchases. He later had to inform some creditors that he was unable to redeem those notes. In June 1878, a year after he began to have financial problems, Wanamaker sold a printing plant for $46,130 to buy back one of his notes.[29]

By July 1878, with the economy of the country picking up, Wanamaker turned a financial corner. Sales rebounded. He increased his advertising budget, and he bought Kelly Street, which allowed him to connect his Market Street property to the block of stores facing Chestnut Street. The real breakthrough came during the 1878 Christmas season, when he did an "immense business," allowing the credit agencies to increase his rating.[30] By 1880, Wanamaker was out of trouble. The Grand Depot was the largest store in the United States and one of the most profitable. All his stores had a net worth of $2,152,300 after liabilities and had total sales of $7 million—$5 million coming from the department store.[31]

Although the Wanamaker empire appeared to grow dramatically during the early 1880s, he did not escape the pitfalls of retailing and at times he seemed on the verge of bankruptcy. The main problems with the financing of a retailing operation continued to be low profit margins, the methods of financing purchases, and the close relationship between business success and the economy. Throughout his retailing career, Wanamaker took a one-third markup on his goods, giving him a 10 percent profit after expenses were taken into account. Such a profit depended primarily upon his ability to take the 5 percent discount offered by wholesalers for cash. Severe competition, especially in hard economic times, could wipe out this margin. When the sixty- or ninety-day grace period elapsed, he had to come up with his payment or lose the discount and the profit. Slowness in payment beyond the grace period meant a loss of credit and ultimately failure. Wanamaker had another problem: he depended on short-term debt, which forced him to rely on his sales to pay his bills. Therefore, a bad season could lead to ruin. Since economic downturns were frequent and sometimes severe, the 1882-83 and 1887-88 recessions left Wanamaker unable to pay his bills.[32]

During these downturns, the credit he extended his customers hurt his cash flow. Wanamaker gave thirty days' credit to his most affluent customers. Credit allowed Wanamaker to compete with his rivals who allowed customers to charge. Credit also encouraged impulse buying among the shoppers in his store. Some customers bought goods beyond their means and were unable to pay their accounts during the grace period. In 1883, consumers owed $800,000—a sum that hindered Wanamaker's ability to repay his creditors. Wanamaker often had difficulty collecting large accounts held by many important people in the city. Some of his worst offenders were clergymen and business people who had received a 10-percent discount on the goods in the first place. He wrote to one recalcitrant credit user, "The taking of the discount reduces the goods to the average cost, and to wait six months for the money is an actual loss of about 5 percent." Wanamaker realized the dangers of credit both to himself and to the borrower. The availability of credit while vast quantities of goods were available could act as an addiction for some individuals.[33]

Once Wanamaker survived his initial financial distresses, he devoted his great energy to the drab building which had served as a freight depot for the Pennsylvania Railroad, turning it into one of the greatest retail show palaces in the United States. In creating the atmosphere in the Grand Depot, Wanamaker proved himself to be a master of department store showmanship. In the words of John Appel, a long-time associate, "He was a merchant who 'staged' his stores, dramatizing them, making them living panoramas of commerce, colossal productions of the thought and craft of man; with lavish exhibits and decorations and display rooms."[34]

To achieve this goal, Wanamaker rebuilt the Depot, which occupied a square block facing Market Street, and bought up all stores facing Chestnut Street directly behind the Grand Depot but separated from it by Kelly Street. Because of legal problems, it took until 1884 to close the street and build a single two-block structure. With the acquisition of the Chestnut stores, he had the largest store in the world, with more than 3,000 workers and a total sales area of more than eleven acres. Divided into forty-eight departments, Wanamaker's had ladies and men's washrooms, restaurants, art galleries, jewelry shops, and furniture exhibitions.[35]

On the evening of November 11, 1878, in preparation for the Christmas season, he opened the expanded Grand Depot for visitors to look but not buy. One reporter viewed the display enthusiastically, writing, "The elite in fashion, the solidity and wealth, the youth and beauty of the city poured through the points of entrance to the Grand Depot in a steady stream of humanity that was at times resistless in its onward rush."[36]

Not only did the store undergo a great physical change during this period, it underwent a technical revolution as well. Wanamaker was constantly looking for advanced technology that would allow him to increase the size of the store and alter its appearance. Nothing gave him greater publicity than his dramatic installation in January 1880 of electric lights, making him the first retailer to use Thomas Edison's invention. Initially, the store had four dynamos installed and sixty-four lamps. Two years later, Wanamaker added 125 lamps, but he bought this electricity from the Brush Electric Company's plant several blocks from the store. Although gas supplemented electric lighting to prevent a blackout, the new source of light was cleaner and gave a steadier glow. Wanamaker visited Edison at Menlo Park in northern New Jersey in 1883 to organize the lighting for his expansion of the store into the basement. By 1888, Wanamaker had 355 arc lamps and 80 incandescent lamps.[37]

Wanamaker followed the electric lights with other electric devices, including fans for ventilation. When the store expanded to a second floor, Wanamaker added an elevator. A ventilating system cooled the store 10 to 12 degrees from the outside temperature during the summer. A giant engine pumped one million cubic feet of fresh air into the building each year.

This electric revolution was a "show stopper" for the Grand Depot. Thousands of people came to the store just to view the lighting displays, to ride the elevators, or to cool off during the summer. It was a window on a future time when incandescent lighting would be available for middle-class homes. Wanamaker had learned from the Centennial Exposition the appeal technology had. They came to the fair by the thousands to use Alexander Bell's telephone. Now they wandered through the Grand Depot to view what Edison and his colleagues had created.[38]

With tourists and urban dwellers alike attracted to the Grand Depot, Wanamaker in the 1880s experienced some of his most successful years. As the largest retailer in the country, he benefitted from a national financial upswing. His success produced great profits and a large reputation in both the city and the nation. His philanthropy became legendary, particularly his contributions to Bethany Church and to other Christian causes. Like many other members of the new upper class, Wanamaker spent parts of his summers in Europe. Sometimes Mary and the children went with him. These trips were important business experiences, allowing him to build contacts and view the latest European retailing styles.[39]

Society columns began to cover the comings and goings not only of

John but also of Mary and their four children. In 1887, when Rodman Wanamaker married Fernanda Antonia Henry and Thomas Wanamaker married Minnie Loebar Walsh, a granddaughter of John Walsh, a former ambassador to England, newspapers reported the weddings as the biggest social events of the year.[40]

Wealth and publicity did not, however, gain Wanamaker entrance into the pre-Civil War aristocracy which continued to control Philadelphia social life. As sociologist E. Digby Baltzell has pointed out, the Philadelphia elite, composed primarily of families with inherited wealth from the Colonial era, remained closed to newcomers. The Biddles, Cadwaladers, and Ingersolls used their money in a private way. Living away from Philadelphia in the suburbs, they largely abstained from politics. Unlike the situations in New York and Boston, Philadelphia's new men of wealth carved out positions for themselves by creating new institutions. Wanamaker's two sons went to Princeton, a Presbyterian school, rather than the University of Pennsylvania, long dominated by the old elite. Wanamaker's evangelical ties also set him apart from the old families, who were largely Episcopalian or Quaker.[41]

Wanamaker did not have the same aloofness from party politics that characterized the old families. Still in his 40s, Wanamaker began to develop political ambitions. He became active in politics by contributing money to Republican candidates and was mentioned as a Republican nominee for Congress and for mayor. Wanamaker viewed his success in the store as a basis for having a greater impact. "I hope in a manner my stores will be a pulpit for me and that I will have an influence for good through them as well as profit on the business side," he wrote. Wanamaker's attitude toward politics was similar to that of the founders of Philadelphia's elite families. They were almost exclusively merchants, who controlled most of the political offices in the city. Like other members of the rising business class, he may have also seen politics as a way of claiming power from the older ruling class. In fact, after he entered politics in a big way in the 1890s, Wanamaker's most important political battles were against Boies Penrose, whose family was part of the old elite. Penrose, unlike most members of his class, chose to become a professional politician.[42]

For Wanamaker, civic virtue and empire building went hand-in-hand. He believed that a businessman had an obligation to promote his city. But the economic and social well-being of Philadelphia also resulted in large profits for his enterprises. An important part of his plan was to turn the Grand Depot into the ceremonial center of the city. The Grand Depot became tied to what anthropologists call "rites of intensification," civic functions designed to bring inhabitants together to celebrate a common political heritage. Wanamaker was always involved with the celebration of July Fourth, the most important civic holiday in the nineteenth century. In 1882, he was also on the planning board for the celebration of the 200th anniversary of the founding of the city by William Penn. Many visitors came into Philadelphia for the ceremonies, which centered on the new city hall. Wanamaker turned his store into one of the landmarks in the celebration by placing a representation of the painting "The Landing of William Penn" in one of his windows. In 1887, to celebrate the 100th anniversary of the Constitution, he built several historical exhibits, including a complete replica of a store that stood at Pine and Water Streets at the time of the Constitutional Convention. To celebrate the Pan American Conference that met in Philadelphia during the centenary, Wanamaker paraded 68 delivery wagons and 121 horses.[43]

Heavy newspaper advertising remained the core of his efforts to reach the public. Wanamaker wrote, "I can only say that no large business can be done ... without a suitable system of advertising, and I believe almost all the money spent for this purpose outside of newspapers is thrown away." The layout of the newspaper advertisements evolved gradually. At first they contained crude drawings and other visual illustrations. But as technology evolved, Wanamaker hired a staff of artists who worked on the layout.[44]

Wanamaker's large expenditure on newspaper advertising was a major factor in his retailing success. His spending and that of other department stores contributed significantly to the rise of the Philadelphia press in the late nineteenth and early twentieth century. More than anything else, daily advertising from department stores helped to finance the expansion in size and numbers of these journals, and as a result significantly shifted control over the metropolitan newspaper. Before the Civil War, most newspapers were organs of the political parties and existed because of patronage from those parties. After the war, the department stores, with their large expenditures for advertis-

ing, gave the newspapers a high degree of independence from politicians and allowed for the rise of the non-partisan press.[45]

More than once, newspaper editors acknowledged Wanamaker's
contribution to their financial development. Wanamaker also benefitted. His relationship to the press played an important part in supporting his image as a public figure. Newspapers defended Wanamaker and
other retailers from periodic attacks on them for underpaying employees and engaging in unfair trade practices.[46]

Probably nothing made a greater contribution to Wanamaker's
retailing achievements than his reputation for personal honesty in
dealing with customers. No matter how big the Grand Depot became,
Wanamaker in his advertising and in his relationships with his customers tried to maintain his image as an honest country storekeeper whose
only real interest was the consumer. This type of salesmanship was very
important in a large city whose population came from rural backgrounds. Because of the impersonal nature of the city, the trust factor
became a very important part of retailing. To keep this personal touch,
even though he had a staff of thousands, Wanamaker was always
available to customers and was seen constantly walking around the
store. His letterbooks from the 1880s show that he wrote more than
300 letters a month, many of which answered customer complaints or
inquiries, even though he had a full staff in the store including a large
complaint department. Many of these letters are addressed to "Dear
Friend," especially those going to women. One typical letter reads, "We
endeavor to serve our customers faithfully and have to ask their
indulgence sometimes if our hands are not obliging."[47]

Before his death Wanamaker attributed his success in retailing to his
"Golden Rule—fair value, courtesy, and satisfaction." Much of the
store advertising went toward creating a feeling of trust. "Storekeeping
at Right Angles With the Public. It cannot be done by conceit that
wearing the names of successful predecessors is sufficient. It cannot be
done by deceit in advertising and instruction of employees with
statements that the store has everything 'just as good as ever.' It can
only be done by a fixed purpose to adhere to the good that remains in
old foundations, and building anew upon them, according to the needs
of the times."[48]

By creating the image of honesty and trustfulness, Wanamaker brought consumers to a large store that they might otherwise reject for a smaller establishment whose owner they knew. John Appel, Wanamaker's New York manager, wrote, "The buying public never for a moment forgets that it is dealing with John Wanamaker instead of a cold, impersonal institution." To maintain this trust, Wanamaker maintained a constant effort to promote truth in advertising. In one letter he wrote his advertising director that, "Your sole business as a writer of our advertising is to find out the truth regarding the merchandise and to tell it in plain words and as briefly as you can."[49]

The Grand Depot also prospered because of Wanamaker's skill as a merchandiser. Displaying a vast exhibition of domestic and imported goods, Wanamaker turned the department store into a consumer palace unique in the United States. Of the major department stores in the late nineteenth century, Wanamaker's was the only one to maintain a European headquarters. His European agent, Andrew D. Butler, and five buyers worked in France. They were constantly on the lookout for materials, dress patterns, and ready-made clothes. Before the opening of the Grand Depot, Philadelphians often went to New York City, but as Wanamaker wrote, "They are no longer content to take the leavings of the ladies of New York, but insist on having stocks supplied direct from foreign markets." Wanamaker purchased a workshop in Berlin to make clothing, particularly coats and wraps. Wanamaker's European buying served the dual purposes of bringing upper class European goods to the United States and purchasing merchandise that was cheaper than high-cost American goods.[50]

Although consistent with the emergence of the Grand Depot as the premier department store in the nation, Wanamaker's policies as an importer were inconsistent with his commitment to the protective tariff as the backbone of American industry and production. Although his rivals often questioned Wanamaker's inconsistency, he never really answered their questions. He had separated his private ambitions to make the Grand Depot the largest store in the United States from his public commitment to Republican ideology.[51]

While bringing in large quantities of imported goods, Wanamaker constantly expanded the lines of merchandise offered his customers. When Wanamaker entered a new consumer line, he did it on a large scale, preempting the merchants who had traditionally sold those goods by offering a larger selection at lower prices.

Nothing illustrates Wanamaker's often ruthless merchandising efforts better than his entrance into the book market. Before 1880, door-to-door peddlers played a major role in the book trade. Large publishers sold subscription sets through these sellers, giving them exclusive contracts and barring bookstores from encroaching on their territories. Price-fixing was also quite common.

The bookstore in the Grand Depot became the largest seller of books and magazines in the country. Wanamaker even published *Book News*, one of the first literary digests in the country, as a venue to advertise new books in his collection. To expand his offerings, Wanamaker decided to enter the lucrative subscription book business.[52]

To allay criticism that he had acted in a high-handed or illegal way in driving out the peddlers in selling subscription books, Wanamaker defended his right to sell the books without publishers' authorization. Wanamaker wrote, "Each of us have a perfect right to any business that we undertake, and if the particular business that we choose has drawbacks to it, such as referred to in my advertisement, it would seem better to try to improve the system rather than abuse the people who call attention to its imperfections." Wanamaker charged the book peddlers with using dishonorable and fraudulent methods to sell their books. He wrote: "The book peddler's a hindrance. He takes the poor man's money and gives him what makes him ashamed when the school master comes, or the minister calls, or his boy or girl away at school comes home over night."[53]

As he often did when defending his business practices, Wanamaker took the highest moral ground, accusing the traditional merchants of dishonest practices. Justifying his actions in moral terms rather than strictly economic terms, many of his rivals in Philadelphia attacked his approach as sanctimonious.

These booksellers regarded Wanamaker as a monopolist who was trying to put them out of business. It was a clash between traditional businesses and new methods of retailing. Because of his attempt to break this system, publishers often sued Wanamaker for infringement of copyright. These cases, which the courts usually decided in his favor, dealt a death blow to the old ways of organizing the book-selling business in the city.[54]

The key case involved the sale of the *Memoirs* of Ulysses S. Grant. Grant, who was dying during the writing of his recollections, produced one of the great best-sellers of the nineteenth century. The book was sold on a subscription basis by Charles L. Webster, Inc., but Wanamaker attacked this process by offering 500 copies of these volumes through his bookstore. When Webster tried to block the sale of the *Memoirs* through a court injunction, the Philadelphia merchant won his case and the right to sell them. This produced a response from Samuel L. Clemens, a partner in the Webster Company, who said that Wanamaker was trying to rob Mrs. Grant of her little pension. Clemens called him "that unco-pious butter-mouthed Sunday school-slobbering sneak-thief John Wanamaker, now of Philadelphia, presently of hell." Clemens, who wrote under the name Mark Twain, had a financial stake in the subscription system and knew that Wanamaker's victory spelled an end to this way of selling books.[55]

With the consolidation of various businesses into the store, by 1887 Wanamaker had almost 6,000 employees. In an era of bitter strife between labor and management, the Philadelphian managed to maintain harmonious relationships with his workers. Labor conflict was out of the question in a retail business dependent upon public good will. Wanamaker's goal was to "remove the antagonism of labor and capital, adding to the sum of human happiness." The Wanamaker labor system was a far cry from the prevailing situation among retailers earlier in the century. Employees, usually young men worked for low wages and worked twelve to fourteen hours a day for six days a week. Many stores had living-in systems; in some cases, the workers lived under the counters.[56]

Harmony between management and employees began with a careful selection of workers. Drawn from the communities Wanamaker knew best, his employees were primarily Philadelphia Protestants, which excluded most of the newer immigrants from employment in the store. The Bethany Sunday School was his most important source of new employees, but he also hired individuals recommended by religious acquaintances and other Philadelphia friends. These young employees learned evangelical values at Bethany that emphasized hard work and obedience to the employer. He also had a long-term relationship with Peirce Commercial College and drew clerical employees from this school. Tradesmen would often move from a business near Wanamaker's to a job in his store.[57]

With the opening of the Grand Depot, Wanamaker developed a paternalistic system to minimize discontent while often paying low salaries to remain competitive with his rivals. He took the position that all his employees were members of a community and dependent upon each other. Wanamaker wrote in an advertisement in 1919, "Living together as we do in our daily work, it is our duty to think of and care for each other by making as agreeable as may be our business relations and thereby enjoy the honor of honest labor and add to the happiness of each other." Drawing upon this community model, the retailer argued he acted fairly toward his employees, writing, "I employ all told five thousand persons. How could I live among them if I taught one thing on Sunday and did another thing on Monday?"[58]

Clerks often entered the work force as teenagers. The lowest salary of $2 per week ($3 after six months) went to cashboys who carried money to a central cash register and returned with a receipt. Sales clerks, most of whom were women, made $3, $4, or $5 per week to start. Although often earning no more than factory workers, Wanamaker's employees had better working conditions and fringe benefits. All employees joined a mutual aid society at the time of employment and remained in it through their stay at the store. Costs for enrollment were 20 cents a month and an additional 20 cents when an employee died. To keep the fund solvent, Wanamaker added money from time to time. Administered by an elected committee, the fund provided sickness and death benefits. Wanamaker complemented this program with a retirement scheme for longtime employees that gave them about half their salary at the time they left the store. Wanamaker also provided cheap lunches, a medical dispensary, and a library.[59]

For Wanamaker, the most important benefit offered by the store was the opportunity it gave for an education and for advancement in business. Because clerks came to the store with little education, Wanamaker offered training and even formal classes to improve their business skills. Since promotions came largely from within the store, he used his classes to identify promising candidates for promotion.

Wanamaker wrote that he tried to create a climate to provide every opportunity for an employee to advance, "making it possible that there shall be nothing between a man and success, but himself." Subsequently, he created a little "civil service" for his employees, putting them on a step promotion system. Becoming a national advocate of business education, Wanamaker argued, "America has been far behind other nations in business education. We are all in too much of a hurry to reach the top, and the want of training to hold positions taken is the constant cause of failure."[60]

One circular sent out to the salespersons in New York was called a "Creed." It pushed the "Golden Rule" for relations in the store, "that its daily application and observance would make all other rules and regulations unnecessary for me." The community operated on several principles, the most important being "holding loyalty on a par with honesty; recognizing that my progress is of my own making, I would hitch my wagon to the star of persistent, patient industry, always busy, cheerfully busy, but never too busy to be considerate of my fellow employees...."[61]

In 1887, Wanamaker began profit sharing for employees who had seven years service. Although several stores in New York and other cities shared profits, Wanamaker's announcement produced a good deal of favorable publicity. During the first year, he distributed about $100,000 to eligible employees. Between 1888 and 1899, Wanamaker distributed almost $700,000 among his employees. Despite the wide-scale publicity and its approval from workers, he later replaced the profit sharing with sales commissions and bonuses after he found the system unwieldy and lacking in incentives.[62]

Wanamaker also opened a hotel at Broad and Brown Streets, the Hotel Rodman, where 80 young women employees lived. The Philadelphia *Press* praised the home because of "the service rendered in solving one of the most perplexing of modern problems—the housing in protected comfort of the woman who works." In creating the Hotel Rodman, Wanamaker imitated a highly publicized experiment by Alexander Stewart in the 1870s to open a boarding house for his female employees. By providing housing, Wanamaker answered charges against department stores that low wages paid to their salesgirls and lack of adequate cheap housing forced them into prostitution.[63]

Despite the favorable working conditions compared to factory employment, Wanamaker could be a harsh taskmaster. Lateness or misconduct resulted in fines. Mistakes might also be costly. One woman in the accounts department misplaced $9 and paid the money back out of her own salary, though $9 was more than she earned in a week. Wanamaker admonished her, "You are expected to make up what your failure in duty has lost." Misconduct also resulted in dismissal. In firing one employee, Wanamaker wrote, "While we try our best to take care of our people, yet even the employment of good hands depends on full service to our customers, if we fail in this we will have no employment for anyone." Although Wanamaker tried to distance himself from the industrial model, his mention of the term "good hands," a term used in factories and railroading, shows how he depended on it at times when dealing with his employees. Fired employees had to leave the job immediately without severance pay.[64]

Despite these firings and occasional problems with discontented employees, Wanamaker had few problems with his employees. Believing unions created divided loyalties within the work place, Wanamaker refused to let labor organize in his stores. In 1886, Wanamaker rejected an effort by carpenters working for him to join a chapter of the Knights of Labor, arguing that labor unions did not benefit the working class. Although he refused to allow unions, during this period of intense labor unrest Wanamaker escaped any strikes. He went out of his way to appear to be favorable to the demands of organized labor. He even received an award from the pro-worker Henry George School of Baltimore for his work in promoting the welfare of his employees. But simultaneously, he suggested that a speaker at an Independence Day celebration tone down his praise for labor because it would have a negative effect on conservative listeners.[65]

By the mid-1880s, Wanamaker's, as the Grand Depot was now called, was functioning as a full-operation department store, the largest in the United States. It was part of a retail empire which also included the original Oak Hall Men's Clothing Store and its branch stores in Philadelphia. After the death of Nathan Brown, Wanamaker made John Houghton, a master tailor who had worked for Wanamaker from his first day in business, his limited partner. He was replaced by Andrew D. Butler briefly during 1877 and 1878 while Wanamaker reorganized the store. Wanamaker also relied heavily on his brother William to manage first Oak Hall and then the Grand Depot. Robert S. Ogden joined Wanamaker in 1879 to manage Oak Hall. Ogden, originally from Philadelphia, had spent many years in New York City working for the David Devlin clothing firm and was a prominent Christian layman in the city and very active in the Sunday School movement.[66]

In 1885, Wanamaker decided to concentrate all his efforts on the Grand Depot and turned Oak Hall into a stock company controlled by his brother William. The new business, in which John took little interest, eventually changed its name to William Wanamaker & Co. and operated men's stores in several eastern cities until late in the twentieth century. Wanamaker also turned over operations in the Sixth and Chestnut store to his other brother Sam, but he remained a special partner in the business. With William Wanamaker now at Oak Hall, Wanamaker brought Robert Ogden to the Grand Depot to become his partner.[67]

Ogden was a fine organizer who kept the store running smoothly, meeting with the staff on a daily basis, collecting and collating inventory and sales reports. He was also a talented merchandiser and publicist. His outside activities gave him a national reputation, particularly as president of the Hampton Institute in Virginia, which had been set up during Reconstruction to provide schooling for African-Americans and Native-Americans. Ogden's activity at Hampton and Wanamaker's own patronage of the institute helped to increase the Wanamaker enterprises' reputation for philanthropy.[68]

After Thomas Wanamaker graduated from Princeton in 1883, he took over a number of managerial functions at the store. Thomas had a good understanding of finances and organization but lacked his father's merchandising skills and his ability to deal with people. He became equal with Ogden as one of the three managers of the Wanamaker business and a partner in its operation. When Wanamaker went to Europe in June 1886, he left Thomas in charge of the Grand Depot for the first time.

By January 1887, with Ogden and Thomas Wanamaker in place, John had considerable time to devote to long-term planning for the store and for outside activities. Although other stores in the city still had financial difficulties in the 1880s, these were some of the most profitable years for the Grand Depot. Enjoying the best of times, a generally favorable press, and a national reputation as the most innovative retailer of his time, Wanamaker began to contemplate a political career. His political ambition came to dominate the next decade of his life.[69]

CHAPTER FOUR

Politics

1880-1905

*B*y 1888, Wanamaker was widely known in Philadelphia as a businessman and philanthropist, but he was little known outside the city. This changed during the next ten years. Wanamaker entered politics as the Republican Party's national treasurer, as a member of President Benjamin Harrison's cabinet, and as an unsuccessful candidate first for United States senator and then for governor of Pennsylvania.

In Wanamaker's political life as in his retailing, there was a close connection to his religious life. His campaigns for office were often moral crusades in which he branded his opponents as personifications of evil. Bringing religion into politics, however, proved to be more difficult than winning converts at Bethany or bringing Christianity into retailing.

Although these forays into politics often left him little time to run his retailing empire, Wanamaker believed that as a citizen he was obliged to participate in public affairs. In early America, merchants had played an important part in the political life of the republic, but they had been replaced by lawyers and professional politicians. Wanamaker thought his business success made him equal or superior to the lawyers who ran the nation and who had never had real experience in practical economics. "The business man whose capital is his own hard earned savings, in daily contact with his neighbors who are pioneers like himself, comes into a knowledge of economics not gathered theoretically from essays or books," Wanamaker said.[1]

Politics came naturally for Wanamaker because it involved the same skills that had made him a successful businessman. He had a knack for self-promotion and was a born showman, a prerequisite for a late nineteenth-century politician. Motivated by burning ambition, he had the resources to make himself a presence on the political scene. His sense of independence was a handicap, however, since the bosses who ran the political parties demanded absolute loyalty.

As with his business ventures, people were seldom neutral about Wanamaker. His allies had only the warmest things to say about his ethics in politics; his opponents considered him a holier-than-thou hypocrite. During one of Wanamaker's campaigns against Pennsylvania boss Matthew Quay, a minister wrote, "Next to his glorious forty-year work in Bethany [stands the] signal service he is now rendering to the cause of pure & honest government." After watching Wanamaker for more than a decade, another minister-turned-journalist concluded, "I have felt obliged to portray the wretched political failures of this ignorant but rich shopman of New York and Philadelphia."[2]

Wanamaker's guiding principle was the idea of civic virtue that had been prominent early in the century. "Every individual should think and talk on questions of Government," he argued, "and that every man will not fail to vote and influence his neighbors to vote. It's only a hind quarter of a man that growls at the state of the times and throws away his vote by absence, quibbling or neglect." His belief in civic virtue came not only from his belief in republicanism, but also from his Christian beliefs. In preparing a statewide Sunday school program, he put in the requirement that each student devote "at least two lessons in each year upon good citizenship and the duties of Christians in relation thereto."[3]

In the antebellum period, there were several efforts to create a Christian Political Party, something that Wanamaker and like-minded evangelicals carried over into the late nineteenth century. As part of a great network of evangelicals that operated through the Sunday School movement, the YMCAs, the tract societies, the Bible societies, and the overseas missionary societies, Wanamaker pushed their Christian agenda of temperance, strict regulation of all activities on Sunday, and bringing morality into politics.

Wanamaker, who neither drank alcoholic beverages nor smoked, advocated temperance in politics. He wrote in 1922, "Personally, I believe in Prohibition, because in a long experience I have seen the evil and degrading effects of the liquor traffic and do not believe that it can be safely played with any more than can dope or dynamite."[4]

As a Lincoln Republican, Wanamaker advocated African-American rights. His attitudes about race dated to his experiences before the Civil War, when he met African-Americans at his father's brick works, and he maintained contacts with a number of prominent African-American leaders, including Frederick Douglass and Booker T. Washington. Blacks worked at Wanamaker's, and despite criticisms, he hired African-Americans in the Post Office when he served as postmaster general. After coming under attack for meeting with Washington, Wanamaker wrote, "It was a matter in which every Christian man, whatever his color, might have rejoiced instead of condemning."[5]

Taking a traditional Republican position on the tariff, the major issue dividing Republicans from Democrats, Wanamaker said that while as a merchant he did not directly benefit from a high protective tariff, like everyone else, he benefitted from prosperity. Downturns in the economy were directly related to the tariff because a low tariff took jobs from the poor. "Every bolt of goods made by American weavers earns American money, to be spent in America, and every bolt of goods bought in Europe carries away American gold to foreign workmen, who keep it in their country," Wanamaker said. But while he continued to justify the principle of protection in his speeches, Wanamaker bought more bolts of woolen goods in Europe than any other merchant.[6]

In the early 1880s, the Republican Party controlled government in Philadelphia, in Pennsylvania, and in the nation. In Pennsylvania, Wanamaker allied himself first with Senator Simon Cameron, the state political boss, and then with his son and successor, Donald Cameron. On the local level, Wanamaker began to distance himself from the Republican machine headed by James McManus. Harassment by local officials, who were always looking for bribes, led Wanamaker into an uneasy alliance with reformers who had been trying to change the city since the 1870s. Many reformers came from old money families, which were suspicious of the new men of wealth.[7]

Many businessmen like Wanamaker felt threatened by the machine politics of the late nineteenth century. First, both state and local bosses had developed independent sources of money, making them less responsive to business needs. Second, political leaders using this power began to extort money from businessmen by demanding bribes and raising taxes. Simultaneously, they failed to provide the municipal and state services that businesses needed to be profitable.[8]

To these business needs, Wanamaker added his concerns as a religious leader that corruption and immorality had overcome the political system. Particularly, in his fight against bossism in the mid-1890s, Wanamaker championed some of the same themes which the Christian Progressives would echo in the early twentieth century.

Aligning himself with younger business leaders such as Thomas Dolan, head of the United Gas Improvement Corporation, and Rudolph Blankenburg, a small manufacturer, Wanamaker saw himself as a moderate reformer trying to change conditions in the city, but not proposing change for change's sake. "I have no sympathy with the ridiculous fault finding that is so much against our officials who are doing the best they can with the means at their disposal," he wrote in 1883. Not entirely happy with the older elite reformers in Philadelphia led by Charles Lea, a professor of medieval history at the University of Pennsylvania, Wanamaker often found himself with a foot in each camp, not always successfully.[9]

In June 1882, several Philadelphia newspapers proposed Wanamaker as a candidate for Pennsylvania's at-large seat in Congress. The vacancy occurred when Tom Marshall, the Republican nominee, withdrew from the race after reformers criticized his ties to the Camerons. Party leaders asked Wanamaker to replace Marshall to cover up the split within the party. Although Wanamaker had the support of the Philadelphia delegation to a special convention to choose a successor, several newspapers attacked him as a tool of Donald Cameron. Responding to this newspaper assault, Wanamaker declined the nomination. This political storm, his first introduction to electoral politics, caused him a kind of pain he had never experienced before, and he retreated to the safety of his businesses. This was not the last time this would happen.[10]

Between 1883 and 1885, Wanamaker worked with William Bullitt, a Philadelphia member of the state assembly, to secure a reform charter for Philadelphia through the Pennsylvania legislature. But in the discussion of charter reform, Wanamaker kept his independence, threatening to oppose reform if the legislature made too many changes in the old charter. In 1884, Wanamaker split with the reformers by supporting James G. Blaine for president while they joined the "mugwump" wing of the party in refusing to support him.[11]

Wanamaker kept his centrist position in 1887 when the charter went into effect. Wanamaker refused to join other reformers in running an independent, non-partisan ticket against Mayor Edwin H. Fitler. The anti-machine leaders even offered to run Wanamaker for mayor, but he declined to run. Wanamaker did feel some guilt over not participating in a broad-based reform effort. Writing to a leader of Philadelphia reform, he said, "I felt very anxious to see my duty and I hope I have made no mistake in the decision I have reached."[12]

In 1886, Wanamaker became involved in a controversy involving the municipally owned Philadelphia Gas Works. A New York company proposed buying PGW, which had a reputation for corruption, poor service, and charging higher prices for gas than other cities—all of which deterred business from settling in the city. To ward off an outside takeover of the plant, Wanamaker offered to lease PGW for twenty years, paying $1 million per year and leaving ownership with the city. The city council rejected Wanamaker's offer, however, and kept the old system for another ten years.[13]

Because he depended on mass transportation to bring people into the central business district, Wanamaker was active in developing an urban transit system. In 1887, he served as president of the Consolidated Rapid Transit Company. During the transit strike of 1895, he helped negotiate a settlement, even helping to pay some of the costs of the agreement. As part of the labor contract, the Union Traction Company, one of the trolley companies serving the city, agreed to take the men back and to allow them to join the union. But the transit company went back on most of the settlement provisions, leading to criticism of Wanamaker for his role in ending the strike.[14]

While gaining prominence in local politics, Wanamaker began to play a part in national politics as well. Because of his wealth, prominent Republicans courted Wanamaker as a source for campaign funds. By 1887, Wanamaker entered fund-raising in a big way, donating $1,500 to support the Republican senatorial candidate in Virginia, John Wise. In return, Wanamaker pressed his interests with state and national representatives.[15]

In Pennsylvania, while supporting urban reform, Wanamaker during the 1880s allied himself with the bosses. As early as 1880, Wanamaker had a working relationship with the Camerons and their ally and heir, United States Senator Matthew Quay, who by 1885 had become the most powerful political figure in Pennsylvania. Quay, who came from western Pennsylvania and was the son of a Presbyterian minister, was one of the state bosses who dominated the Republican Party at the end of the century. Using his control of national and state patronage and of money contributed by banks and railroads dependent upon friendly state government, Quay controlled Pennsylvania to a greater extent than earlier leaders, even taking over Philadelphia and Pittsburgh.[16]

In 1888, Quay ran Benjamin Harrison's presidential campaign and secured an appointment for Wanamaker as a delegate to the Republican national convention in Chicago and as treasurer of Harrison's presidential campaign. Approaching his job with the same gusto he dedicated to his business, Wanamaker raised enough money to make the 1888 campaign the most expensive on record. Wanamaker, with his friend Thomas Dolan, personally contributed $100,000 to a fund that totaled more than $400,000. Wanamaker raised the money so quickly that the Democrats never knew what hit them. With this money, Senator Quay reversed Republican fortunes in New York and Indiana, where the party had lost in 1884. In Indiana, Quay used the money to buy votes, assuring that Harrison carried his native state. Quay created directories of voters in New York City to challenge Tammany's voter lists, enabling Harrison to win New York State.[17]

Wanamaker's activities in 1888 helped to revolutionize the use of money in campaigns. In the post-Civil War era, presidential campaigns cost less than $100,000. Wanamaker's fund-raising activities were part of a long-term trend that increased the power of business leaders in politics. Senator Quay and bosses in other states, such as Thomas Platt in New York, used patronage and funds raised by control over the revenues of their states to run their political organizations. These methods reduced their dependency on the business community. By raising large sums of money in 1888, independent of the regular Republican machine, Wanamaker helped increase the influence of the economic elite in the party. Businessmen also began to run for office instead of just contributing their money. The changes that began in 1888 reached an apex in 1896 with the choice of Mark Hanna, a Cleveland businessman, as Republican national chairman. Hanna also served several terms in the United States Senate, where he joined other businessmen.[18]

Soon after Benjamin Harrison's 1888 election to the presidency, rumors circulated that Wanamaker would receive an appointment in the new administration. Wanamaker had never met the president-elect, but in January 1889 he traveled to Harrison's home in Indiana, staying for several days for an interview. After the meeting, Harrison made Wanamaker postmaster general, touching off a furious reaction among Pennsylvania's political bosses. Harrison had not followed the usual practice of clearing the appointment with the nominee's home-state senators. This action left Senators Matthew Quay and Donald Cameron angry at being presented a *fait accompli*. By appointing Wanamaker as postmaster general, Harrison hoped to separate himself from Quay, who had developed an unfavorable reputation as a political manipulator. Quay, who believed Harrison owed his election to him, advised Wanamaker against accepting the appointment and broke with Wanamaker when he took the job. Wanamaker's appointment led to a break between Quay and the administration, and the Pennsylvania senator lost much of his patronage clout. Wanamaker further infuriated Quay by removing one of Quay's aides from his post office job.[19]

Wanamaker's appointment to the position stirred considerable controversy because of his fund-raising for the Harrison campaign. Although a few businessmen had served in presidential cabinets before Wanamaker, the positions usually went to professional politicians. Grant had appointed several industrialists to office, but his attempt to nominate Alexander Stewart as secretary of the treasury lost in the Senate. The postmaster general's job, with its vast control over patronage, usually went to an experienced political operator who used that job to advance his party's fortunes.

Newspaper barbs in 1889 were just the start of Wanamaker's encounter with criticism. Journalists and cartoonists had a field day with the rich and portly Philadelphian. Wanamaker did not react kindly to the attacks. Having just entered the political scene, he had a thin skin for that rough-and-tumble game. "I am terribly sick of being abused and maligned," he said in 1891, reacting to newspaper criticism.[20]

His selection as postmaster general gave Wanamaker the national prominence he previously lacked. During his service from 1889 to 1893, because of his dominant personality, his recommendations for change in the postal system, and the controversies in which he became involved, he became one of the best-known members of the administration. Retaining his prominence after his years as postmaster, he subsequently was mentioned for other major positions, including president.

Wanamaker had a particularly close relationship with Harrison. Both men were Presbyterian elders and thought alike. Harrison was sympathetic to Wanamaker's efforts to make his department more service-oriented and to his desire to clean up the party. Harrison also was impressed by Wanamaker's great wealth. Wanamaker often accompanied the president on campaign trips, and the Harrisons visited with the Wanamakers at their summer cottage in Cape May, N.J. Before he left office, Wanamaker bought the president a house at the summer resort.[21]

In Washington, Wanamaker bought a large mansion from the outgoing Secretary of the Navy, William C. Whitney. Because of the size of the house and Wanamaker's ability to entertain on a scale more lavish than most politicians could afford, his house became a social center in Washington, despite his refusal to serve alcohol. After Mary Wanamaker returned in the summer of 1889 from Europe, where she had been with her two daughters Minnie and Elizabeth, she took over the social roles required of a cabinet member's wife. Although most observers felt she was retiring and shy, she fulfilled the duties imposed upon her.[22]

Back in Philadelphia, the bulk of the burden for operating

Wanamaker's store fell upon his son Thomas and Robert C. Ogden, both of whom had become partners in the 1880s. However, Wanamaker spent part of each day on store business, visited it on most weekends, and even moved back when one of his partners was on vacation.[23]

During his first year in Washington, Wanamaker was beset by financial problems. Finding themselves unable to meet all the demands for money at the height of an economic boom, bankers raised interest rates and called loans that had been issued earlier at lower rates. Forced to pay off a $1 million debt, Wanamaker found himself hard pressed by an unprofitable $2.5 million investment in a wholesale business and a $3.5 million credit account owed by his customers. Wanamaker decided to get rid of the wholesale business. Even so, by the middle of December 1890, rumors abounded that Wanamaker was about to fail after he lost money in the stock market on Reading Railroad stock. Wanamaker's membership on the board of directors of the failed Keystone Bank in Philadelphia in 1890 also led to losses and newspaper criticism. An upturn in business in 1891, saved him from potential failure.[24]

Using his political position to keep abreast of business conditions, Wanamaker sometimes compromised his ethics. Although a strong proponent of protection, Wanamaker was one of the largest importers in the United States. Consequently, he kept a keen eye on the administration's efforts to pass a high protective tariff. When the bill seemed certain of passage, he urged his son Rodman, who operated his Paris importing house, to ship all his French purchases to Philadelphia by August 31, 1890, when the new duties would go into effect.[25]

The Philadelphian brought his full energies to his new position, just as he had done in his business. Although most cabinet officers did not get to work before 10 a.m., Wanamaker often arrived at 7:30 and spent several hours at his desk before his clerks arrived. He spent these mornings personally answering each of the hundreds of letters he received from citizens suggesting ways to improve the postal service. He also devoted time to studying postal laws and practices in foreign countries. From these reports, he formed many ideas for reforming the system.

The post office department in Washington, which had twenty

employees, supervised about 150,000 people in the United States, making it the largest agency in the federal government. Traditionally, the post office department was the center of the patronage machine for the party in power. Wanamaker did little to change the system. Although he believed the government needed to improve personnel, he rejected a radical civil service reform approach, fearing it would damage the party. Although he made some promotions by examinations, he generally buckled under to Republican legislators on appointments and removals of postal officers. Because of his party loyalty, Wanamaker became an open opponent of Theodore Roosevelt, a civil service commissioner and advocate of merit selection.[26]

Compared to the store, where his decisions were instantly obeyed, Wanamaker's job in Washington was frustrating. Although President Harrison let Wanamaker handle department affairs, Wanamaker felt restrained by Congress, which considered itself the real master of the department and did not expect cabinet officers to initiate changes in their organizations. These were to come from the appropriate congressional committees. Congress even regarded the president as an executor of laws, rather than as an originator of new legislation. Writing at the end of his term, Wanamaker reflected on his loggerheads with Congress: "I hardly know of anything more difficult than to get such legislation through Congress. I have been laboring for four years with many highly meritorious projects to benefit the postal service, and it is a fact that very few of these have had the attention of a committee."[27]

Although Wanamaker failed in most of his efforts at postal reform, the post office department gave him a platform to espouse his views about the future of the United States. He viewed the country as one national entity linked by cultural, economic, and commercial ties. Farmers in the Midwest would wear the same clothes, read the same books, and play the same piano music as workers in the East. Protected by tariff, they would all participate in the economic gains that this arrangement produced. In antebellum America, Henry Clay had called such regional interdependence the American System. Wanamaker built upon Clay's Whig vision for the realities of late nineteenth-century America. He conceived of the American System as part of a greater European world community. As an importer of European products, he believed that Americans could learn from that part of the world and simultaneously profit from penetrating its markets.[28]

Many of his reform proposals also reflected his own frustrations as a large retailer who looked to a national market for his products. Although he never maintained a catalog department equal to Marshall Field's or Sears & Roebuck, he sold goods by mail from his earliest years in men's wear. Even if he never operated a great mail-order concern, he had an affinity with businessmen who sold merchandise nationally.

To carry out his ideas, Wanamaker tried to change the post office operations so that they would be more businesslike. He wrote, "I had profound belief that the post office business could be promoted the same as any other business by giving conveniences of deliveries and collection of mails by boxes and by thousands of places convenient to the people like the drug stores and cigar stores where they could get postage stamps."[29]

Believing that rapid mail service in large cities was "as important to business as good blood circulation to the body," Wanamaker felt that the department had not kept up with changes in technology. He introduced pneumatic tubes in New York City and Philadelphia to speed mail delivery between the post office and downtown office buildings. In St. Louis, Wanamaker experimented with a streetcar post office, in which postmen sorted the mail on the move. As an urban advocate, he increased the annual budget of the New York post office from $7 million to $10 million but failed to get Congress to improve the facilities in the city.[30]

Wanamaker's most notable effort to aid business through improved postal service was his proposal for a parcel post system. Costs for sending merchandise through the mails were almost prohibitive. Packages were limited to four pounds at sixteen cents per pound; meanwhile, international agreements allowed packages of up to eleven pounds to be sent overseas at a rate of twelve cents per pound. Wanamaker's plan for a parcel post was opposed by the five express companies (American Express Company, United States Express Company, Adams Express Company, Wells Fargo Express, and the Southern Express Company) and by local retailers. The latter feared that the metropolitan department stores would destroy their local businesses.

The measure languished until long after Wanamaker left office. In 1912, with Wanamaker's support, Congress passed the measure. On January 1, 1913, Wanamaker sent the first package to President William Howard Taft from the main Philadelphia Post Office.[31]

In a second measure to improve mail services for business, Wanamaker proposed rural home delivery. The postmaster urged the measure "because it is so easy, and, second, it is so widespread, and it seems to me so patriotic." Congress authorized the experiment, originally operating from forty-six post offices, in 1890. The Cleveland administration ended the program, but President McKinley revived rural free delivery in 1897. By 1910, delivery expanded to 41,118 rural routes costing more than $37 million. With both parcel post and rural free home delivery in place, mail-order companies came to dominate rural retailing.[32]

While postmaster, Wanamaker also pressed for a subsidy program to promote the building of merchant ships in the United States. Congress authorized the subsidy in 1891 and, to the dismay of subsequent postmasters general, the post office department carried it as part of its budget.

The strangest proposal to come from Wanamaker was his advocacy of nationalizing the telegraph and telephone services under the post office department. The proposal, which copied a European practice, grew out of his feeling that these natural monopolies should be run for the good of all Americans rather than for the private profit of a few. "Public interests, private needs, and the popular will call for these agencies to perfect the great postal system of this country," he said. "The electric current belongs to the people by right, and is bound to become their servant, not of a class nor of one-sixty-fourth part of the population, as at present." In his fight against Western Union, Wanamaker was also grinding his own ax against a monopoly that he believed had long overcharged him and other businessmen. He had often expressed outrage at the rates that he paid Western Union as a businessman. As a cabinet member, the high rates Western Union charged the government disturbed him. Although Wanamaker's proposal for socialism in telecommunications never received a real discussion, it fit into his belief that nothing should interfere with the smooth interchange of goods and ideas in the United States.[33]

Wanamaker also advocated creating a postal savings system. Having earlier pioneered a savings plan for his employees, Wanamaker believed Americans were hoarding at least $4 million at home, which did not help the economy. If depositors put this money into a postal savings bank, which would pay two percent interest, the money could then be placed in circulation by neighborhood banks, thus making it available locally. Although Wanamaker failed to secure a postal savings plan, the Wilson administration approved the system in 1914.[34]

Wanamaker's religious beliefs influenced some of his actions as postmaster. Since the 1830s, evangelical religious groups had tried to eliminate all mail deliveries on the Sabbath. Wanamaker was a strong advocate of blue laws. His own stores were always closed on Sundays, and he never advertised then. Writing to a Chicago merchant, Wanamaker argued, "I would give up a business that compelled me to break God's law." So, in one of his first orders as postmaster general, Wanamaker ended Sunday deliveries.[35]

Wanamaker also launched an attack on state-run lotteries, particularly the Louisiana lottery, the largest in the country. Wanamaker, who opposed gambling on both religious and economic grounds, helped push an act through Congress in September 1890 to outlaw the sale through the mails of both domestic and foreign lottery tickets. Once the law was in place, Wanamaker vigorously enforced it, sending several lottery operators to prison.[36]

While frustrated at the slow pace of government, by the time he left office Wanamaker was satisfied with his accomplishments. "The clear conscience I take away" also pleased him. His satisfaction did not last, however. After Wanamaker left office, he was frustrated with Washington again when his policies were reversed, particularly his program of house-to-house mail pickup by postal workers.[37]

When President Harrison ran for re-election in 1892, Wanamaker participated in the campaign, donating $10,000 in startup money and an additional $50,000 to the re-election committee, headed by Cornelius Bliss. Overall, the campaign went poorly, and the death of the President's wife during its closing months further hindered it. With the loss of the White House to Grover Cleveland, Wanamaker returned to Philadelphia. During the next five years, he remained active politically while managing the store through the trying depression of 1893.[38]

After he left the cabinet in March 1893, Wanamaker tried to work out his differences with Senator Matthew Quay. His meeting with Quay received a good deal of press coverage, leading many friends to attack him. In his discussion with the party boss, Wanamaker had his eye on the United States Senate seat held by Don Cameron, whose term would end in 1897. Cameron had lost a great deal of his power to Quay, who decided to replace the senior senator with someone else.[39]

Although he professed continued friendship toward Cameron, Wanamaker hoped to replace him and courted Quay for the nomination. Privately, he tried to undermine Cameron, praising the work of a journalist who, "smashed the hopes of the Cameronians." But at the same time, he wrote Cameron, "I trust our old friendship still stands & if there are any broken links, that some of my friends & yours-will make clear to you that there ought not to be."[40]

Since 1896 was a presidential election year, and a year in which Cameron's replacement would be chosen, Wanamaker kept a low profile during the contest for president. Although he preferred Harrison for another term, he realized William McKinley had the Republican nomination. Wanamaker went abroad in January and did not arrive home until mid-June, having traveled to Cairo, Paris, London, Carlsbad, and Hamburg. He had left his political friends working for his nomination for senator.

Coming home from Europe, Wanamaker received the unwelcome news that Quay was supporting someone else—Boies Penrose, a Philadelphia state legislator—for the senatorial nomination. In the nineteenth century, senators were not elected directly by voters, but were chosen in a joint meeting of the two houses of the state legislature. Thus, elections to the legislature often became referendums on the person who would sit in the upper house of Congress. In Pennsylvania, Republican and Democratic conventions selected their party's candidates. Legislators met in January after the November election to choose a senator. Before the contest, Republican legislators met in a secret caucus to ratify the vote of the state convention. Because most Republican legislators were indebted to Quay, his choice of a candidate usually won.[41]

After Quay endorsed Boies Penrose, effectively blocking Wanamaker's political ambitions, the retailer turned against his former ally and entered the race against Penrose. As part of his campaign, Wanamaker demonized the senator, blaming him for corrupting American politics. Wanamaker wrote to the Rev. B.F. White, "I need hardly to add that the degradation of Pennsylvania was never so conspicuous as it is now and that the need of a rising up on the part of religious people against the greed of corporations and the tyranny of machines never as timely." He kept up this moral attack on Quay until the political boss's death. Wanamaker was frustrated because Quay opposed him for high political office, but his hatred of Quay became obsessive and at times almost without reason. Wanamaker was engaged in a crusade against Quay which resembled his attacks on peddlers and small merchants earlier.[42]

Wanamaker had allies who also distrusted the Pennsylvania senator. Wanamaker's main base of support was the Businessman's League of Philadelphia, with Rudolph Blankenburg as executive secretary. Blankenburg and other members of the league had long opposed boss rule in Philadelphia and turned against the Quay machine as the source of bad government in both the city and the state. Wanamaker and his friends were members of the new business elite whose fortunes were tied to a vibrant Philadelphia and who saw the time and money invested in reform as investments. Like Wanamaker, many of these men were active in Christian activities and in commerce. In Philadelphia these reformers would provide the backbone for the Progressive Movement in the city during the early twentieth century.[43]

Wanamaker launched a campaign to convince Republican members of the Pennsylvania Senate and General Assembly to dissociate themselves from the Quay machine. To accomplish this, he campaigned during the fall legislative elections, trying to persuade candidates for election to commit themselves to him rather than to Penrose. To develop grassroots support around the state, he made speeches in forty counties and met with most of the Republican legislative candidates who would have the final say. He warned one wavering newspaper editor against allowing Quay to pick the second senator. "If the State of Pennsylvania is better satisfied to have a Senator with two votes and is moved by personal political considerations rather than the interests of the people, I suppose there is nothing to be done but to submit to one boss rule," he said, "but I should protest against it and work for something else as long as I live."[44]

Quayism was the main theme of the campaign. Wanamaker charged that the machine and its leader had made Harrisburg the corruption center of the state. No citizen could pass without paying tribute to the boss. He charged that Pennsylvanians paid taxes 35 percent higher than needed to feed the machine. In a speech, Wanamaker charged, "The degradation of Pennsylvania was never so conspicuous as it is now and . . . the need of a rising up on the part of religious people against the greed of corporations and the tyranny of machines never as timely."[45]

Quay and Penrose counterattacked, charging that Wanamaker's election would be a victory for wealth. "It would mean that in the future none but multi-millionaires need present themselves as candidates for the United States Senate in Pennsylvania," they said. "It would mean that no poor man need apply."

Wanamaker's role as an importer came under fire in a very protectionist state. One editor charged that "Wanamaker was a free trade man, tied to the importing of goods for his stores." Another weak spot for Wanamaker was a federal fine he paid for violating the contract labor law by employing an immigrant who had been hired in England to work in the Philadelphia store. The Penrose forces charged that this evidence showed that Wanamaker opposed restriction on immigration and was no friend of labor. The United Mine Workers accepted this argument, supporting Penrose because "the working people of this Commonwealth do not want a millionaire to represent them, and it has in the past been proven that the fewer number of capitalists in office the better it has been for the working classes." Although Wanamaker had technically violated the law, the man hired by Wanamaker's staff was a professional hatter. Congress passed the law to prevent the immigration of large numbers of unskilled laborers who worked for low wages under the direction of contractors.[46]

A low point in the campaign for Wanamaker was his involvement in a bribery charge. Christian Kauffman, a legislator from Columbia County and Wanamaker's campaign manager, approached many assembly and senate candidates to line them up for Wanamaker. In some of these contacts, Kauffman offered campaign financing from the merchant in return for support in the election. When this correspondence fell into the hands of the Washington Post, the newspaper charged that Wanamaker had attempted bribery. "Can we believe that this holy man, who speaks . . . of faith and hope and charity on Sundays, and who, during the week, sacrifices himself a thousand times a day by selling drawers at half their real value to his needy fellow Christians—can we believe that he would engage in such a deal as this?" the newspaper asked. These attacks left Wanamaker unnerved: "I do not enjoy the fight and there is much in it far from pleasant but I am in it and must stick at it until it ends," he wrote. "I fear defeat as it will be a miracle to win against Quay and all his machine now bitterly moving against me."[47]

Wanamaker lost the Senate fight when the Republican caucus met on January 5, 1897, and voted for Penrose, 133-75. Wanamaker then asked that his name be withdrawn from consideration by the legislature. Although obviously disappointed by his defeat, Wanamaker remained optimistic. Believing the ground he had gained against Quay was almost a miracle, Wanamaker reasoned that defeat at the hands of an entrenched machine of thirty years' duration was not unexpected. He felt that "there is much to do in Pennsylvania to recover the state from those who are preying upon its vitals."[48]

After the election, Wanamaker and his friends suffered another blow when McKinley, the newly elected president, turned over patronage in the state to Quay and Penrose. Wanamaker failed even to have one of his neighbors appointed to a fourth class post office near his home in Jenkintown. Because he contributed $10,000 to the McKinley campaign, Wanamaker believed he had a say in patronage. He wrote, "It was not the politicians, but the business men that elected Major McKinley, and they mean to continue to have a hand in politics of the country." After this defeat, Wanamaker did not make further patronage suggestions to the new administration.[49]

Out of frustration with the McKinley-Quay alliance and his exclusion from federal patronage, Wanamaker decided to break with McKinley, attacking him on May 14, 1897, in a speech at the Business Men's League. Warning that McKinley was not moving fast enough to repair the damage done by the depression, he concluded, "The people betrayed and disheartened, would no longer have faith in the party, and would turn to any leadership that offers better times." He even predicted "a revolution that will give birth to a new political party." This speech led many writers to believe that he was ready to leave the Republican Party. He tried to clarify his intentions with one journalist who wrote, "We all with one accord regret to see you go." Wanamaker, however, said that his purpose was not to leave the party, but to try to make it live up to its platform.[50]

During 1897, Wanamaker maintained a close relationship with the Business Men's League and often consulted with Blankenburg and with other leaders in the group. Wanamaker worked through a few friendly newspapers to spread the league's activities to other parts of Pennsylvania. With an election for governor coming up in 1898, Blankenburg and other friends urged Wanamaker to run against Senator Quay's candidate, William Stone. Wanamaker played the reluctant candidate. To a professor at Swarthmore, Wanamaker wrote, "I can only say I am greatly perplexed to find my duty and am quite averse to holding the office of Governor. Yet I am borne down by a conscience that insists upon doing a duty whether one likes it or not."[51]

The reformers followed through on their plan, nominating Wanamaker for governor on February 2, 1898. At a meeting of several hundred businessmen, the reformers urged Wanamaker to show that "the honest people of this State are in the majority and when once aroused, they will demonstrate their power in such a manner as was never shown before." After waiting three weeks to reply, Wanamaker accepted the nomination, writing that he had no desire to be governor, but, "I have really one purpose and that is, to afford a rallying point for men like yourself who wish to protest against ring rule." Personally, he felt "involved in a political contest going on in the State sacrificing myself utterly as a protest against machine government."[52]

Wanamaker's candidacy attracted national attention among nascent reformers who were beginning to organize against boss rule. A.K. McClure, editor of *The Philadelphia Times*, wrote, "You cannot be strong against Quay unless you show at the outset that you propose honest reform by honest methods and demand it imperiously not only of Quay but of your friends as well." McClure asked Wanamaker to support a movement to reform all politics. This movement was more than Wanamaker had undertaken. His was a crusade against an individual whom he pictured as a ruthless opponent who had strayed from the virtues of the American political system. Wanamaker did not support the larger movement for reform envisioned by people like McClure. He was disturbed by the damage such a reform movement might do to the traditional Republican Party.[53]

During his campaign for governor, Wanamaker made sixty-seven speeches in seventy-two days, attacking the excesses of the Quay machine. He declared, "The people are tired of it all, and are joining the forces to overthrow the usurpers of their rights." Charging that the machine had manipulated all patronage in Pennsylvania for its benefit, Wanamaker accused Quay of also using the banking system to benefit the machine. Five million dollars in state money was deposited in state banks interest-free, and banks receiving these funds were the largest contributors to the Republican Party. Wanamaker also charged that loose banking regulation led to the failure of People's Bank and the Guarantee Finance Company of Philadelphia. "Voters of Pennsylvania, are you dumb and are you blind?" he asked. "You will risk your life to defend your homes and your property from thieves at night, yet you applaud the robbers who by day take millions that belong to you."[54]

Stone got the Republican nomination at a convention in May, a few weeks after the war with Spain began, which may have helped Quay in maintaining the *status quo*. Although Wanamaker conceded the nomination just before the Republican meeting, he continued to give anti-Quay speeches around the state through the summer and fall. Although he resisted supporting either the Democratic ticket or a Prohibitionist candidate against Stone, Wanamaker sought to generate enough opposition to Quay to deny him renomination to the Senate when his term expired in January.

In all, Wanamaker gave 140 talks during the campaign, many to audiences of up to 10,000 and in the open. By the close of the campaign, he had traveled to all parts of the state, including central and western Pennsylvania, the heart of Quay territory. The merchant even reached out to groups that might be hostile to him because of his wealth. In Tioga County, a mining area, Wanamaker tried to allay the fears of the miners, who were probably the most anti-capitalistic group in the state. He told them, "I have become intensely interested in the relationship existing in Pennsylvania between capital and labor."[55]

Quay did not take the attacks sitting down. His supporters broke up anti-Quay meetings. At the Media courthouse, Quay supporters attempted to turn a Wanamaker speech into a debate, but Wanamaker refused. Pro-Quay newspapers accused Wanamaker of corruption and with prejudice in hiring. When Senator Penrose made an attack that Wanamaker considered libelous, he consulted with lawyers about suing Penrose, but reconsidered.[56]

By the end of the contest, Wanamaker could barely speak, and his voice never completely recovered from making so many speeches to so many audiences. The following year, Wanamaker summed up what he was trying to do: "I want to see the state start anew out of the wilderness of political corruption into a land of economy and justice, of hope and prosperity." For Wanamaker, and for many of his supporters, the fight against Quay became a crusade to rid the country of an evil and to restore it to its lost virtue. Wanamaker's efforts did not satisfy everyone. One newspaper editor argued that he embarrassed the reform elements, who had never counted him among their members. The editor claimed that Wanamaker was only running for governor to capture Penrose's Senate seat in a few years.[57]

While campaigning for governor, Wanamaker became involved in the military preparations for the Spanish-American War. At the start of the war in late April 1898, Wanamaker raised a regiment of 1,000 men that cost him $50,000 to equip. Since Wanamaker did not see action in the Civil War, he looked forward to fighting in the war with Spain. His ambition for high political office probably also played a part—Presidents Grant, Hayes, Garfield, Harrison, and McKinley had all been war veterans.[58]

Wanamaker's involvement with the military upset Mary who had been long disturbed by her husband's political career. She was constantly complaining about how badly the store looked with John continuously on the road. Now with the outbreak of war, she objected to how everybody expected an attack on Philadelphia by the Spanish fleet. "War is the all absorbing topic, it all has seemed so useless, that this great nation, with its 'Arbitration of Peace' should be at such business. It's sad beyond words when you think of what our men may suffer."[59]

Although the United States government gave Wanamaker's regiment official recognition, it was not called up, probably because McKinley did not want to turn one of his opponents into a war hero. After the war, Wanamaker's officers criticized him—they felt they had been cheated, and they demanded compensation.

After the election for governor, Wanamaker had mixed feelings about the future. He spoke bitterly of the campaign: "They [the people] have preferred the Quay brand of politics, and the wasteful extravagance and dishonesty at Harrisburg that we have had." Simultaneously, he worked to deny Quay re-election to a Senate seat by getting the Democrats and the anti-Quay Republicans in the legislature to work together. He defended this attempt at fusion, saying, "Republicanism is the best of all politics if it is faithfully adhered to upon the old lines of Lincoln, and Grant, and Garfield, but its interpretation by the Quays and others like them cannot be accepted."[61]

Although Quay received support from the Republican caucus, nineteen dissidents refused to attend, leaving him several votes shy of election. He also had five indictments against him growing out of alleged misuse of bank deposits, charges made during the campaign. Despite a serious illness, Wanamaker went to Harrisburg to campaign against Quay and to work out a compromise between the nineteen Republican dissenters and the Democrats. His strategy only partially succeeded. The full legislature rejected Quay, but deadlocked when the Republican minority and the Democrats each nominated their own candidate.[62]

In April, a court acquitted Quay of the banking charges. On the same day, to Wanamaker's dismay, the governor chose Quay for the Senate. "I am not discouraged," Wanamaker wrote to a political friend, "but troubled to think of the hard work that lies ahead."[63]

Wanamaker was not finished with Quay. He mounted a campaign to force the United States Senate to reject him. Before the beginning of the next congressional session on December 3, 1899, Wanamaker put together an anti-Quay advertisement signed by a number of prominent people in the state. Wanamaker wrote, "I regard this as religious work. So long as Quayism rules even Elders of our Churches, and Sunday School Superintendents are elected to the Legislature and are corralled by the Quay influence, nullifying the Church work." Wanamaker even convinced former President Harrison to use his influence to get the two senators from Indiana and the members of his administration who were in the Senate to vote against Quay's seating. In a surprising vote, with several Republicans joining the Democrats in the Senate, Quay was refused his Senate seat on the ground that his selection by the governor was illegal. The Senate took this action, removing a member who had served for eighteen years by a 33-31 vote, because Quay had become a political embarrassment for the Republicans. But for Quay, it was a temporary setback. In 1900, Quay was nominated by the Republicans to the still-vacant Senate seat.[64]

While campaigning against Quay, Wanamaker bought the *North American*, the oldest continuously operated paper in the United States. He paid $200,000 for the paper in 1899, purchasing it from Morton McMichael, who sold it to Wanamaker despite his ties to Senator Quay. To avoid the charges of conflict of interests, Wanamaker sold the paper to his son Tom, who ran it until his death in 1908, at which time the paper passed into Rodman's control. From 1899, the *North American* was the major reform paper in Philadelphia and one of the major Progressive journals in the country. Both Tom and Rodman tended to run the paper independently of their father, which sometimes led to conflict with him, as when they created a Sunday paper or when Rodman supported Teddy Roosevelt in 1912.[65]

Wanamaker had intended to abstain from politics during the 1900 campaign because of serious respiratory problems, which debilitated him during the summer. He was absent from work for four months, including a month visiting the Paris Exposition. But with Quay up for election, a presidential contest, and a race for mayor, Wanamaker decided to play a role. The chance to deal a blow to Quay led him to make a series of speeches around the state. These efforts prevented him from fully joining Blankenburg, who was trying to elect a reform mayor in Philadelphia, but he did contribute money to the campaign.[66]

While he maintained a low profile, Wanamaker donated money to the McKinley-Roosevelt national ticket. When Quay won election by one vote in the legislature for the remaining four years in the term and the reform campaign in the city failed, Wanamaker was desolate at seeing all his efforts fail. After Quay's return to the Senate, Wanamaker lost interest in politics. In reply to a letter from Congressman Joseph Throop, who was trying to put together a reform organization,

Wanamaker lamented his inability to defeat the machine: "[I] can only believe that some other person than myself is necessary to the organization which you so clearly define."[67]

In October 1901, Wanamaker found himself at the center of another controversy. The city Republican Party distributed a letter written by Wanamaker to a woman. In the letter, he invited himself up to her apartment at a late evening hour. Wanamaker denied any romantic involvement. The woman was the widow of an employee, and according to Wanamaker, he paid a visit to comfort her.[68]

While combating this slur on his reputation, Wanamaker also nearly lost his son Rodman to appendicitis. The dual strain drove him from politics for a number of years. In December 1901, he suddenly left for Europe during the busy season, leaving Tom, Rodman, and Robert Ogden in charge of the stores. When he arrived in Europe, he went to Italy and then took a boat through the Suez Canal and to India. He spent the better part of six months on this arduous journey. He did not inform Mary Wanamaker of his destination until at sea. In India, he established several missionary centers, perhaps as penance for his embarrassment.[69]

When he returned to the United States, Wanamaker made a conscious effort to refrain from politics. In late 1902 while ill, he took a retrospective glance at the political battles of the previous four or five years. He informed some of his colleagues of his desire to leave politics behind, for he believed that "some other leadership might be more successful."[70]

From 1901 until 1912, Wanamaker kept a comparatively low profile in politics, although he supported several anti-machine candidates for mayor of Philadelphia. Wanamaker remained alienated from the leaders of the Republican Party. The murder of McKinley in 1901 and the subsequent death of Matthew Quay from a heart attack in 1904 did not bring Wanamaker out of the political wilderness. Although he was not close to Theodore Roosevelt, Wanamaker supported him against Judge Parker, the Democratic candidate. Despite Wanamaker's support, the president gave control of patronage to Boies Penrose, who inherited the Quay machine and held power in the state until the early 1920s.[71]

Wanamaker's entrance into elected politics had been costly. He never achieved his goal of being elected to the United States Senate, and his reputation as a Christian businessman had been tarnished by charges of bribing legislators. He had entered politics in order to improve civic affairs, but he had become deeply ambitious and had lost his balance through his personal vendetta against Quay.

At the same time that Wanamaker's crusade against Matthew Quay went down to defeat, the country was in the midst of its worst depression. This economic collapse left Wanamaker with severe business problems at a time of his greatest distraction. But the depression also provided him with an opportunity to expand his business operations and fulfill a business dream.

CHAPTER FIVE

Merchant Prince

1890-1902

*D*espite Wanamaker's political career and the financial panic, the 1890s were important years for the Wanamaker concept of retailing. His ideas about retailing had largely matured by the time he left for Washington, so Wanamaker and his partners spent these years implementing the ideas, drawing ever-larger numbers of people into his store. Because these were hard times for most store owners, Wanamaker needed every trick he had developed in order to survive. When the depression ended after 1897, he was in a position to take advantage of the new prosperity. Rather than retrench because of financial panic, Wanamaker made one of the most audacious moves of his career. He expanded into New York City, buying the A.T. Stewart store, which had failed during the depression.

Although Wanamaker turned 60 in 1898, he retained his high energy level and ability to remain active in different spheres. His major physical disability as he approached old age was a growing sensitivity to colds, which left him unable to speak for weeks at a time. His arduous campaign speaking tour in 1898 may have set off his problems, but his illness seemed to go back to a much earlier time, perhaps even to his respiratory difficulties in the late 1850s. Wanamaker sought relief in vacations at the shore, often at Atlantic City or Cape May. He also used a European vacation as a way to break away from Philadelphia.[1]

In the 1890s, the Wanamakers lived the lifestyle of the American commercial aristocracy, with homes in Philadelphia, in Cheltenham Township (a Philadelphia suburb), in Cape May on the New Jersey shore, and in Paris. The family's suburban residence, Lindenhurst, about 10 miles north of the store, was a fifty-room house located on seventy-seven acres. Wanamaker built his house on farmland purchased in the early 1880s. Besides the main house, Wanamaker built an adjoining art gallery which housed 800 paintings worth several million dollars, a stable with high-price horses, and Mary's pride, a beautiful garden that was featured in *House Beautiful Magazine*. The estate was near a railroad and Old York Road, a major road tying Philadelphia to New York City. Wanamaker's sons and his son-in-law Barclay Warburton also bought houses in the area. Although isolated from Philadelphia, Wanamaker had a constant stream of visitors during the summer months, some of whom remained several days or more.[2]

Wanamaker used the house from April through October, when he moved to his Philadelphia home. In 1892, Wanamaker bought a property at 2020 Walnut Street at a sheriff sale for $30,000. On the site near Rittenhouse Square, the longtime residential neighborhood for the elite in the city, Wanamaker built one of Philadelphia's largest urban mansions. This house allowed Wanamaker to maintain his strong ties to the Philadelphia community. Members of Bethany Church, evangelical ministers, political friends, and business associates visited the house frequently.[3]

Wanamaker traveled often to the spa at the Congress Hall in Saratoga Springs, New York, and to spas in Europe. Many times, he traveled alone, leaving his family for up to six months. During the summer months, Mary Wanamaker vacationed in Europe or in the New England mountains with one or both of her daughters.[4]

Despite these separations, Wanamaker took a Victorian view of family life, writing, "The home makes or unmakes the character of each member of the family—it was the first church and the father was the first priest. Whoever makes the homes of the people, makes the history of the nation." He always expressed a good deal of sentiment toward his wife, writing to her after one extended separation, "Blessing on you for never losing the way yourself & for always helping me along the rising path."[5]

Observers described Mary as composed and quiet. In 1889 she was 52 years old, but looked much younger because she had little grey hair. She was quite plump, but attractive. She was five foot four inches, with brown hair and blue eyes. Her clothing was of the richest materials, but both on the street and at home she wore drab colors: grays, blacks, and dark blues. She also wore only one type of shoe, a leather boot with a modest heel. She was much adored by her two boys. Tom in 1889 was 27 and Rodman 25, Minnie and Lillie were 20 and 18. Rodman had the only grandchild called Nina, named for her mother.[6]

Although Mary usually kept a hands-off policy regarding the store, she occasionally played a role through John or one of her two sons. At times employees, particularly women, wrote to her to ask for help with a problem they had in the store. From time to time, after walking around the Philadelphia store, she urged changing some personnel or suggested rearranging counters or merchandise to increase business.[7]

During the 1890s, Wanamaker turned over a large part of the Philadelphia store's operations to his oldest son, Thomas Brown Wanamaker. When John was out of town, particularly during his years in Washington and during his political campaigns, Tom along with Robert Ogden ran the store. Nevertheless, John maintained tight control over decisions. But as he approached 60 and saw his friends die, Wanamaker thought increasingly about turning his assets over to his two sons. "The years of us old fellows are creeping on," he wrote to his son Rodman in 1898. "We must give place to the younger generation."[8]

Rodman Wanamaker, who graduated from Princeton in 1886, did various jobs at the department store before becoming manager of the woman's clothing department. But in 1888, he touched off a family crisis by deciding he did not want to remain at the store. To prevent the problem from ruining Rodman's relationship with his father, Mary persuaded John to send Rodman to Paris as the resident buyer. Rodman's father-in-law had emigrated from France, so Rodman's wife, Fernada Henry, easily fit into the social scene. Rodman, who spoke French, had a strong sense of merchandising and was a creative manager of the Paris operation.[9]

Rodman's arrival greatly broadened Wanamaker's European presence. John sent his managers from the glove, dress, and jewelry departments over to be trained by Rodman in current fashions and to buy merchandise. Rodman, who visited such major stores in Europe as Bon Marché, became the idea man for the Philadelphia store. He believed that "the real task of winning people to appreciate fine merchandise and avoid the cheap and gaudy lay in the education of buyers."[10]

The two surviving daughters of Wanamaker were Minnie Wanamaker Warburton and Elizabeth Wanamaker MacLeod (one daughter died at birth and another, Mary, died when she was five years old). Although active in some of Wanamaker's religious activities, they were not involved in the store. From their earliest days, both women were also socially active, and they married into prominent families. Elizabeth's husband, Barclay, owned the Philadelphia *Record*, giving John an important newspaper connection that increased after he purchased the *North American*.[11]

Like other wealthy Philadelphians, John Wanamaker had many financial interests generally tied to the growth of the city. He developed a long-term commitment to the Reading Railroad, which had a terminal across from his store, and at one point he considered taking on its presidency. Wanamaker was responsible for extending the West Jersey Railroad from the Delaware River in New Jersey to Cape May Point, where he held property. He also had an ongoing interest in Philadelphia real estate, constantly buying and selling property, particularly in the central part of the city.[12]

As with his business interests, most of Wanamaker's philanthropy had a Philadelphia accent. As a leading figure in Philadelphia, Wanamaker was constantly solicited to contribute to individuals and charities. Usually turning down private requests for charity, Wanamaker concentrated his donations on charities that had their greatest impact on the city. For Wanamaker, money spent in Philadelphia contributed to his goal of building the community closest to him, the community that had been responsible for his wealth. In this respect, Wanamaker's philanthropy was similar to that of other retailers, like the Straus family in New York and Marshall Field in Chicago, who gave to local institutions. Wanamaker contributed money to the University of Pennsylvania in Philadelphia to support its archeological activities. With these contributions, Wanamaker helped make Philadelphia a major center of archeological research in the United States and helped develop a museum that attracted thousands of visitors to the city.[13]

Although Bethany remained the centerpiece of Wanamaker's philanthropic work, he increasingly supported Protestant overseas missions, particularly in India, where he created missions in Allahabad and Calcutta. Wanamaker wanted to bring news about the "Lord's coming" through missionary work. "The heathen cannot receive the Gospel," he said, "until it is brought to them in some way." In Philadelphia, Wanamaker created the Friendly Inn, a refuge for homeless men. Run by the Rev. Thomas Horney, the Inn housed hundreds of men per week, providing food and shelter.[14]

Although Wanamaker was almost hyperactive in rushing between his political, religious, and philanthropic activities, the store required a good deal of attention while he was in Washington. The Panic of 1893 ushered in a long depression with many business failures and high unemployment. Wanamaker sensed the difficult economic situation after leaving the cabinet. Writing Rodman, he warned that before good times returned there would be "a general liquidation." By August 1893, business in the country was off 25 percent from 1892. With many of Philadelphia's factories closed, Wanamaker felt the worst was yet to come. Although he continued to make small dress purchases in Paris, Wanamaker was cautious in spending for the Christmas season and even had difficulty paying a $50,000 city tax bill. Christmas season in 1893 was quite poor. He did better than his rivals, but low sales forced him to reduce spring orders by 50 percent.[15]

By 1896, at the height of the downturn, Wanamaker had 100 applicants for every job he advertised. As is common with modern economic downturns, this depression was accompanied by much labor and political upheaval. Strikes were common and farmers organized a powerful political movement that challenged both political parties. Money was extremely tight, and Wanamaker found it difficult to borrow except for short terms and at high rates.[16]

The depression created severe problems for Wanamaker but provided opportunities as well. From 1893 until 1898, business was flat. Since he served an upper-middle-class clientele, however, the effects were less disastrous for him than for other merchants in the city. Wanamaker's total sales declined from $13,163,553 in 1892, to $12,981,344 in

1893, and $12,926,182 in 1894. By 1895, sales rebounded to $13,639,097, although a December transit strike that deterred many women from shopping downtown hurt business. In 1896 and 1897, however, Wanamaker's Philadelphia business continued to have problems. In early 1897, Wanamaker drew $125,000 from his personal account in order to cover his unpaid Christmas bills.[17]

Poor economic conditions resulted in intensified competition. Strawbridge & Clothier, Wanamaker's chief rival for the carriage trade, hired an agent to reside in Paris. To counter this new competition, Wanamaker upgraded the store, relying upon Rodman to pick up ideas in Paris. Rodman's innovations included the introduction of escalators, which he first saw in a Paris department store. Wanamaker also faced increased competition from Gimbel's, whose Philadelphia store generally sold a merchandise line priced below Wanamaker's. "The Gimbels are audacious and unscrupulous as copyists & bidders for our best people," Wanamaker wrote to Rodman.[18]

In early 1897, the city's business district suffered another serious loss when a fire swept along Market Street, wiping out many small stores and burning part of the facade of Wanamaker's. For Wanamaker, it could have been worse because the merchant had canceled all his insurance, believing the companies had overcharged him. Wanamaker attributed the little damage done to his store to the "unseen hand that came to the rescue."[19]

To cope with the economic problems, he closed his men's store at 818 Chestnut Street after twenty-eight years of ownership. This expedient resulted in layoffs of employees, some of whom had worked for him for many years. Although he tried to find work for them, he held that he had no obligation to place a worker. To one laid off worker, he wrote: "While long time association in business increases confidence and respect, it does not always form a foundation for either increased salary or a continuation of an old salary."[20]

Wanamaker's greatest opportunity of the depression came from the failure of the Alexander T. Stewart Company in New York City. The Stewart store, occupying the block between Astor Place and Broadway and Ninth and Tenth Streets, was built in 1863 at a cost of $3 million. When Stewart died in 1876, his business, including several stores and a wholesale business, went to his executor, Judge Henry Hilton, and

Stewart's partner, William Libbey, who played a very large role in Wanamaker's career. Stewart's business went through much turmoil during the next twenty years and often seemed on the verge of a dissolution. The depression of 1893 left Hilton unable to repay a $1 million loan, forcing his failure in August 1896. At bankruptcy time, the Astor Place store had a value of about $700,000.[21]

The Astor Place store, constructed of cast iron inside and out, had steam heating and steam-operated elevators. A great chandelier lit by gas but ignited by electricity graced the interior. Many considered it the most beautiful store in the world.

Wanamaker was very much influenced by Stewart. He wrote a letter to William Libbey in 1876 expressing his sadness at Stewart's death, and he assembled a scrapbook containing newspaper stories about him. Wanamaker often acknowledged Stewart as the inspiration for his own success. His sentiment toward the store where modern retailing began may have led Wanamaker to purchase it. With two sons, the Philadelphian also saw a second store as an easy way to divide his estate. Finally, Wanamaker was very eager to keep his leadership in retailing. New York was the retailing capital of the United States; Wanamaker may not have been satisfied with a grand reputation in Philadelphia, the third city in the country.[22]

When the store became available in August 1896, there were many reasons not to buy. The economy was still quite bad, the country was in the middle of one of its most crucial elections since the Civil War, and Wanamaker was in the thick of his campaign for the Senate. But Wanamaker seized the opportunity to buy Stewart's, writing to Rodman, "The Hilton failure is the excitement and we can get the place now if we want it and could raise the money. It is a big undertaking."[23]

The New York City venture disturbed Mary Wanamaker. She felt the Philadelphia store was falling apart and did not have a complete stock. She was not sure how John, Tom, and Ogden could manage the new operation and maintain the old one. "I really feel that I am quite in the business, as I talk to one & the other. This splendid *business!* but it wants encouragement," she wrote to her son Rodman.[24]

Despite Mary's opposition, Wanamaker clinched the deal for the Stewart store in the middle of October 1896. Wanamaker envisioned the New York store as a joint venture between Robert C. Ogden and his son Rodman. He urged Rodman to return from Paris to take over. "I want your help here in the New York business & want it badly," he wrote to his son. "I feel we are to use our Paris office more than ever but we shall not need any Paris office at all if we cannot organize and drive our business immensely & well both in NY and here." Several years elapsed, however, before Rodman returned to the country, and almost a decade passed before he took over the New York store. Ogden, who had spent twenty years in New York as a retailer, took primary responsibility for putting the New York store together, arranging its displays and hiring personnel. Until Ogden's retirement in 1908, Wanamaker's in New York remained under his control.[25]

The New York Times greeted Wanamaker's opening in New York on November 16 enthusiastically, editorializing that "the revival of this great business meant work for factories that would have otherwise be shut down; . . . and it means in the face of all the grumblings about hard times there has been one man so well convinced of the renewal of prosperity that he takes unto himself a duplicate business." Although favorable to Wanamaker because he had opened an empty landmark, New York critics were not impressed with his efforts to blitz the New York papers with advertisements. Wanamaker lacked experience in this market. One reporter wrote, "The Wanamaker advertisements in the New York papers look just a bit out of place as yet. We are not able to shake off the curious impression that we have picked up, by mistake, one of the Philadelphia dailies."[26]

The first months of Wanamaker's adventure in New York were unsuccessful. At first, the store was packed with former Stewart's customers and persons drawn by curiosity, but a boom in New York never materialized. In early December, the New York store made only $25,000 a day, a sum much lower than the Philadelphia Wanamaker's. The Christmas season proved a distinct disappointment. "Business is severely cut by something and nobody knows what." Wanamaker wrote to Rodman, "If all were not complaining I should be more worried."[27]

Between the falling business and political problems, Wanamaker wore himself out and developed a very bad cold, which put him on his back for most of December. Some of his political friends visited him at his house. He was in such bad shape that he had to bypass the Christmas dinner at Tom's home, Meadowbrook.

By the end of the Christmas season, however, Robert Ogden was more pleased with the New York results. He felt the store needed a shakedown period to weed out incompetent staff, redesign the building's layout, stock new merchandise, and build the best delivery system in the city. To control personnel, Wanamaker moved his Philadelphia manager, William Daggett, to New York. He also upgraded the store's first floor, giving it a more artistic appearance. As a result, business picked up in 1897. Beginning with January sales of $394,180, business rose to $1,330,520 in December, with total receipts for the whole year of $7,426,567, about one-half Philadelphia's results. With an overhead similar to Philadelphia, the New York store lost money.[28]

Ogden and Thomas Wanamaker were full partners at this time, and Wanamaker generally consulted with them on most major issues. In 1898, with Wanamaker involved in politics for the better part of the year, the New York operation was almost completely in the hands of Robert C. Ogden. Tom handled the Philadelphia store.[29]

At the top of the managerial pyramid, under the partners, were two managers who controlled the clerical and accounting ends of the business. In 1895 the two senior employees in Philadelphia were William Daggett and William Brewer, but Daggett's move to New York left Brewer as the manager of the store. Brewer, who had spent his whole career in Wanamaker's employ, did all the hiring except persons directly employed by a buyer. Firing of employees also rested with Brewer or with the heads of departments. Wanamaker's managerial staff also included George Sidebottom as chief financial officer for both stores and William L. Nevin, Wanamaker's personal lawyer, who assumed responsibilities in the store below the partners.[30]

The key persons below management were the buyers, who had charge of purchasing for their departments and had control over all other departmental matters, including the hiring and firing of employees. Wanamaker deferred to them to maintain discipline within their departments. He also counted upon the buyers to control the stock and held them responsible for overbuying. To Wanamaker, control of inventory was the most important act in the life of a merchant: "It seems to me so childish to be loading up stuff that eats up capital in interest and loses its bloom and value and requires scientific surgery to cure."[31]

Buyers were often known outside the store through their active participation in national trade associations and in city business groups. Wanamaker's organization resembled many of his competitors. Generally, buyers were the central figures in the great department stores at the end of the nineteenth century. These giant emporiums resembled a collection of small specialty shops, controlled by a boss who bought the goods, set up the displays, and ran the sales force.[32]

Perfection of this organization allowed the Wanamaker business empire to operate at a high level during the 1890s. Through the leadership of Thomas in Philadelphia, Ogden in New York, and Rodman in Paris, backed by the 150 or so buyers, managers, and advertising directors, the Wanamaker operation was innovative and competitive. Despite the depression and the distraction of Wanamaker's political campaigning, the stores in the 1890s perfected Victorian merchandising techniques. Once recovery began after 1897, the two stores along with their rivals in Philadelphia and New York held a dominant position in retailing which they retained until the next great depression, in the 1930s.

At the time Wanamaker purchased the New York store in 1896, Bon Marché in Paris was the largest store in the world, with sales greater than Wanamaker's. In 1898, the two Wanamaker stores eclipsed the venerable French house. Together, the Wanamaker stores held $6,850,000 worth of merchandise, making them at least by composite the largest world emporium. Wanamaker employed 4,000 to 5,000 workers in Philadelphia, and daily sales in the Quaker City during the Christmas season exceeded $100,000. Yearly Philadelphia receipts in 1900 were $16,824,000, increasing to $17,332,620 in 1901. By comparison, in 1911 the eleven largest Paris *grand magasins* together only employed 11,000 clerks or an average of nine hundred per store.[33]

Wanamaker meant to have his Philadelphia store act as an anchor for the city's business center. Individuals, particularly women, would be drawn into the metropolis, would mingle with other consumers, and would taste the myriad delicacies of the city. They would encounter the finest merchandise, the finest art, and the best music which civilization had to offer. While in the store with its shops and restaurants, they would receive an education in a highly sophisticated ambiance. After such exposures, visitors to Wanamaker's would develop newly exalted tastes that they would carry over to their homes, changing the lives of not only themselves, but of their husbands and children as well. To Wanamaker, "The results of this are felt in the artistic assemblage and display of finer kinds of merchandise brought from foreign parts and its distribution into thousands of American homes to the betterment of taste, and refinement in appreciation of the beautiful."[34]

By 1896, Wanamaker's early dream of a large emporium which sold everything was fulfilled. He wrote, "This is an aggregation of large stores. We have a book store, for instance, which is as large and complete as any one in the country. We aim to keep everything that is published. We have one of the largest shoe stores in the city. It is the same with clothing and other things." For Wanamaker this collection of stores differentiated him from most of his rivals, who had departments devoted to many types of consumer goods but lacked a comprehensive merchandise display. He believed that only Marshall Field in Chicago had created a similar type of store.[35]

Besides being a consumer's paradise, Wanamaker's had other facilities which turned it into a center for the life of many ordinary Philadelphians. With heating in the winter and large steam-operated fans in the summer, the store became a refuge. Philadelphians could escape their cold winter houses without central heating and hot summer homes without cooling systems. By the middle of the 1890s, Wanamaker's had become an important tourist attraction, drawing suburbanites, rural residents, and out-of-town visitors. One newspaperman in Chester, Pennsylvania, urged his readers to journey to the store: "There is every arrangement made for the country visitor, facilities that tend to make the day one of entire pleasure and the item of fatigue a minimum quality." For the non-urban shopper, escaping from the imagined dangerous city streets into the safety of the store was important. The store had "a certain air of comfort that makes the stranger within the gates quite at home," the Chester newspaper reported. The visitor was given a place to rest, to put the baby to sleep, to write a letter, and to get rid of packages. Finally, "when luncheon time arrives a spacious dining room answers all the requirements necessary at that hour." Further romanticizing, the Chester newspaperman concluded, "The Philadelphia dweller has no idea what a delightful place Wanamaker's must seem to those who come long distances to secure those benefits."[36]

For Wanamaker, the store was more than a place to sell merchandise. Although Philadelphians wandering through the store for one of its events, enthralled by the displays of merchandise, might become his customers, Wanamaker saw the Grand Depot as the center of civic life for the city. It was an educational institution, a center of patriotic festivals, and an entertainment palace. Wanamaker compared it to such other Philadelphia educational centers as the Franklin Institute and the Centennial Fair, as each made an "appeal to the intelligence" and made it "with such directness as to be appreciable even by young minds."[37] In the late nineteenth century there was a decline in the large-scale civic street activities which characterized the American city before the Civil War. For Philadelphians, Wanamaker reconstructed these ceremonies inside the store.

Simultaneously, the store would further the "education" of employees and customers alike, expanding their awareness of the fine arts and the greater world. In accomplishing this civic vision, Wanamaker was the constant impresario, bustling to make it all happen with fanfare and flair. Wanamaker created elaborate programs for patriotic holidays, particularly Lincoln's Birthday. Other events at almost every time of the year complemented these days. People came to hear lectures by eminent men of science and letters, see movies, or tour industrial exhibitions. With frequent exhibitions, the store at times took on the look of a museum. Individuals who might have been intimidated by a museum got a view of culture at Wanamaker's. Displays depicted the signing of the Constitution, an Indian village, Napoleon's life, early shoemaking, a celebration of the French Revolution, and the visit of the Czar to Paris. Visitors to the store also saw moving pictures and photographs of the funeral of Edward VII, films showing Paris fashions, the first exhibit of radium in the United States, salon paintings every year from Paris, and the largest collection of tapestries ever displayed in an American store.[38]

Using the store as a museum was Wanamaker's way of drawing people into his consumer palace. Once inside, they had the opportunity to buy goods from all parts of the world. Wanamaker portrayed these products as instant keys to a place in the new middle-class society. By promoting both older and newer classes of merchandise, Wanamaker helped to define the tastes of the new consumer. Although the more affluent members of Philadelphia society were the targets of these displays, everyone had the privilege of walking into his public space. Many people who could not afford to buy from Wanamaker took advantage of his festivals and civic celebrations. In the process, they saw new lines of consumer goods.

For various complex reasons, middle-class Americans sought release from a "stultifying" Victorian code of morality that reinforced a rigid personality geared to self-control. They began to find various forms of intense experience more satisfying, more continuous with an increasingly-felt fluid sense of self. These long-term changes in America were created partially by rising levels of income for the middle classes, which helped trigger a desire to spend money on consumer goods previously considered luxuries. At the same time, as historian Jackson Lears has shown, manufacturers with surplus goods created demand with advertising that used subtle messages tying consumer goods to better health and a sense of psychological well-being. Women, who did much of the buying, were particularly manipulated by these advertisers into believing that they would gain greater independence and fulfillment through their purchases.[39]

Part of the excitement of department stores was that they began to respond to this powerful impulse by giving people what they "needed." Materialism, reinforced by conspicuous consumption and image manipulation, was the unintended consequence of sincere actions deemed beneficial to all. Wanamaker believed he was providing Americans with the means to live fuller, more satisfying lives. Wanamaker wrote that the store had a special place in the city, "smoothing the paths of commerce, sowing the seeds of courtesy and kindliness in trade, and doing its best with all its might for the honor of the city and the welfare of the land." He was involved in a vast, impersonal process of change. He may have found ways to satisfy his own and his customers' psychological needs in his retailing innovations. He was not so much in command of his aspirations and impulses, let alone those of his customers, that he could fully comprehend and cynically manipulate these aspirations and impulses to gain profits.[40]

One new product in the 1890s that played to consumer dreams and aspirations was the bicycle, the first item to draw mass consumer attention as the depression ended in the middle of 1897. Although bicycles came in all prices, Wanamaker sold only higher-price models, ranging from about $75 to over $100. Concerned about his liability for repairs and accidents caused by inferior quality, Wanamaker discovered that even his more expensive vehicles generated large numbers of complaints because of mechanical failure.[41]

Wanamaker also had trouble with manufacturers, such as the Humbar Company, who often dealt shabbily with their dealers. To get quality bikes, Wanamaker reached agreements with the manufacturer of his most expensive line to sell its bikes as an exclusive agent. Even after agreeing to advertise the product, he often found his contract undermined by agents who had sold the bicycles to one of his rivals. On all the contracts, Wanamaker conflicted with small agencies that also had been given the right to sell this new consumer delight. Like his earlier battle with booksellers, Wanamaker pleaded his case as a large seller against the agent: "The public is willing to pay a fair price for any article, and they know we treat them fairly, and this gives us a large outlet that no manufacturer can, in interest to himself, close his eyes upon."[42]

Because of the difficulty of dealing with these manufacturers, Wanamaker began selling bikes under his own label, "Road Flyer," allowing him to buy from any manufacturer who was willing to meet his specifications. Since he guaranteed all the goods in the store, he did not have to worry about manufacturers' warranties or about name brand advertising.[43]

In Wanamaker's efforts at enhancing Philadelphia's middle-class culture, nothing was more important than women's fashions. Although the art exhibits and concerts attracted substantial audiences, the Paris fashion shows were the major cultural and retailing events in the spring and the fall seasons. Wanamaker advertised that these shows had as their purpose "to guide women to dress better, more simply, more graciously, to make themselves more attractive by wearing well-bred clothes that express them . . . to make their own the Frenchwoman's century-old fascination and daintiness of dress."[44]

France had long been the fashion center of Europe, setting trends for the rest of the continent, even for England and Germany, which were ahead of France in technology. Wanamaker's had established a Paris connection as early as 1879, when one staff member went there as resident buyer. Soon after that, Wanamaker opened a large office to buy French goods. With Rodman Wanamaker as the head of this division, buyers from both stores attended the fashion shows in Paris, keeping on good terms with local designers. Once the French developed a fashion theme for the year, Wanamaker had his buyers bring it home to Philadelphia and New York. Wanamaker's was the first American department store to follow this practice. The fashion theme became the motif not only for the dress shows but for the fall season in the store as well. One year the Second French Empire became the motif not only for the major fashion exhibit but also for an art exhibit. In other years, the fashion themes were Egypt and then Greece. Another year, Wanamaker held the "*Fete de Paris*," an event that celebrated the Napoleonic Era and featured a gown worn by Josephine and "mantles and hats that reflected the militarism of the Emperor," according to a Wanamaker advertisement.[45]

Art was also an important part of the middle-class ambiance at the store. Wanamaker wrote that "Art goes hand-in-hand with commerce." He featured art supplies for consumers engaged in producing their own art and displays of decorative art for the new collector class. As with fashion, the merchant's ties to Paris, the art capital of the world, were important. In the 1890s both Rodman and John frequented the Paris salons, spending large sums of money on artwork for sale at the two stores. Between 1898 and 1900 they brought 600 paintings to the United States. Rodman even set up the American Art Academy in Paris to provide a place for the training of young American artists who had already shown promise. It provided classrooms, social facilities, and scholarships for these students and for many years became the home for aspiring artists from the United States. The academy helped give the Wanamakers an important connection with the French art community.[46]

Although most of his French paintings were traditional nineteenth-century art, Wanamaker bought modern art as well. As would be expected, much of the art and many of the artifacts displayed in the store were either religious or patriotic. The pictures that received the most publicity were paintings by Michael Munkacsy, a Hungarian artist. Wanamaker bought his "Christ Before Pilate" and "Christ on Calvary," exhibiting them in the store before starting a tour of the United States.[47]

In a sense, art for Wanamaker meant more than an art department or an exhibition of fine paintings. Everything in the store was art. The merchandise on the counters and the goods displayed in the windows were arranged according to the latest artistic rules. Wanamaker wrote, "The results of this are felt in the artistic assemblage and display of the finer kind of merchandise brought from foreign parts and its distribution into thousands of American homes, to the betterment of taste, and refinement in appreciation of the beautiful."[48]

Music also dominated the department store, which Wanamaker often turned into a public performing hall. Wanamaker claimed that the musical performances at the store were part of his effort to return a part of his profit to his fellow citizens. He believed that his two bands, composed of employees of the store, performing at many of Philadelphia's patriotic functions benefitted the city as a whole.[49]

Wanamaker's concerts were the backdrops for one of the largest musical retailing enterprises in the United States. In 1899, Wanamaker opened the first department store piano shop. Becoming the largest vendor of pianos in the world, Wanamaker introduced a time payment system for his pianos, making the instruments affordable. Wanamaker advertised the idea that pianos were a necessity for middle-class homes. He sold music's virtues as a basic part of the education of children, particularly girls. Wanamaker wrote, "It is fair to treat of the Wanamaker Piano Stores under the heading of EDUCATION—for they are vital forces in the musical and educational uplift of the world."[50]

For Wanamaker, the piano he received as a wedding gift had been his symbolic uplifting into the solid middle class. Piano playing became symbolic for millions of other urban dwellers. Especially for women, pianos became important parts of their new culture. Family and friends gathered around while songs were played on the piano. The place of the piano was as central to middle-class homes at the end of the nineteenth century as the television set became in the late twentieth century.[51]

Merchandising was just one prop upon which Wanamaker's retailing acumen rested. Advertising was another. As a founder of modern retailing, Wanamaker recognized the importance of advertising to his success. From April 1861, when he took the profits from his first sale to advertise in the *Philadelphia Ledger,* until his death, the Philadelphia merchant paid great attention to the image he projected to the region's consumers. The store, rather than individual merchandise, was the centerpiece of Wanamaker's advertising. Wanamaker's ads made individuals think about the environment that they were entering. The department store was the center of a new urban space created by Wanamaker and his competitors in the nineteenth century.

Wanamaker used his advertising to create the image of an honest merchant whose word could be trusted. To one customer, he offered to give $100 to the poor children of the customer's town if he could present evidence of a deception in a purchase. "I am just as particular about an advertisement as the Pennsylvania Railroad Company is to run its trains on schedule," he wrote. To one of his directors of advertising, he urged, "Your sole business as a writer of our advertising is to find out the truth regarding the merchandise and to tell it in plain words and as briefly as you can." In this respect, Wanamaker became a crusader for better advertising as a means of uplifting the public's taste.[52]

This technique won applause from many professionals in the advertising field. S.S. McClure, a Philadelphia editor who went on to fame as a crusading Progressive journalist, wrote, "Mr. Wanamaker is the best advertiser in the world. He is the best advertiser because he is an honest man."[53]

Although the major part of Wanamaker's advertising budget was spent on newspapers, he published an array of catalogues and other materials that he sent directly to his customers. A 140-page fashion magazine sent throughout the United States was published twice a year. He also published a book catalog listing 8,000 titles and *Everybody's Journal,* which contained advice, fashion articles, and product advertisements and was distributed free in the store.[54]

In 1890, Wanamaker spent over a quarter-million dollars on newspaper advertising. His contract with the *Philadelphia Record* gave him one full page per day, except Sunday, for $100,000 per year. Because advertising was such a large expense, Wanamaker constantly negotiated for the best rate possible. Recognizing the segmented character of the city, Wanamaker shifted his advertisements to papers his customers read to gain the most from his spending. He abandoned one paper whose readers lived in the Kensington section of Philadelphia and never shopped downtown.[55]

Throughout his career, Wanamaker wrote and edited advertisements, and even when his staff became quite large, he took time to personally supervise the work of the advertisement department. Although his advertising manager would often correct his grammar, Wanamaker had a unique style that other retailers around the country copied. Whether written by himself or by others, Wanamaker advertisements were long-winded and folksy. They tended to be more like heart-to-heart talks than the down-to-business advertisements used by most of his rivals. This type of advertisement proved to be successful even in New York City, where many of its detractors thought it would fail.[56]

Sometimes these down-to-earth advertisements drew unexpected criticism. In one piece, Wanamaker announced that he strictly adhered to the one-price system, eliminating the antiquated practice of having the customer "Jewing down a price." When Jewish leaders criticized the ad, Wanamaker responded that he had no intention of attacking the Jewish race. He said he had employed Jews for many years and had made a deliberate effort to hire Jews for the New York store, "showing I had no sympathy with the old regime there." Stewart had made it a practice not to hire Jews for his stores and had owned a hotel in Saratoga that excluded Jewish guests.[57]

With high-volume advertisements from department stores, the major newspapers in Philadelphia grew and their circulations increased. The papers were sometimes accused of doing the political bidding of their advertisers. Wanamaker broke with the *Record* for several years in the mid-1890s, after the paper's management did not support his political campaigns. After leaving the *Record*, Wanamaker advertised in four other Philadelphia dailies—the *Ledger*, the *Press*, the *North American*, and the *Times*, which also supported him politically. In 1899, Ogden, disgruntled with editorials in the *New York Evening News*, suggested dropping all Wanamaker's advertising from the paper. But Wanamaker feared the paper would make political capital from such a move. Instead, he took away some advertising to warn the editors that they did not have as close a relationship as before, giving them cause for alarm, but not cause to complain. In an early 1900s New York state campaign, the Democratic Party candidate for governor attacked department stores, including Wanamaker's, as monopolies which endangered the well-being of consumers, competitors, and the female clerks who worked in these stores. The New York metropolitan newspapers almost universally came to the defense of these stores who had largely supplied them with the better part of their revenue for the previous twenty years.[58]

Although Wanamaker's merchandising and advertising successes were the major factors in his retailing rise, his ability to hire and train his employees gave him the edge over his rivals. In 1896, the Wanamaker store in Philadelphia was one of the largest employers in the city, averaging 3,450 workers during the year and 5,452 during the Christmas season. The store employed as many women as men, and the workers included 233 boys, who averaged 14¼ years of age, and 52 girls, who averaged 15 years of age. The men had an average age of 30, while the women's average age was 25. Wanamaker estimated his weekly payroll at $34,500 and his annual yearly payroll at $1,794,000, meaning that his workers averaged about $10 per week. The lowest-paid person in the store was the young boy or girl who ran errands and normally made $4 per week but might make $6 after a training period. Wages for buyers, for heads of advertising, or for other top managers often exceeded $20,000 per year.[59]

Wanamaker's salary schedule was competitive with other retailers and equal to industrial work. Ten dollars per week or $520 per year was the base wage for an unskilled male worker. Great inequities existed in this salary range. Despite Wanamaker's public statements that the $4- or $6-a-week jobs were held by boys, grown men often worked at these jobs. One complained about his low salary for carrying bundles through the store. Wanamaker said that men sometimes worked at these jobs when nothing else was available.[60]

Women workers often had the same problem. Wanamaker assumed that his most poorly paid female employees, the cashiers who earned $6 per week, lived at home. For those who rented rooms at boarding houses that charged from $3 to $5 per week, not much remained. But some women had to take these positions, despite the low pay.[61]

Most of Wanamaker's employees were American-born and Protestant. He hired salespersons only if they spoke English as their native language. Although Wanamaker contended that he accepted individuals of all creeds and religions, many of his employees were either from Bethany or had recommendations from a minister. A few Jews worked in the store, but almost no Italians or Southeastern Europeans. To a great extent, his workforce was second-generation English, Scotch, and Irish. As if to emphasize the homogeneous nature of his workers, Wanamaker held prayer services from noon to 12:30 every day, giving his employees extra time at lunch to attend. Thus, although Wanamaker had a strong sense of community, his community was largely limited to persons who had been in Philadelphia when he started in business and excluded the newest immigrants.

As a liberal Republican on racial matters, Wanamaker felt an obligation to the African-American community in Philadelphia, employing blacks usually in behind-the-scenes jobs, in workshops and service positions. Explaining his hiring practices to an African-American whom Wanamaker's had rejected for a job, he wrote, "We have quite a number of colored people in our employ and I have no prejudice such as you speak of."[62]

In his dealings with his employees, Wanamaker assumed that a community of interests existed between capital and labor, although he largely defined the terms of this community. In a talk to his employees, he said, "We are not simply a store. We have always said that. We are a family. We are in a sense, so far as we could thus far arrange it, in a kind of loyal partnership." Wanamaker emphasized the important role his employees played in the success of the enterprise. "I insist that workers shall have proper recognition. I will not have people called 'shopgirls,' I will not have people called 'help.' We are men and women living our lives, doing our share, doing it with dignity."[63]

This view of labor, which echoed the artisan rhetoric of labor common earlier in the nineteenth century, contrasted sharply with attitudes toward labor relations in the industrial sector. Service employees dealt directly with customers; discontented workers would hurt sales. Industrial employers valued workers primarily for faster activity along the assembly line and for absolute obedience to their supervisors.

A strike in a department store would harm the only capital an owner really ever had, a good relationship with his customer.[64]

Perhaps the most important manner in which Wanamaker carried out his idea of the store as a family was in providing job security. Although the depression of 1893 greatly affected the Philadelphia economy, leading to massive unemployment and causing a drop in Wanamaker's business, Wanamaker kept his core of 3,500 employees on the payroll. His policies did not protect carpenters who were members of an outside union. They were not considered part of the regular staff, and if no work was available for them, Wanamaker laid them off.[65]

Over the years, Wanamaker shifted the hours his employees worked. The original store hours were from 7 a.m. to 7 p.m. during the week and from 7 a.m. to 10 or 11 p.m. on Saturdays. (On Sundays, the store was always closed.) But the nature of work had changed since the early nineteenth century, when proprietors of family enterprises lived in the shop, opening at 6 a.m. and staying open until 10 or 11 p.m. Wanamaker introduced changes in his store that reflected the changing work habits of the city. He pioneered shorter hours, cutting the workday to 8 a.m. until 6 p.m. He also began half-holidays on Saturdays in 1886. Shorter hours not only gave Wanamaker's workers more leisure but also allowed them to live in more remote parts of the city. After they had been at the store for one year, he granted employees two weeks' vacation in the summer.[66]

While Wanamaker was proud of the part he played in reducing hours for his employees, he took offense at any interference by the state. In 1897, the Pennsylvania legislature passed a law restricting employment to sixty hours per week for minor children and women, which Wanamaker's employees exceeded during the Christmas season. Wanamaker attacked the legislation, asking, "Has the Legislature the right to regulate and restrict the employment of people to such an extent that they might by legislation deprive them of employment for one day a week?"[67]

The educational component of Wanamaker's benefits package probably had the most lasting influence on his employees. From his days as a Sunday school teacher, Wanamaker had an interest in teaching. Herbert Gibbons, Wanamaker's earliest biographer, noted in a private letter, "John Wanamaker was pre-eminently a teacher. He never gave up interest in teaching the Bible. In his business he was a teacher not only to his staff but also to the customers." The merchant had an array of educational programs aimed particularly at children, who often came to Wanamaker with little education. In 1882, under the leadership of Mary Brewer—who later became a famous Philadelphia physician and whose brother was a store manager—Wanamaker created a school for cashboys, the John Wanamaker Commercial Institute.[68]

In 1891, Wanamaker expanded his educational activities so that training became available for all his employees, young and old. Elementary education was provided early in the day, while a night school provided commercial courses on a secondary or even collegiate level for older children and adults. Wanamaker believed his work in educating his employees had lasting benefits not only for his business but for the nation as a whole. He wrote, "We are planning that the United States shall reap a harvest of Healthy, Educated, contented men and women, fit for conditions peaceful and prosperous, instead of leaving them to Socialistic anarchies, ignorance and poverty that breed discontents and crime."[69]

As part of the Commercial Institute, Wanamaker's ran a military camp at Island Heights, New Jersey. Young Wanamaker employees received two weeks of military training during the summer months, participating in water recreation and some introduction to military science. These employees received pay while attending the camp. Like many other Americans of his age group, military idealism of the Civil War influenced Wanamaker. He sent troops from the Commercial Institute to the Spanish-American War, the American intervention in Mexico, and the First World War. Wanamaker wrote, "Never was money better spent or better invested. But the results have not come in advertising: they have been in Americanism."[70]

For the store, the education system provided Wanamaker with a constant supply of middle and upper management. For the young recruits, the education they gained at the store gave them the promise of advancement. By the 1890s, many of Wanamaker's buyers and executives were individuals who had spent their whole careers at Wanamaker's, although buyers and managers also still entered from the outside. Boys who came in at the lowest levels were encouraged to work hard and move up in the organization. These younger employees were first evaluated for promotion in these classes.[71]

Wanamaker did not envision the same route for girls. Women buyers came from outside the store, often having picked up their expertise as independent merchants. Except in advertising, no women occupied administrative positions. Wanamaker's practices were similar to situations women faced in other stores throughout the country. Although women buyers earned salaries generally lower than men in comparable positions, a few earned more money than in other nineteenth-century professional positions for women.[72]

The Wanamaker Commercial Institute influenced the wider community as individuals trained in the store as children went on to business and political leadership in the city. Wanamaker's trainees showed up among the managers of departments at all his rivals as well as in other aspects of the retail and wholesale trade. Several of Wanamaker's employees went on to hold major political positions including a mayor of Philadelphia and a member of Congress.[73]

To deal with the large number of employees, Wanamaker developed a professional employment department through which most employees received their initial interview. At the start of the twentieth century, this department handled more than 5,000 applicants every month. Each applicant was carefully considered. Although Wanamaker occasionally made recommendations for jobs, he usually sent people over to the buyer or manager of a department. He was always careful to give the manager the right of selection. Wanamaker always personally interviewed potential buyers. For a New York position, Ogden also participated in the selection. Discipline was largely left in the hands of departmental managers, who also were left in charge of firing employees for cause.[74]

With his employee policy set and with his achievements recognized by his customers and rivals, Wanamaker was set to face the new century. Wanamaker wrote in a widely quoted essay that "the merchant must be big enough, broad enough, far-seeing enough to survey the whole field and then stand as a bulwark amid the confusions, heresies and fears of his times." To a great extent, he fit this description. Wanamaker's in Philadelphia had become the retail standard by which other stores in the country were judged. It sold an endless array of foreign and domestic goods and advertised lavishly in local newspapers. His employee relations were also held up as models of amicability in an era of strikes and labor boycotts. But even standing as "a bulwark amid the confusions . . . of his times" did not prevent Wanamaker from being threatened by the changes in retailing taking places as 1900 approached.[75]

Like much of the 1890s, the last few years of the nineteenth century were fraught with problems for Wanamaker's stores. During the Christmas season after McKinley took office, the business showed its first substantial upswing since 1893. Most political problems were behind the country, and the new president inspired a good deal of business confidence. But just as Wanamaker expected a good year, the war scare and then the Spanish-American War shut things down. Losses at the store were offset, however, by sales of clothing and equipment to the military.[76]

The store was further disrupted in 1898 as Wanamaker remained away for much of the year, trying to raise a regiment and running for governor. Mary complained that the store was being allowed to run down. "Your Father is well and busy—wandering off in the clouds after something all the time," she wrote to her son Rodman.[77]

Wanamaker turned his attention back to the store by 1900 and with that, combined with the rebound that followed the depression and the war, his two stores returned to operating at capacity. Sales and profits were good, but the competition became more intense. In Philadelphia, rival department stores sprouted all over the central business district, contributing to the ambiance that marked the early twentieth-century city. Electric lighting, automobiles in the streets, tall office buildings, and beautiful store windows made the downtown an exciting and attractive spot for residents and visitors. Although Wanamaker's was Philadelphia's first true department store, its rivals were beginning to catch up. Strawbridge & Clothier, opened at Eighth and Market Streets by two old Quaker families, boasted an ornate exterior and large displays of European and American goods. It was a formidable rival for the carriage trade.

Jewish immigrants opened other rival stores that sold goods aimed at the lower-middle and working classes. The most important of the newcomers was Gimbel's, built by a family which had earlier established itself in Milwaukee. Lit Brothers' and Snellenburg's concentrated on lower-priced goods; nevertheless, the Lit's store was the most impressive iron construction building in Philadelphia. Another new rival, Blum's, created a women's store at Tenth and Market, aimed at providing a more exclusive atmosphere than the department stores. Next to these rivals' new buildings, Wanamaker's—still located in the Grand Depot, a reconstructed railroad barn—was beginning to look a little shabby.[78]

In New York, Wanamaker was the interloper who had to prove himself against such formidable rivals as Macy's, now owned by the sons of his former lessee, the Straus brothers; Siegal-Cooper, which had rebuilt its building; Lord & Taylor, and Arnold Constable. Wanamaker's old Alexander Stewart Building was off the beaten path at Eighth Street and Broadway as the new titans of retailing relocated near the Pennsylvania Railroad Station at Thirty-fourth Street and Fifth Avenue.

Wanamaker was beginning to feel the heat from these competitors. He particularly disliked Gimbel Brothers, which seemed especially aggressive in trying to gain sales. Gimbel's often went after merchandise from manufacturers or other retailers in trouble, buying goods at deep discounts and then reselling the items greatly marked down.[79]

Wanamaker became convinced that he had to enlarge both the Philadelphia and the New York stores to keep up with the competition. Agreeing with his boss, Ogden began negotiating for property to add to the New York store. In Philadelphia, Wanamaker began searching for a grand design for a new store to replace the Grand Depot. He envisioned a building that would dominate the rising skyline in a reconstructed Philadelphia.[80]

All of the illustrations on the following pages are used with the permission and courtesy of The Historical Society of Pennsylvania, Philadelphia.

John Wanamaker, twenty-five years old.

Photograph of John Wanamaker, circa 1876.

Wanamaker as Postmaster-General.

Middle aged Wanamaker standing—around 1910.

Older Wanamaker (seated in wicker rocker) in 1921.

Wanamaker family portrait taken at Meadowbrook, the home of Rodman Wanamaker, on Christmas Day 1900.

The site of the John Wanamaker store, Thirteenth and Market Street in 1875.

The members of the Centennial Exposition Board of Finance in 1876 (Wanamaker is top center).

Bird's-eye view of the interior of the Wanamaker Grand Depot (1877).

President Benjamin Harrison (center) at Lindenhurst, Wanamaker's home in 1889.

Wanamaker at Bethany Presbyterian Church taken from Frank Leslie's Illustrated Newspaper, *April 13, 1889.*

Mary Wanamaker, wife of John Wanamaker in 1895.

Wanamaker's window in 1895—"Evening With Music at Home."

Wanamaker's department store decorated for Easter, circa 1900.

Exterior of John Wanamaker's in 1902.

Store decorated with lilies in 1903.

Wanamaker's hat department in 1903.

Construction of the new Wanamaker's building in 1904.

Wanamaker dedicating the cornerstone of the new building, June 11, 1910.

An exhibition of French gowns at Wanamaker's in 1910.

President William Howard Taft at the dedication of the new store in 1911.

French perfumery shop in the Grand Court of the new Philadelphia store.

Grand Court decorated with Dutch scenes around 1912.

Grand Court of Wanamaker Store with the Eagle in fore-ground decorated with flags, around 1912.

John and Rodman Wanamaker meeting with Native-Americans in the Philadelphia store on February 24, 1913.

Wanamaker sending first parcel post package from Philadelphia, 12:01 am, January 1, 1913.

Wanamaker and friends preparing to sail in 1914.

Wanamaker seated at desk in 1917.

"Red Cross Day" during World War I.

Wanamaker with General John J. Pershing, the commander of the American forces in France during World War I, on September 12, 1919.

General Pershing in front of Wanamaker's on September 12, 1919.

Wanamaker with a group of children in his office, circa 1920.

CHAPTER SIX

Rebuilding the Stores

1903-1912

*A*t the start of the new century, John Wanamaker was at the height of his fame. The *Dry Goods Economist,* the leading retailing trade journal, in November 1899 acknowledged Wanamaker's accomplishments, writing that Wanamaker deserved "the credit for originating and first adopting many of the modern methods of retailing." But Wanamaker still had his greatest accomplishment ahead of him: the building of a new store which, other than Independence Hall and City Hall, would be the most famous building in Philadelphia. More importantly for visitors and local citizens during the next ninety years, this store became the physical and ceremonial center of Philadelphia. For many of these people, going to Philadelphia meant going to Wanamaker's.

Although he remained at most times quite vigorous for someone past 60 years of age, Wanamaker continued to suffer debilitating, long-lasting winter colds that left him bedridden or unable to talk. To try to avoid them, he headed to Europe, particularly to the German spas adored by the trans-Atlantic elite. Arriving in the off-season to almost empty hotels, Wanamaker rested his voice. He also took side trips to warmer climates in Italy and even India. Before coming home, he was sure to visit Paris for his annual buying trip, meeting with his buyers as they prepared for the fall fashion season. The cross-Atlantic trip, which took over a week, brought Wanamaker and his family into close contact with other elite sojourners to Europe.[1]

During these early years of the century, Wanamaker's prominence in religion continued to parallel his achievements in retailing. By 1900, he was one of the best known Protestant spokesmen in the United States. Because of his wealth and prominence, he participated in a myriad of state and national evangelical activities in addition to running Bethany, the largest Presbyterian church in the United States.

Corresponding with ministers around the world, Wanamaker was the center of a network of persons with similar religious beliefs, such as H.J. Heinz, the Pittsburgh industrialist, and Morris Jessup, the New York financier. His core connection was with the Moody Institute at Northfield, Massachusetts, which he had endowed, and he continued to maintain a relationship with Moody's son and widow. These contacts became an interlocking network for many of Wanamaker's philanthropic endeavors. Several ministers at Bethany, including William Chapman and William Patterson, came from the Moody Institute.[2]

Active in the Sunday School Association, Wanamaker was president of the Pennsylvania association, which had its headquarters about a block from his Philadelphia store. He regarded the Sunday school as one of the moving forces in his life. Wanamaker believed that "Christianity in this new country would not stand where it does but for the Sunday School, which has been a Christian college to the young people and the pioneer of tens of thousands of churches." As the driving force behind the Philadelphia Evangelistic Committee, Wanamaker brought prominent revivalist preachers to the city, including the English minister Reuben A. Torrey in 1905 and Billy Sunday in 1915.[3]

After his visit to India in 1903, Wanamaker became quite committed to foreign missionary work. He wrote to Hugh Cork, the secretary of the Pennsylvania Sunday School Association, that there was the greatest possibility to bring about the "Lord's coming through missionary work. The heathen cannot receive the Gospel until it is brought to them in some way." Active in the foreign missionary movement, he served on the advisory committee for the Presbyterian Board of Foreign Missions, donating $25,000 to build missionary schools in Calcutta and Allahabad, India.[4]

Despite Wanamaker's growing outside commitments, Bethany remained the center of his religious activities. He handpicked most of the ministers of the church. Its lay board of trustees was loaded with his friends, including Judge Hugh Black, whom Wanamaker had befriended when he was an orphan, and Thomas Coyle, who was Wanamaker's insurance broker.[5]

When in Philadelphia, Wanamaker got to the church early in the morning to run the Brotherhood, a group of 400 men devoted to Bible study. He then took charge of the Sunday school, whose 5,172 members made it the largest in the country. He also lectured to the Bible Union with 1,000 adults present. Wanamaker's intent was to produce a show that would attract people to church. Once there, he hoped, they would buy religion. As a showman, Wanamaker knew the dynamics of public ceremony and how to achieve a perfect blend of sights and sounds. He changed anything that distracted from an unblemished appearance until the effect was perfect—a technique that he applied to business as well as religion.[6]

In addition to spending time on the business of Bethany, he also socialized with its parishioners. In 1908 while on holiday, he sent cards to each and every one of the 1,300 members of the Bethany Brotherhood, even though it took him one hundred hours to complete this task. While in Philadelphia, he often visited sick members of the congregation or had his wife do so. He made suggestions as to doctors to see at Presbyterian Hospital and sometimes picked up doctor bills for patients who could not do so. By his constant interest and generosity, Wanamaker had an impact on the family lives of many of Bethany's parishioners. One woman wrote in 1904 that her husband had not had a drink for six months thanks to the influence of Wanamaker. "I feel very grateful to you for the change and I wish to thank you again for the interest you have taken in him."[7]

The church under Wanamaker's leadership sponsored a number of special days, a technique he had used so successfully in his stores. One of the most important was Mother's Day, which became an important retailing device for the store. Bethany first celebrated Mother's Day on May 17, 1908, after Ann Jarvis suggested it to Wanamaker. He was later condemned by several ministers for turning the day into a great business event. Writing to them, Wanamaker replied, "My idea of advertising is much higher than merely to sell goods. It is to educate our own people and, to some extent, whoever reads what is upon our page."[8]

It's quite clear from reading Wanamaker's letters to the ministers at Bethany, that he regarded the services as a show which attracted people to church. Once they were there, they would come to buy religion. Especially important for this show was an interesting sermon, so Wanamaker brought popular visiting evangelical preachers to the church as part of their visits to the city, which he usually helped sponsor.[9]

Because of his age, Wanamaker reduced his commitments at Bethany, allowing a gradual but not always smooth transition to younger leadership. In 1903, he resigned as president of the First Penny Saving Bank, which served the Bethany community in the area below South Street between Broad Street and the Schuylkill River. In 1904, Wanamaker gave up the presidency of the Board of Trustees of Bethany to Robert Coyle, his insurance broker, and turned over the Brotherhood to Thomas Horney, who also ran the Friendly Inn, the Wanamaker shelter for homeless men. However, Wanamaker never completely withdrew.[10]

The most serious problem facing him as the founder of the church was its survival. By 1904 the neighborhood around Bethany had changed substantially as African-Americans, Jews, and Italians became the dominant residents. Most of the Bethany parishioners were living in West Philadelphia. Wanamaker helped plan and largely financed the building of a new church in that section of the city. Construction of this facility came at the same time Wanamaker was engaged in the rebuilding of both his stores.[11]

When well, Wanamaker continued to expend on his businesses the same amount of energy he gave to his philanthropic enterprises. Despite having turned over command of the two stores to Tom and Robert Ogden, he supervised operations in both the Philadelphia and New York stores, taking a hands-on approach, roaming the aisles, and changing layouts and even menus in the restaurants. Writing to Rodman, he summarized the reason for his constant activity: "We must not leave a single stone unturned to get better service. The whole hurt of the business is the lack of satisfying our customer by avoiding blunders and preventing complaints by not making promises that we cannot fulfill."[12]

Wanamaker was a transitional figure. He was an old-style, hands-on entrepreneur who built his empire from the ground up. But he also contributed to the new style of managerial capitalism by granting key subordinates, such as his buyers, autonomy and decision-making power. Delegation of control, Alfred Chandler argues in *The Visible Hand,* was necessary if firms were to coordinate production (or purchasing) and distribution successfully in a vast, impersonal international market. If Wanamaker in some respects recognized and acceded to the managerial revolution of his day, he seems to have been very reluctant to relinquish control. His bustling through the department store, rearranging things and setting things up anew, was evidence of his reluctance. His hands-on, old-style methods may have put him at risk when he found himself overstocked during times of economic downturns. Despite his "modern" innovations—his use of advertising, his sensitivity to European trends, and especially his dazzling showmanship—Wanamaker was compulsively old-style.[13]

Although Wanamaker had turned over most personnel matters to subordinates, he kept tight control over his buyers. He had long conversations with his partners about the sixty key people in each store, constantly discussing their physical and psychological health and suggesting vacations and other ways of keeping them active and innovative. In an often paternalistic way, he showered his employees with favors. Once, he paid for a five-week trip for one of his New York buyers because he felt she was doing a much better job than her counterpart in Philadelphia. He wrote to one buyer, Florence Stowell, when she completed 11 years in the New York store that "I want you to know that I feel that your eleven years of business life, shows not only a record of successful work, but of continuous influence for good, through your unassuming and faithful example of the fineness of real womanhood." While praising his successful buyers, Wanamaker kept track of buyers who did not fulfill their promise, and he would not tolerate buying practices that led to a loss of profits.[14]

At times Wanamaker felt almost helpless when encountering incompetent staff because he was so dependent on them. He apologized to one customer who felt she had been mistreated by a member of

Wanamaker's staff, writing, "it is the extreme opposite of satisfaction to me to feel so dependent upon human beings imperiling my business and their own employment by inaccuracies and carelessness, for which you are the sufferer." Wanamaker indicated he would get rid of the people who were responsible."[15]

Although Wanamaker engaged in many economic activities, the two stores remained the base of his wealth. With a boom during the first five years of Roosevelt's presidency, the Philadelphia store prospered. By 1905, the two stores reached $38 million in business annually. From this revenue, the Philadelphia store made a profit of $1,377,305, down from $1,413,992 in 1903, but ahead of the profits in 1907, a recession year when the store made $834,675. A turnabout in 1908 resulted in net profits of $1,150,486.[16]

Business in New York, on the other hand, grew more slowly, although for most years the store showed a profit. By 1899, business in the store was greater than in Stewart's heyday. In 1903, although twenty-five of the sixty departments in the store showed a loss, the store showed a small profit. In the recession year of 1907, the New York store lost $76,087. Although profitability returned in 1908, Wanamaker faced sophisticated competitors with better locations. Wanamaker's in New York never achieved the success the merchant had hoped.[17]

The stores' earnings gave Wanamaker wealth beyond his greatest aspirations when he had been a young man entering the retail business. In 1904, Wanamaker received $1.5 million in profits and interest on his $10 million invested in the business. His ability to draw this sum at a time when his average worker made about $500 per year allowed the Philadelphian to maintain a lavish lifestyle. During the early twentieth century, Wanamaker's personal expenses ran between $200,000 and $475,000 per year. His two sons and Robert Ogden, Wanamaker's formal partners, also benefitted. Thomas Wanamaker received $450,000 in 1904, while Rodman received $320,000. Robert C. Ogden received $250,000 for running the New York store.[18]

Until 1906, Wanamaker maintained the store as a proprietorship with his two sons and Ogden as limited partners. Preferring to maintain private control, Wanamaker resisted all efforts by Ogden, Rodman, and Tom to persuade him to incorporate the business as the best means of ensuring its survival. Like many of the rugged individualistic founders of department stores, he resisted sharing power even with his eventual heirs. The idea of limited liability implied by incorporation also meant limited power. He conceded in 1906, creating two corporations, one for each store. He turned over a few shares of stock to his two sons and to Ogden to meet legal requirements, but he kept almost all the stock in his own hands. Thus, Wanamaker eventually accepted the corporation as the safest method of ensuring the survival of his business, just like most of his rivals.[19]

To prosper, he had to continually update his merchandising techniques. Although Wanamaker's merchandising methods had been unique when he opened the Grand Depot in 1876, by 1900 the United States had 8,970 department stores, many of them doing more than $1 million per year in business. These emporiums dominated retailing, significantly reducing the ability of small stores to survive. In Massachusetts, for example, the ratio of stores to population decreased from one store for every 115 people in 1875 to one for every 142 people twenty years later.[20]

In a time of intense competition, store owners had to stand above the crowd with their product lines, their advertising, and their general sense of merchandising. By out-advertising and out-performing his rivals, Wanamaker could usually distinguish himself. His display of foreign goods exceeded any other store in the country. Wanamaker advertised, "Surely, there is romance in merchandise to those who have eyes to see. A tour through Wanamaker's is a tour 'round the world." He boasted that the store contained fine illustrated books from Scotland and England, bound in London in the finest leather, while a visit to the linen department, "is like a tabloid tour of other lands, and especially suggestive of Erin, lovely emerald of the Northern seas." To persuade Philadelphia's elite that they did not have to go to New York to shop, Wanamaker created a department that was the largest retailer in gems, high-priced jewelry, and silverware in the city. He also had several brands of his own cosmetics with catchy names like St. Mary's to compete with the two leading advertised brands, Hudnut and Colgate. Selling his own private labels gave his shops an exclusiveness but, as he wrote Rodman, "You can make much more, of course, on your own goods than you can on the other lines."[21]

Although he encountered greater competition in New York,

Wanamaker's store had a similar major display of luxury merchandise. To meet this competition, Wanamaker tried to train his salespeople as expert merchandisers. In a letter to Rodman, he stressed the need to find persons who "do something more than simply ask 'size' and 'about what price' or 'how would this suit you.' We have got to have people that the customers will recognize from their manner that they have an idea of what a refined lady should wear. We have got to have people who will not simply hand out an article that the customer asks for but will introduce pretty goods that the people will buy without intending to when they come in, attracted by the nice manners and by the exceptional beauty of the goods, especially the foreign goods." Wanamaker urged "We must not leave a single stone unturned to get better service. The whole hurt of the business is the lack of satisfying our customer by avoiding blunders and preventing complaints by not making promises that we cannot fulfill."[22]

Wanamaker became the biggest seller of pianos in the United States. His major manufacturers were small but quality producers who were prone to failure in the intense competition, sometimes forcing him to purchase the firms to continue their lines. When the failure of Mason and Hamlin, manufacturer of one of his biggest sellers, left him with a $300,000 inventory that might have become worthless, Wanamaker in October 1903 paid $147,500 for the company.[23]

For Wanamaker, new technologies and improved middle-class goods were always important keys to success. Following his pioneering work with bicycles in the 1890s, Wanamaker introduced automobiles in 1903. Always fascinated by advances in science, Wanamaker used an automobile himself to travel to Lindenhurst and to Cape May. However, his experiment in selling the new device proved quite sobering. Wanamaker became the agent for Searchmont cars, but they did not sell, and he tried to dispose of them in Paris. Cars also posed a difficult service problem. Because of their tendency to break down, Wanamaker was under constant pressure to live up to his guarantees. He got into still deeper trouble when he sold used cars, even then a dangerous occupation for a man known everywhere as "honest John." Although Wanamaker persisted for several years in selling cars, even securing the first Ford dealerships on the East Coast, he eventually realized the difficulty of selling cars out of a department store, sold his agency, and got out of the business. Because of his Ford dealership, he was forced to defend himself legally against manufacturers suing the Detroit automaker for infringement of patents. Servicing automobiles also proved difficult for a downtown department store with more profitable services to provide in limited space.[24]

In the early years of the new century, Wanamaker felt the increased competition from his rivals. In 1904, Marshall Field's new store in Chicago passed Wanamaker's Philadelphia store in total sales, doing $3 million more business. Moreover, the competition in Philadelphia was intense. He was always on the lookout for attempts by other owners to undersell him or to capture a part of his market. Regular comparisons were made by store employees about the state of the other stores in Philadelphia. Gimbel's was the usual first stop on an itinerary. Wanamaker was particularly incensed when he felt one of his rivals had engaged in what he believed was unfair advertising. He became particularly upset with Frederick C. Strawbridge, who visited him at the New York store after what Wanamaker regarded as a misrepresented advertisement. He wrote Rodman, "I had to spend a little time with him to be polite, though I felt like unfolding to him the 'fake' advertisement of rugs he had in the paper and giving him the facts we had; that some of the rugs they were advertising as coming to them from the Persian Consul were rugs they had bought of us." Wanamaker felt most threatened by Gimbel's. The threat became greater in 1899, when Gimbel's began to build a larger and more modern building.[25]

Feeling this competition, Wanamaker wrote to Rodman that he had to replace the Philadelphia store, "this queer old patchwork building that has a threefold charm about it—utility, great strength, and incomparable economy." He also feared Wanamaker's was a fire hazard that could have been a tomb for thousands during the Market Street fire in 1896. The store, which often held 50,000 people, had only eight doors and a large window at the top of the store that could shatter during a fire and spray the people below with glass.[26]

Wanamaker was also moved toward the rebuilding of his two stores by a dramatic change in the city at the turn of the century with the creation of a new urban skyscraper. At about the time Wanamaker responded to the rebuilding craze, many of his contemporaries including Marshall Field's in Chicago, Macy's in New York, and Filene's in

Boston also reconstructed their stores using one of the new urban architectural firms for their designs.

Wanamaker committed himself to the project in September 1902, when he took specifications for a new store to the Art Institute of Chicago for a meeting with Daniel H. Burnham. Burnham, a leader of the Chicago school of architecture that had helped to redesign the American city, was responsible for the Marshall Field department store, which greatly influenced Wanamaker.[27]

Despite Burnham's reputation, his choice as architect came under fire because Burnham was not a Philadelphian. The *Real Estate Record* attacked Wanamaker for going outside the city: "If there is a single man on God's earth who has a right to stand for all that loyalty means to the city in which he has made his big money through the earnest support and patronage of its citizens, it is Mr. John Wanamaker."[28]

After the Chicago meeting, Burnham accompanied Wanamaker back to Philadelphia and began sketching the new enterprise, which was to be built in marble drawn from quarries in Maine. Built on the same site as the Grand Depot, the project was broken into three phases so that parts of the store could always stay open. The work included digging into solid bedrock to give the new store an extra-heavy foundation with wide steel supports. "This kind of construction for strength, fire-proofing, conveniences, and other accommodations for the public must necessarily be slower than common building," Wanamaker wrote in 1904, the year construction began.[29]

In reading through correspondence generated by his building plans, the reader is struck by Wanamaker's careful attention to details. In handling the complicated legal negotiations, Wanamaker had an eye to legal problems which might arise almost as calculating as a good lawyer. On the architectural details, Wanamaker understood what the plans meant. He of course relied upon professionals to fill in the details and handle the final closing.

Because of the three-phase construction, the new building took almost ten years from Wanamaker's first meeting with Burnham to be completed. Work on the first section, at the corner of Market and Juniper Streets, began on April 24, 1904; that section opened for business on March 12, 1906. Final dedication of the whole building took place in December 1911.

The building's construction period also was prolonged by labor problems. Most of the contractors were from the Philadelphia area, and to avoid picketing and bad publicity, all workers were from labor unions. Problems arose anyway from jurisdictional disputes between unions in October 1905, after the first section of the building was completed. The dispute delayed work on the second section and launched Wanamaker into an angry diatribe against the workers: "The greater fact is in the unfinished building itself in the very heart of the city, held up by disagreements and irreconcilability of the various branches of work people, who have left it as an object lesson to warn all enterprising people against undertakings dependent upon the present rule and regulation of labor organizations."[30]

Although Wanamaker had excellent counsel in Burnham and in William G. Haddock, who was in charge of physical plant in Philadelphia, the project ran into unanticipated delays. After work started in early 1904, Wanamaker wanted the first floor completed by October, in time for the fall selling season. However, the discovery of water under the building complicated and delayed construction until long after Christmas. It was the first setback for Wanamaker in what proved to be a prolonged agony over construction problems. Elevators posed another problem. Even after builders completed the first section, Wanamaker could not use it during the 1905 Christmas season because the elevators failed. When the first section opened in 1906, Wanamaker had logistical problems as he had to keep the remaining buildings open, moving stock from the section about to be torn down, while keeping on a construction schedule for the second part of the building.[31]

Because Wanamaker was in New York, he worked through Haddock. With the two sections facing Market Street completed by 1906, Wanamaker struggled to complete the last section facing Chestnut Street, which comprised one-half the whole job. He originally hoped to have the store built in 1908 and opened for Christmas, but because of zoning problems, he could not get final approval for the design until July of that year.[32]

While Wanamaker was hiring Burnham and letting contracts for the Philadelphia building, he also was planning to expand the New York store by constructing a second building. Renting land across from the Stewart building, Wanamaker chose a location facing Astor Place and

Lafayette Park. Besides building a new eight-floor building at Astor Place, connected to the Stewart store by a bridge, Wanamaker planned to add three floors to the old building.[33]

In retrospect, despite the good transportation facilities, rebuilding the New York Wanamaker's was a mistake. The New York business center had moved to Herald Square, the city's prime transportation area near the Pennsylvania Railroad terminal and several subway lines, including one to New Jersey. Although Macy's and Gimbel's built their stores on this prime location, Wanamaker turned down several offers of real estate there. Trapped by his strong feelings toward Stewart, Wanamaker failed to see the potential in the new uptown site.[34]

As in Philadelphia, the New York project suffered delays. In New York, the problems were political. The planned opening of the new building in New York was delayed from October 1905 until October 1907, when City Council repealed an ordinance requiring the use of fireproof wood in a new building.[35]

Wanamaker also suffered a series of personal and financial problems that threatened his rebuilding. In December 1904 after returning from the St. Louis Exposition, Wanamaker came down with one of his long-lasting colds. It persisted through the whole Christmas season, and he suffered a relapse when he went out on Christmas Day against the advice of his doctors. Wanamaker's doctors finally ordered him to leave the city, so he went to Palm Beach, Florida. When he felt well, he left for a German spa, staying there from April until late June, when he passed Rodman and Mary in the Atlantic. Since they did not return from Europe until October, John did not see them for more than five months.[36]

After Wanamaker's recovery, his son Thomas took ill. He had long suffered from several illnesses, including gout, but in June 1906 he became critically ill, forcing John and Rodman to cancel trips to Europe. In December 1906, Tom decided that because of his failing health he would have to leave the business. Although he rebounded during 1907, participating in a limited way in the business, he never fully returned to the activities in the store.[37]

In February 1907, soon after Tom quit, Robert C. Ogden suffered a heart attack and dropped out of the business as well. Wanamaker partially blamed himself for Ogden's condition. "I fear that I must blame myself for not giving him in some way the relief he needed," Wanamaker wrote to his son Rodman. With Tom and Ogden gone, John at almost 70 years of age found himself in charge again, assuming control of the New York store. He even bought a house in the city. Because he was considered an outsider by many in the management, who were loyal to Ogden, he had problems assuming control and several of his department heads quit.[38]

While he ran the New York store, Wanamaker put Rodman in charge of the Philadelphia store, although Rodman consulted him about managerial changes and purchases. Rodman, who had headed the Paris division until the death of his wife in 1899, worked with Ogden in New York after his return. Although Rodman had less business sense than his brother, he was a merchandiser like his father. With artistic sensitivity gained partially from his years in Paris, Rodman became known for putting on even more lavish exhibitions than his father. In 1909, trying to revive the stores from doldrums, Rodman staged one of the most spectacular Wanamaker displays. The "Hiawatha" exhibition in the New York and Philadelphia stores drew upon an 1908 expedition to the West by Dr. Joseph Kossuth Dixon, a minister and photographer who recorded and photographed the customs of Indians. John Wanamaker financed eleven Dixon expeditions. Although the photographs won prizes, modern critics of the treks regard Dixon as a charlatan who posed the Indians in costumes aimed at playing upon American stereotypes. Nevertheless, Dixon drew the Wanamakers into Indian affairs. In 1910, John became the moving force behind an attempt to build an Indian monument on Staten Island. In 1924, Rodman played a leading role in the movement to get citizenship for Indians.[39]

After Rodman took over the store in Philadelphia, William Nevin, who was chief counsel for the stores, became his second in command while Joseph Appel, who headed Wanamaker advertising, assumed a role in the management of both stores. William McCaugham, who was active at Bethany and acted as Wanamaker's personal secretary, also traveled between the two stores to keep an eye on things for Wanamaker. To coordinate this new managerial team, Wanamaker met with a council of buyers regularly.[40]

Despite the many delays, Wanamaker on October 1, 1907, opened the new building in New York City on Astor Place with a ceremony that was a typical John Wanamaker event. Five thousand dignitaries attended, and a 100-piece band led the spectators in singing "America." Although Ogden had advised that New Yorkers were too sophisticated for such Philadelphia methods, 210,000 visitors came to the store during the first three days it was open. Although New York City headed into a recession, the improved store had more business during its first months than during the previous year, averaging about $60,000 per day.[41]

The New York store presented customers with an elegant image. Wanamaker put great emphasis on the first two floors, which customers saw as they entered. The focal point of the Stewart Building was a rotunda encircled by large aisles. This became a place for special sales, announced in newspapers as occurring under the rotunda. The elegance of the store was enhanced with ceiling lights, rather than lamps. Famous European and American artists regularly gave concerts on the store organ, which was the largest in the city.[42]

Wanamaker created a store in New York to appeal to upper-middle class and elite women. He even advertised the men's shop as a place where a woman could shop for a man. This was the new middle-class culture in which men worked long hours in offices while women used their new-found leisure to shop for the family. As with Wanamaker's in Philadelphia, Wanamaker advertised it as more than a store: "It gives a vastly greater public service-gives it cheerfully, and leaves no trail of obligations upon the recipient of its courtesies." Wanamaker's tried to influence consumer taste through sights, sounds, and smells. In a single emporium, customers could find the best pictures, fashions, furniture, music, foods, and perfumes. The store aimed to create an especially warm, non-threatening environment for its customers. Customers wandered through these sensual delights without much interference from the sales clerks, whom Wanamaker instructed to be courteous, not pushy.[43]

The upper floors of the remodeled A.T. Stewart Building featured twenty-one specialty shops for women's fashions, and Wanamaker noted that "those who have been used to the Paris Shops will be surprised and pleased to be at home in them again without having to take a ship across the ocean to get to them." The store also had several restaurants, each aimed primarily at attracting female diners. The menu designs carried through the European motif in the store. For example, a 1913 menu featured a reproduction of a French drawing of a girl with a mirror.[44]

In keeping with the new elegance of the store, Wanamaker revitalized the jewelry and silverware departments, creating a glamorous Diamond Room. The store also featured imported foods such as Camee candies made from Paris recipes. Wanamaker advertised, "When a new bonbon appears there, it appears here almost instantly-made from samples sent us by our Paris House." Wanamaker capitalized on upper-class desires to adopt European manners and European goods. The men's, women's, and children's shops featured "Red Leaf-London Fashions." Other imports included Tyrolean cloth, Burges lace bedspreads, Louis Vuiton of Paris luggage, and men's ties from Tribout of Paris.[45]

Home furnishings dominated the rest of the Astor Place building. For individuals with modest incomes, the New York store featured a home furnishing section called "The Little House that Budget Built," consisting of two complete small apartments. Wanamaker advised his customers, "Don't waste time on uninteresting furnishings, don't waste money on ordinary furnishing. Come to Wanamaker's and find the pleasure of expressing your own personality through buying on a prearranged plan." For the upper classes, the Astor Place annex featured "The House Palatial," which reproduced a $250,000 Fifth Avenue mansion with forty-four furnished rooms, allowing "home-makers to select proper furniture and house adornments, and to enable them to individualize their homes from the mere commercial furnishing way."[46]

Wanamaker's advertising for his "House Palatial" reflected a shift in emphasis. The Grand Depot had been a store to be trusted for the needs of a middle-class household. Wanamaker now appealed to customers to develop their personalities, offering them a wide spectrum of goods oriented toward their individual tastes.

At the time of the opening of the New York store, the United States was in the midst of a severe financial panic. Because of his heavy construction costs, Wanamaker came nearer to suffering a business failure than at any time since 1877. When he committed himself to the rebuilding, the country was enjoying an economic boom that lasted through 1906. In Spring 1906, business in New York ran almost 20 percent ahead of the previous year. But the economy quickly fell apart because of a money crunch, and Wanamaker found it hard to find the credit he needed to pay his bills. Wanamaker's first inkling of impending financial problems occurred in February 1906. Judge Horace Russell, the executor of the Hilton estate, which held the first mortgage on the Stewart Building, demanded its repayment—a step which would cause the cancellation of the $500,000 second mortgage held by the New York Life Insurance Company. Because Wanamaker had committed his cash reserves to rebuilding the New York and Philadelphia stores, he was caught without funds in a tight money situation. Although Wanamaker was able to consolidate the two loans, he did it with great difficulty and some panic.[47]

The business downturn hit first in New York City but quickly spread to Philadelphia. At first the panic was largely confined to the money markets, but it soon spread as businesses that were unable to raise capital laid off employees, who in turn stopped buying. Although this downturn was not as severe or as long as the decline in the 1890s, it took a heavy toll and lasted until 1910.

In late 1906, Wanamaker had trouble paying his construction bills on time. In October 1906, he delayed payments to the American Bridge Company for the steel in the Philadelphia building. He did not apologize, but wrote instead, "We feel free to do exactly what your company did in furnishing the material, for the want of which our building has been behind a number of times." Wanamaker said he would send portions of the money in "fairly good promptness." Another contractor threatened to sue him if $3,114 was not in the mail. Infuriated by the letter because he already had paid $149,316 on the contract, Wanamaker sent the check but with an angry response. Wanamaker wrote one correspondent, "Like others, I am meeting the stringency of a very unusual money market." He indicated he owned real estate he would like to liquidate at this time, if he could. Wanamaker responded to some bills from old contractors in uncharacteristic ways. He tried to put the best foot forward and at times blamed billing mistakes when he did not pay on time.[48]

Several firms, fearing the worst, attempted to take notes issued by Wanamaker to commercial banks to ensure their repayment. One firm that had received a Wanamaker note to the Burnham Company reassigned it to the Chemical Bank of New York, to the chagrin of Wanamaker, who charged that such an assignment was illegal. In December 1906, a furniture firm assigned a bill for about $35,000 to the Philadelphia National Bank to guarantee its payment when due in February and March 1907. The bill was for merchandise Wanamaker had just ordered.[49]

Expenses at the stores were high, and the rebuilding required large sums of additional money, usually raised through short-term loans. The Philadelphia store had to generate $2,400,000 per year in profits to pay its taxes and other expenses. Wanamaker made an almost fatal financial mistake by trying to finance the rebuilding without resorting to outside funds. He also used his available cash to retire $3 million in short-term notes rather than pay high rates of interest. Now caught in a financial bind and unable to pay for the construction out of his own funds, finding money became harder. In July 1907, Charles Dunn, who did most of Wanamaker's banking, had a difficult time disposing of $250,000 worth of Wanamaker's notes. Dunn wrote, "We are getting to the 'end' of this long siege, by the forces of clammy, malice, & lying which we have all been trying to combat, for the past five weeks." Tom Wanamaker, who dealt with the failing finances before he left the store, was particularly disturbed by the banker's failure to secure the loans. "Dunn has acted like a yellow dog & literally taken to the woods," he wrote to his father.[50]

Sagging sales made it more difficult for Wanamaker to generate the needed money. Sales in 1907 fell below 1906, and sales for 1908 were also disappointing. In June 1908, Wanamaker ran sales in New York, but the discounts did little to attract consumers hurt by the recession. To further reduce expenses, Wanamaker laid off employees from the two stores. They were the first Wanamaker workers laid off since the depression of 1893, when Wanamaker closed his Chestnut Street men's store.[51]

Quite clearly, Wanamaker was overstocked, despite his belief that the death of a merchant came from overstocking the store. As the economy faltered, many departments appeared to have too much merchandise. The Philadelphia piano department had a $300,000 stock, enough to turn a profitable department into a losing one.

Bicycles were another problem, as the store had leftovers from the previous year.[52]

Wanamaker's crises were not limited to business. Two fires hit his country estate. On February, 8, 1907, while Wanamaker was in Atlantic City nursing an unusually severe winter cold, the house burned down. The house, worth $1.5 million, was a complete loss; most of its contents, including rare rugs and furniture worth another $1 million, also were destroyed. Servants saved Wanamaker's paintings, which were stored in an adjoining gallery, and piled them in the snow in front of the mansion. Some of this art, along with the stables on the estate, was destroyed in a second fire in July.[53]

On May 18, 1908, after the fires at Lindenhurst and during the financial difficulties that almost led to the collapse of his stores, Wanamaker transferred $517,134.92 from the insurance on the house and stable to his wife, Mary. These transfers protected money from Wanamaker's creditors in case he should fail financially.[54]

The mysterious nature of the fires, coming during Wanamaker's most dire financial predicament and generating needed cash from his insurance, has led to some suspicion that he burned down the house. In the context of his whole life, such an act seems out of character, and no evidence exists to document such a charge.

Lindenhurst's destruction was a sad moment for Mary. She reflected to Rodman, "My but it all seems strange—I did want my earthly possessions for my children—I enjoyed them long—*It is all right*—I have you & the dear children. We will never let any thing come to mar the love that is in our hearts for each other." Mary urged her husband not to worry too much about the rebuilding because he had enough concerns. The house had been her particular haven with its lush gardens and lavish porches where she loved to spend the summer. She wrote John one of her more affectionate letters, telling him how much she appreciated all he had done for her. Since the children all had their own homes, she felt the rebuilding was unnecessary. "You certainly provided . . . my comforts and luxuries have been great—sufficient to have made me very selfish—which I dread it has," she wrote, "I bless & thank you for all, more than you know." In 1911, after Wanamaker was out of the woods, he rebuilt a slightly smaller Lindenhurst with Rodman supervising the operation. The new Lindenhurst, sold after

Rodman's death, was torn down after the Second World War to become a camp for the Boy Scouts of America. The land has since been developed for suburban housing.[55]

While the family was recovering from the fire, Tom contracted his final illness in November 1907. Mary returned from Europe that month and went to a cottage she had at Lakewood, New Jersey, to nurse her son. Tom was both physically ill and in a depression brought on by his illness. Mary remained with him during November and December. They kept several servants, and visitors and doctors dropped in from time to time.[56]

In January 1908, Mary convinced Tom to accompany her on a vacation to Europe. Although his gout was so bad that he could not walk, Mary believed that he would get well aboard the ship. She also felt that his smoking, bad diet, and "old habits" (probably alcohol) prevented him from any real improvement. By late January they wound up in Egypt, trying to find warm weather. At times Tom acted irrationally, which sent Mary to her room in tears. He also seemed to need to keep moving constantly. They changed hotel rooms in Cairo several times but could not find a comfortable one. Minnie came with them and proved to be a great help and comfort to her mother.[57]

Tom died on March 2, 1908, at 47 years of age. His death came in Paris, where they had gone from Egypt. In despair at hearing the news, John Wanamaker wrote, "I am living over everything of the dear fellow's life since his childhood, and wishing so sadly that I had been a less busy man that I might have had more of my boys." He felt the whole affair had left him paralyzed and unable to even talk about it. The funeral was Saturday, March 28, in Philadelphia. Both stores closed for the mourning.[58]

At the time of Tom's death, Wanamaker's financial difficulties threatened to halt the work on the Philadelphia store with only half of the building completed. Low on cash, Wanamaker had fallen behind in his payments to some of his contractors and even owed Burnham money that he did not pay until 1912.[59]

The first two sections of the building cost $5 million to complete. Wanamaker went into the money market to find money for the second part of the work, offering the completed portion and the land beneath the store as collateral for a $7 million loan from New York Life, which the company did not grant. The Land Title Mortgage Company eventually loaned Wanamaker $6 million, part of which he used to pay off an indebtedness of $2 million.[60]

While trying to secure the loan in the fall of 1907, Wanamaker faced a serious problem getting supplies for the Christmas season. He tried to put his best foot forward to convince his suppliers that he had passed through his financial stringency. Joseph Williams, the store's chief financial officer, met with the big suppliers to work out ninety-day payments on the goods, while still allowing a discount that usually only went with a thirty-day payment. On November 2, Wanamaker canceled goods that did not meet the terms he requested. In one letter, Wanamaker replied to a payment-due notice, "The brutality of your letter, threatening to sue us for $358.20, which our buyer believes is not due . . . is such that we enclose our cheque herein." Wanamaker canceled all further orders and forbade his buyers to make purchases from that firm.[61]

He also had problems paying newspapers for advertising. Falling almost a year behind in his payments to the *New York Journal,* Wanamaker owed the paper about $28,000 and did not pay his 1907 debts until late 1908. Although the papers resisted cutting him off, Wanamaker reduced his advertising voluntarily.[62]

Because of these tight financial times, Wanamaker was forced to reorganize the operations of his two stores. Wanamaker studied the practices of other department stores that had begun to be transformed by modern corporate practices. The second generation of Straus Brothers reorganized Macy's, and Gimbel's had undergone substantial changes before its New York store opened in 1910. Wanamaker, however, found it difficult to relinquish control over the everyday operations of the business.

To survive the crisis, Wanamaker changed his organization in ways that would have an impact for the remainder of his life. He gave Joseph Williams, his longtime treasurer, fiscal control over the managers of both stores. Wanamaker also ordered the 120 buyers in his two stores to maintain tightened inventory control and get rid of stock that had been in inventory for longer than six months. Wanamaker warned them, "Stock not having been sold as buyers promised in Oct. last is worth less today than it was then." Each department head was responsible for all of his expenses, including advertising, to allow a proper accounting of a department's worth. To prevent a future cash crunch, Wanamaker put controls on future buying. "I have been long conscious of a defect in our system in the care of the goods between the invoice room and the stock rooms and the sale counters," Wanamaker wrote to his son Rodman in 1909, "and I want . . . a plan that we shall be able to audit the stocks that we pay for as carefully as we audit the cash that the sales people turn in as having received for them."[63]

When he made the buyers more responsible for the stock, Wanamaker relieved them of some control over their salespeople. Traditionally, the buyer hired, fired, and disciplined all personnel within a department in addition to making purchases, advertising their products, gauging the needs of customers, and keeping a check on inventory. A brilliant merchandiser might fail as a manager of his department because of an inability to deal with subordinates. After observing his sales clerks on one trip around the New York store, Wanamaker wrote to Rodman, "I am also disagreeable impressed with what seems to me a lack of conscientiousness on the part of a great many of our employees. So many of them seem to have nothing whatever to do." He blamed this situation upon the failure of his buyers to properly control their salespeople.[64]

To improve the efficiency, Wanamaker gave control over departmental salespersons to aisle people, who oversaw general operations usually within several departments and reported to the store managers directly. Wanamaker still allowed buyers the right to remove a salesperson they did not want. The buyers opposed the change, but it gave them more time to control their inventory, which was Wanamaker's major goal.[65]

For Wanamaker and his other managers, nothing was more important in assuring a steady rise in profits than choosing good buyers, retaining successful buyers, and getting rid of buyers who did not work out. Few students of department stores have discussed the work of the buyer, but Wanamaker realized how much success and failure depended upon them. Buyers were an important creative force. Besides merchandising, they managed their departments, established relationships with customers, and advertised and sold their products. Frequently a buyer who specialized in a particular product, such as dresses, brought in his or her own clientele, which could immediately improve a department's profits.[66]

Searches for buyers took considerable time. Although some buyers had been with Wanamaker's from the beginning of their careers, it was not unusual for a buyer to move from one store to another or to a manufacturing concern. With more than one hundred buyers in the two stores, Wanamaker and his managers spent much time evaluating and replacing buyers who had left or had been fired. For example after searching for some time for a buyer in the New York rug department, Wanamaker wrote that he had found a man who had "some of the merchant spirit ... and will have to be let alone until he proves that we cannot afford to let him alone."[67]

Salaries of the top managers compared favorably with the managers in industrial corporations and contrasted sharply with the bulk of Wanamaker's employees, who averaged about $10 per week before World War I. By the time of Wanamaker's death, John and Joseph Appel, who headed advertising and then became store managers, had risen to the upper echelons of the organization. In 1920 Joseph earned $92,555 while his brother earned $87,500. Both men came to Wanamaker after advertising careers outside the store, but a number of other employees had been hired as youngsters and advanced up the Wanamaker ladder to high places in the enterprise. Rodman Barker, who later became a vice president, started in the bookkeeping department in 1901 at $8 per week. By 1905, he was making $25 per week and showed a steady increase so that by 1912 he was making $75 per week. In 1920 he earned $230 per week and in 1926, $400 per week. Another employee, Frederick W. Wilkens, started in 1905 as a cadet making $5 per week. In 1910 he made $8 per week, but by 1915 his salary had been raised to $25 per week. By 1922, as an aisle manager, he made $75, and shortly after that he moved into management, making $230 per week.[68]

By 1900, women had come to play an important role in the operation although they continued to earn less than men. In an era when few women reached higher-level positions in any field, they held 25 percent of the buyer positions. Several women buyers at Wanamaker's earned salaries that were high for the day. A few women earned more than $25,000 per year and fifty made $5,000 annually.

The reason they reached these high salaries was connected to bonuses buyers received for running highly profitable departments. Women ran many of the fashion departments, some of which sold high-price European dresses, hats, and coats which generated great revenue. They also enjoyed other benefits, including foreign travel, usually tied to their buying operation in France, England, or Germany. Several women played major roles in the New York or Philadelphia store. Ida Appel held a senior advertising role while Nancy McClellan was the chief fashion buyer in New York and spent three or four months each year in Paris. Her letters from Paris were used as advertisements in both the Philadelphia and New York newspapers. She also helped plan a display of paintings called the Paris Exhibition. In a letter to Rodman, Wanamaker praised "her wonderful breadth and business analysis of conditions." On another occasion, Wanamaker wrote that she "had ten times the ideas of the head men in the store under her little hat than they had in their whole heads." Yet despite the prominent role of women like McClellan, Wanamaker was reluctant to place women in store-wide decision-making roles. Women never appeared in this inner circle and never made salaries as high as their male counterparts.[69]

During the years before World War I, Wanamaker received a great deal of criticism from reformers about the low wages paid to women, most of whom made $8 or $9 per week, although many made less. Wanamaker defended his wage policies by arguing that women who were educated and had technological skills and used them in the departments in which they were employed received wages competitive with other industries. To answer charges that he was having his "girls" thrown onto the streets because they couldn't afford rent on his wages, he set up a hotel for single girls, the Hotel Rodman, but it closed down after several years of operation.[70]

During 1908, although the economy was better, Wanamaker was clearly not out of the woods. In the spring, when most of his accounts were current, he wrote about his finances in a very positive way. The selling season was good, making up for a drop in the winter season, and his profit margin was healthier than it had been for three years. Still, financial problems forced him to push back demolition of the Chestnut Street section of the old Grand Depot building. He hoped to complete the project in time for the fall 1909 season. To raise money for this push, Wanamaker tried to sell some of his other Philadelphia real estate, but the real estate market was still tight.[71]

On September 18, 1908, with the mortgage money in hand, Wanamaker began demolishing the last section of the Philadelphia store, a job that provided work for 4,000 Philadelphia laborers during the height of the recession. Wanamaker moved all the merchandise from the section under construction, which comprised more than half of the total store space, into the completed part of the building. Nine months later, Wanamaker held a large ceremony celebrating the laying of the cornerstone.[72]

This last construction project coincided with the completion of work on the Philadelphia subway, which was to bring commuters to the central city from the heavily populated suburbs. Wanamaker believed that the rail line, which he had promoted for many years, would produce a rebound in sales. To gain maximum benefit from the new line, Wanamaker opened his new basement at Market Street to connect with it and stocked it with lower-priced goods to appeal to shoppers who normally did not venture into the store. The basement appealed to members of a new middle-class population who had moved to outlying parts of the city and were affluent enough to become shoppers at a Wanamaker's. These people had previously visited the store only for its pageantry. Although the basement store sold lower-priced merchandise, Wanamaker tried to maintain good quality. He wrote, "I have cherished the idea of a certain kind of store, that so far as my knowledge goes does not exist anywhere, and it is I that will stand or fall by the new venture."[73]

To attract customers to the basement store, Wanamaker added a number of services there, particularly a sales-adjustment department and a credit office offering credit to his new customers. Because it was physically separated from the floors serving elite customers, it also served to segregate his new clientele from his old customers.[74]

As the main buying season began in 1908, Wanamaker was quite careful about his purchases. He tried to balance his need for fresh goods against a feeling that sales, particularly in New York, would continue to slide. He met with his salespersons, giving them a pep talk urging them to "Stand up to the duty of the hour & keep step to the music of success." Sales in New York began badly, even in comparison to

1907, a poor year, but December sales were very robust. Two days before Christmas, despite some miserable weather, the store in New York did more than $140,000 in business. The crowds were so large that clerks often were unable to quickly record sales and deliver merchandise to the customers. In Philadelphia, however, sales did not rebound as well as in New York, remaining behind 1907.[75]

Financially, Wanamaker's problems continued through the 1910 selling season, although sales never again dropped to 1907 levels. A March 1910 strike against the Widener Wolf Traction Company by all street transportation workers in Philadelphia complicated the recovery. Even after the strike ended, business remained slow, leaving Wanamaker overstocked. In New York, the failure of the Northern Bank of New York City cost Wanamaker $23,000 in deposits and reduced consumer confidence. The result was a disappointing Christmas season—a decline of about 10 percent from 1909. Even a year later, at the start of the 1911 Christmas season, economic conditions continued to plague the store. With the stock market falling, Wanamaker worried, "These losses make people spend less, as you can imagine."[76]

Construction of the Philadelphia store concluded in May 1911. Eager to spend his remaining years in his home city, Wanamaker placed Rodman in charge of the New York store and returned to Philadelphia. On November 14, 1910, at 8 a.m., he opened the final section of his rebuilt Philadelphia store. "Flocks of people flowed in all day," Wanamaker observed. "I kept on shaking hands until flatteries drowned me and I went off to see callers."[77]

Wanamaker personally supervised the arrangement of first-floor departments to give his store the best possible appearance and to maximize profits. A central part of the new store was a jewelry store facing Chestnut Street. Wanamaker gave the department's head an enlarged budget; he envisioned turning the store into a competitor with the two major jewelry stores on Chestnut Street—Caldwell's and Bailey, Banks and Biddle. He also created the Little Gray Salon for his most affluent customers, which perhaps balanced out the basement shop. Wanamaker advertised that the Salon was "designed for the convenience of women to whom luxury, elegance and exclusiveness appeal." The shop is "thoroughly French in .... tone, being furnished, finished and mirrored like the best Parisian shops."[78]

After the many trials and tribulations of the preceding ten years, Wanamaker got his chance for the event that marked the high point of his fifty years in business—the dedication of his new store. The new building was a culmination of his long study of department stores and their place in urban society. In planning the store, he had visited major department stores in Europe, including Le Printemps in Paris and Teitz of Berlin. He kept pictures of these stores in an envelope in his desk. Even today, his store stands as a monument to early twentieth-century architecture. One journal called it "a concrete demonstration of original thought ... in the new Wanamaker building are centered a group of technical and mechanical features which illustrate the highest constructive skill."[79]

Although Wanamaker later downplayed the structure, arguing that the building mattered less than what was in it, the store was unique. It was twelve stories (247 feet) above the ground, had a basement with a mezzanine and a sub-basement thirty-four feet below the ground. With two million square feet, the building was the largest in the world devoted to merchandising. Its exterior and interior were very ornate. Fire walls divided the store into three sections so that in case of a fire, the parts would remain separate. The building had a framework of steel, with each concrete floor supported independently of the others. Ten dumbwaiters and two large chutes allowed goods to be moved in or out, while sixty-eight elevators embedded into the fire walls carried passengers and merchandise.[80]

At the center of store stood the Grand Court, with a dome rising 150 feet, surrounded by Ionic and Corinthian columns. With a floor of gray Tennessee marble, 112 feet long and 66 feet wide, the court held 25,000 people. At the center of it all was a 2,500-pound bronze eagle, which Wanamaker had purchased for $10,000 from the German Exhibit of Arts at the St. Louis Exposition in 1904. Overlooking the Grand Court stood the largest organ in the world, with 17,954 pipes, which Wanamaker bought at the same time as the eagle. The organ is still played regularly in the store, ninety years after Wanamaker installed it.

Yet, as one visitor to the Grand Court wrote, "the sheer beauty of the scene was not its most inspiring characteristic. That was the animation of the scene unfolded before me from the balcony—the moving, busy, happy, smiling, chatting throng that gave it all a soul. The ideal represented in the living reality that thrilled me was only secondarily the aestheticism of the Greek; primarily it was the dedication to service that has distinguished and edified the Anglo-Saxon."[81]

During the Christmas season the Grand Court took on the atmosphere of a church. Decorated with a great tree and surrounded with angels and other Christian symbols, the court echoed with hymns from the great organ and from choirs singing Christmas songs such as "Hark the Herald Angels Sing" and "All Hail the Power of Jesus Name." People who shopped Wanamaker's received "devotional reminders and religious encouragement." With 14,000 people crowding into the court, the religious congregation was larger than in any church in the city. One patron in the 1950s wrote after viewing the display, that the store's "beautiful decorations honoring Jesus Christ" were "beyond human expression." In the Grand Court, Wanamaker achieved his goal of "bringing into mercantile life much more of Christian organization that would give an uplift to the people."[82]

Another highlight of the store was the Great Crystal Tea Room, which was the largest dining room in Philadelphia and one of the largest in the world. Done in Renaissance style and modeled after a room in Robert Morris's house, the room got its name from the rows of crystal reflecting chandeliers hanging from the ceiling. It was on the eighth floor, and its windows afforded a commanding view of the city.[83]

But the exterior of the store and its internal architecture were only packages for Wanamaker's *piece de resistance*, his merchandising displays. Wanting to create a major public place in Philadelphia superior to any museum or concert hall, Wanamaker filled the building with paintings, sculptures, and antiques. Wanamaker also turned the store into a public performing hall, gaining publicity from the store's musical events. He held daily and special concerts, sometimes featuring star attractions such as Richard Strauss. Wanamaker tried to feature American composers, bringing to Philadelphia such musicians as Victor Herbert. The musical center of the Philadelphia store was the Egyptian Room, which could hold 500 singers at a time and 1,400 persons in the audience. Several smaller halls surrounding it could hold 500 or 600 people. All the halls were quite opulent, featuring elaborate woodwork. During the Christmas season, music could be heard everywhere.[84] In reality, Wanamaker's music was ancillary to the largest music business in the United States. Before World War I, Wanamaker's piano shop was the largest retailer of pianos in the world, selling a record 223 pianos in one day.[85]

The University of Trade and Applied Commerce occupied almost an acre of store space on an upper floor of the building. All the boys and girls in the store were required to attend some schooling at the university, and older employees also took courses. The boys were also required to participate in some athletic program and many also belonged to a marching band that entertained customers in the store and also participated in local civic ceremonies. The curriculum of the university, divided into commercial, practical, and academic subjects, was drawn from department store experiences. At the dedication of the college's new quarters in 1916, Wanamaker wrote, "[W]e are planning that the United States shall reap a Harvest of Healthy, Educated, contented men and women, fit for conditions peaceful and prosperous, instead of leaving them to Socialistic anarchism, ignorance and poverty that breed discontents and crime."[86]

For the dedication of the store on December 29, 1911, Wanamaker invited 25,000 people, including President William Howard Taft. The event was one of the great coups in Wanamaker's advertising career and a pinnacle of a two-month celebration that began with the jubilee affair in the middle of November and continued with the Christmas celebration and the dedication of the new building. It ended a period that was among the hardest of his career. Parades, music, speeches, and visiting dignitaries enlivened the store.[87]

For Philadelphians, the dedication of the store was long remembered and helped to cement the place that Wanamaker's had at the nexus of Philadelphia. With the new subway line extending to the basement of Wanamaker's and with the terminals of the Pennsylvania and Reading Railroads only blocks away, the store was at the center of a greatly expanded metropolitan area, drawing shoppers from the suburbs, rural areas, and distant parts of the United States to shop at America's great emporium.

The new store next to city hall fulfilled Wanamaker's dreams. It was the epicenter of the new Philadelphia. An architectural masterpiece, it was one of the last built by Burnham, who died in 1914. Part of an urban renaissance, the store was but the grandest of many new buildings in Philadelphia built in an urban Gothic style. Wanamaker's was a cathedral for a new middle-class culture of Philadelphia. For the next sixty years, Wanamaker's was the focus for the city's civic culture as people gathered at the store for celebrations and for memorials. Because Philadelphia was later slow to accept the post-Second World War glass architecture, the massive Gothic continued to define Philadelphia's appearance long after other cities accepted new forms.

CHAPTER SEVEN

Last Years

1912-1922

The forty-six acres of selling space in the new store dwarfed the original two acres of the 1876 Grand Depot and was larger than any store in the world. But it was more than just a retail outlet. With its Crystal Tea Room and its concert halls, Wanamaker's was the center of the city, its civic heart. As *The New York World* of March 9, 1928 noted, "The department store today is not merely a place to purchase goods. . . . It is a place to hear lectures, to look at picture exhibitions, to attend musical concerts. It bears directly and favorably upon the social life of the community."

At the opening of the new store, Daniel H. Burnham commented that Wanamaker's "monument is his store—a thing of beauty and dignity enhancing the appearance of the city, a building that the entire community is from this time on to take the greatest pride in, for in a high sense it is theirs and they are to use it." After 1911, Wanamaker, the building, and Philadelphia became largely inseparable in the minds of most Philadelphians.[1]

When Burnham's masterpiece opened, Wanamaker was 73 years old, an age at which most people were retired. He had completed his major monuments, the two stores and new buildings for Bethany. Rodman was his chosen successor and he made sure that his son would get absolute control of his business.

But John lived eleven more years and remained the central fixture in the store and in Philadelphia until his death in 1922. Except for periods of bad health, Wanamaker remained actively creative, constantly moving around the store, rearranging counters and departments. He continued to go over departmental reports and to supervise the work of the buyers. Rodman was in charge of operations in New York, but until the last few months of Wanamaker's life consulted his father on major decisions.[2]

John even took to writing his own advertisements, something he had not done since the 1880s. He felt that the new store lacked some of the intimacy of the Grand Depot buildings. To restore this intimacy with customers, he wrote a series of folksy style columns. Although the ads attracted a great deal of attention for their break with the slick advertisements dominating newspapers at the time, they also generated controversy. Sometimes the ads hit sore nerves with groups in the city. After misstating the facts in a St. Patrick's Day editorial, Wanamaker received complaints that he was anti-Catholic. Wanamaker replied that he had a very high regard for the Catholic spirit and that a large proportion of his employees were Catholic, and many of them Irish.[3]

Even for a younger person, these would have been trying times. Recessions, a war, and a long inflation made the retail waters quite treacherous. Despite his age and the fact that he represented the generation of the founders of the department store, Wanamaker provided continued leadership for the industry, maintained an active role in many religious activities, and even returned to the political campaign trail.

During the last decade of his life, Wanamaker's central religious activity continued to be Bethany. When in the Philadelphia area on Sundays, Wanamaker continued to spend them at Bethany, engaged in activities which took him from 8:30 in the morning until early evening, or just about the same hours he spent at the store on the other days. His most prominent role at the church remained as superintendent of the Sunday school, but he also spent much time as the head of the Brotherhood which consisted of 500 to 1000 men who met early Sunday morning to give testimonials and sing hymns. Although Robert Coyle functioned as the real leader of Bethany, Wanamaker was still the symbolic leader and, when health permitted, gave regular sermons at the Bible Union. When well he continued to attend board meetings and tried to dominate activities at the church.[4]

Perhaps the religious high point of Wanamaker's last years was his participation in Billy Sunday's 1914 and 1915 Philadelphia rally. Starting in December, the meeting went on through March, attracting over one million participants. Although not quite the success of the Moody revival, it did stir up a sensation in a city greatly preoccupied with the European war and its own economic problems stemming from that conflict. While in Philadelphia, Sunday and his family stayed at Lindenhurst with Wanamaker. As a parting gift, Wanamaker gave the evangelist a wardrobe of suits.[5]

When Sunday came under considerable criticism from several Philadelphia newspapers, including the *Inquirer* and the *Bulletin*, Wanamaker wrote these off as papers which were "inimical to vitalized religion." Making a spirited defense of the evangelist, Wanamaker wrote, "I think those who are inclined to belittle 'Billy' Sunday's efforts and discourage what they regard as his eccentricities, are making a great mistake, for 'Billy' Sunday is a real man, a living force, and his sense and knowledge of the truth that he talks in his own way twists people's lives around for good."[6]

While preoccupied with the Sunday revival in 1914, Wanamaker became increasingly involved with the activities of the Salvation Army. Forty years earlier when in London he had attended the first meeting held by William Booth, making periodic contributions to promote its work. Until 1914 his largest donation was $10,000, which went for the creation of the New York headquarters as a memorial to the founder. After Booth's death, Wanamaker became Booth's daughter Evangeline's personal financial advisor, helping set up an account for her at the First Penny Savings Bank, with money left to her after her father's death. In May 1917 he brought Evangeline to Philadelphia for a major revival session. She spoke at Bethany on Mother's Day on the topic "Mother and Home" and at the Empire Theater at Broad and Fairmount Streets. The meetings were part of a congress to stir up interest in the Salvation Army in Philadelphia. Wanamaker also played an active role in her efforts to build an Army headquarters in Philadelphia. When the Army had difficulty raising the money, Wanamaker paid to complete the building.[7]

Although in his mid-70s and fully committed to his business and religious affairs, Wanamaker returned to politics to support President William Howard Taft in his unsuccessful effort to win reelection. Taft's participation in the Philadelphia dedication ceremony brought Wanamaker back into national politics. He supported the president in 1912, when Theodore Roosevelt challenged Taft for the Republican presidential nomination. A reformer in the 1880s and 1890s, Wanamaker was out of step with the Progressive wing of the Republican Party during the Roosevelt years. Never close to the president since they clashed over civil service reform, Wanamaker was also out of step with the younger reformers, including his son Rodman. Wanamaker did join the reformers in supporting his old friend Rudolph Blankenburg in his successful campaign for mayor. For his help, Blankenburg appointed Wanamaker a member of the city's Board of Education.[8]

Several months before the Wanamaker celebration, Taft had invited him to stay at the White House. After talking to the president until 1 a.m., Wanamaker went to sleep in the Lincoln Room, which had been used as an office during Benjamin Harrison's presidency. Wanamaker had a hard time sleeping, thinking of both Lincoln and Harrison. Wanamaker wrote Mary, "I saw a number of the men of the old times and so many are gone that it was almost painful to think of Blaine, Windom, Rusk, Proctor, Foster, Elkins, McKinley, Chief Justice Fuller, Harrison, Mrs. Harrison."[9]

In March 1912, at Taft's request, Senator Boies Penrose asked Wanamaker to represent Pennsylvania in the June Republican national convention in Chicago. Surprised by the offer, Wanamaker wrote to Rodman, "Mr. Penrose is to be a force in this election and must not be ignored. He can show his ugliness if he wants to anyone who fails to recognize his position." Although he agreed to go to Chicago, Wanamaker continued to distance himself from the Penrose machine. Two years later, however, he reached a rapprochement with Penrose, who was up for election, and contributed to the senator's campaign. He did not endorse him openly because he felt it would "jolt" the reformers and hurt his credibility. Wanamaker's renewed interest in national politics was whetted by newspaper rumors that he might replace the ailing Vice President John Sherman on the ticket.[10]

Before his appointment as a delegate, Wanamaker had booked a

European trip. Because of a dock strike in France, Wanamaker almost missed the convention. But arriving back on June 19, he rushed to Chicago for the June 21 convention in time to make a seconding nomination for Taft. Praising Taft as an experienced leader who was best able to pull the country out of difficult economic times, Wanamaker argued that the president encouraged commerce and ran the country with real business principles. "The government, under a thorough analysis, is a business proposition, pure and simple, and in the highest sense," he declared.[11]

Wanamaker's speech attracted a good deal of criticism from papers opposed to the president. One journal attacked him for equating government with business and not understanding the purposes of government. Another newspaper lamented that the great reforming journal the *North American*, which helped elect Rudolph Blankenburg in 1911 as reform mayor of Philadelphia and broke the back of Penrose, had so little effect on him. Rodman owned the *North American*, which he had inherited from Tom.[12]

Pleased with the nomination of Taft but disappointed that Sherman was renominated, Wanamaker also was disgusted at the disorder at the convention. Wanamaker feared that Roosevelt's walkout from the convention would lead to a victory by the Democratic candidate Woodrow Wilson in the fall. At the end of the convention, Wanamaker was so tired that he was unable to go to church the next day.[13]

During the campaign, Wanamaker's physical condition worsened. This illness was beyond his usual cold; he did not return to his office until October 1912. When better, Wanamaker strongly supported Taft, attacking Roosevelt, now the candidate of the Progressive Party, as "a mad man trying to wrest the presidency from the man who, in all fairness, should have Roosevelt's support." A few days after Wanamaker delivered this address, Roosevelt was shot while giving a speech, but survived. Critics attacked Wanamaker for his campaign against Roosevelt and likened him to the slanderers of Garfield who caused his murder. One writer wondered how Wanamaker, a defender of Sunday schools and religion, could have contributed to so vile an act. "I only make this suggestion, your conscience will make the application," he wrote to Wanamaker. Another writer, while praising Wanamaker for his past activities in favor of good government, could not understand his attachment to the reactionaries in this campaign. Furthermore, by supporting Taft, the writer charged, Wanamaker assured the victory of Wilson and free trade. Such an eventuality was cutting his own throat since his Philadelphia customers would be so financially hurt by such a result. The writer of this letter did not understand the alienation which had existed between Roosevelt and Wanamaker for a long time dating back to the Harrison Administration, or the actual philosophy of Wanamaker. The merchant had opposed the bosses in Philadelphia, but had never opposed the national bosses of the party, except for Quay, which was largely personal, and had never endorsed the Progressive Movement.[14]

Wanamaker made his major campaign contribution in a *New York Herald* editorial republished around the country at Wanamaker's expense. Wanamaker called upon business leaders and their workers to support the president. "No new government ought to be permitted to check existing prosperity or to begin new policies that jeopardize the nation's future," he said. If Woodrow Wilson were elected, "the pillage of labor and the ravaging of industry would begin immediately after March 4, 1913." He warned that Wilson would repeat the disasters brought on by Cleveland. In this effort for Taft, Wanamaker repeated ideas he had championed since early in his life. Seizing upon the nineteenth-century idea of mutual interests among workers and capitalists, Wanamaker argued that the protective tariff benefitted both classes. He also played upon the harsh memories many people had of Cleveland's depression in the 1890s.[15]

Wanamaker's defense of prosperity based on the tariff helped to give some shape to what was a floundering Taft campaign. Its ideas were picked up by other Republicans and became the main theme of the election. When Vice President Sherman died on October 30, several members of the Republican National Committee came out in favor of Wanamaker for the position, but the committee declined to nominate anyone.[16]

After Wilson won the election, with Taft running third, Wanamaker wrote letters to both Taft and Wilson and met with Taft, who was traveling by train from New Haven to Washington, D.C. Wanamaker joined him in New York and stayed with him until Philadelphia. In his letter to Wilson, Wanamaker wrote, "There is a citizenship above

Party and an old personal friendship for you that calls out this expression of goodwill." However, on March 3, 1913, the day Wilson became president, Wanamaker wrote, "I am unpatriotic enough to wish a habitation in Sicily or Italy for the next four years."[17]

Wanamaker had had a warm relationship with Woodrow Wilson earlier. Both of Wanamaker's sons had graduated from Princeton, the school where Wilson taught and served as president before becoming governor of New Jersey. As a large contributor to the college, Wanamaker had known Wilson. Both men were active Presbyterian laymen, and Wanamaker had hired the future president to speak at meetings of the Pennsylvania Sunday School Association.[18]

Despite earlier friendships, the change of administrations in Washington created some of the most vexing legal problems of Wanamaker's career. In November 1911, William Loeb, the collector of customs at New York, informed Wanamaker that he was being charged with failing to pay duties on some imported goods. To prevent future problems with an unfriendly administration, Wanamaker settled the claims before Taft left office. But the new collector of customs under Wilson, William Barry, egged on by Democratic Congressman A. Mitchell Palmer from eastern Pennsylvania, refused to accept the agreement. Barry brought the case before a grand jury. The jury accused Wanamaker of receiving packages marked "samples, no commercial value" that contained goods sent to him for sale.[19]

Wanamaker's problems left him embittered. He felt all importers were subject to dangers similar to his. "It is worthwhile to note, however, that this is the way the Government regards the merchants and importers, who furnish the largest part of the Treasury revenues," he said. Wanamaker believed the Wilson administration used the issue to discredit the Taft administration. Wanamaker's difficulties continued into 1914, when he settled with the government for $100,000.[20]

After Wilson became president in March 1913, the economy went into a sharp decline. Lack of confidence by business in the new administration as well as a tight money supply resulted in high interest rates and large-scale unemployment. Lamenting that money was scarcer than in 1907, Wanamaker wrote, "We are poorer than any church mice you ever heard of." Business was very slow. All of the New York stores were in trouble and were selling their stocks. "It is not a time to make profits apparently, if you wish to hold your customers."[21]

Because general economic conditions were poor in 1913, sales for the whole year ran behind 1912. To avoid getting caught without cash as he did in 1907, Wanamaker issued $100,000 in short-term notes to the Chemical Bank. This expedient was something he had not done in twenty-five years, and the interest was about 6.5 percent, much higher than previously. Economic conditions continued to drift during the year, producing a weak Christmas season. By the summer of 1914 conditions had yet to recover. Retailing in New York City was particularly hard hit, resulting in a number of failures. The economy had not yet reversed itself when in August, the European war broke out between the Central and Allied powers.[22]

In his business operations as well as his personal life, Wanamaker held an affinity for Europe. During 1912, 1913, and 1914, Wanamaker spent the early part of each year in Europe recovering from his winter illnesses. His family, including Mary and Rodman, and sometimes his daughters and some of his grandchildren, spent the summer in Europe. Wanamaker often sent his buyers to Europe during the summer vacations to pick up the latest fashion tips to be used back home. In 1914, he sent two buyers to Paris to cool off after a dispute between them.

When war broke out in Europe between Germany and Austria on one side and England, France, and Russia on the other side, Wanamaker and his family had many business and personal contacts in Europe. Like many of the American ruling class, they liked to think of themselves as part of the European business elite. Wanamaker also had strong ties to Germany, France, and England. Because he had met the rulers in all three countries, he could not believe they had any evil motives.[23]

His buyers purchased laces, cloth, and other goods in Germany, and he had an office in Berlin. His favorite vacation spot, particularly in his older years, was Carlsbad or other German spas, where he stayed for a month or more at a time. But Wanamaker's most important contacts were in Paris. He often visited French department stores for new ideas, and he had maintained an office and a home in the city since the early 1880s. Most of Wanamaker's imported goods came from

France. Wanamaker also maintained a headquarters in England, and he had many English friends in Christian missionary work and among political leaders, particularly those interested in international postal reform. He disliked the English climate, however, and generally avoided long stays.

Like many Americans who had ancestors in one of the warring countries, Wanamaker experienced apprehensions about the war. He wrote Rodman: "These are indeed awful times, when the wheat fields of our fathers in Germany, France and Belgium are being turned into cemeteries of the dead, slain in battle." As a businessman, he knew that few men of commerce benefitted from war over the long run. Consequently, business people had long been associated with the anti-war movement. When the war broke out, Wanamaker in a newspaper editorial called for American neutrality so that "nothing shall draw the United States into this wild war."[24]

His feelings at this time reflected a realization that his whole idea of the world was about to crumble. Always, he believed in a society held together by commerce and religion. Initially he applied this concept to the Philadelphia area, and as postmaster general, he looked at the whole of the United States through this vision. In the twenty years before the war, he applied this idea to the world through his purchases of European and Asian goods and his promotion of the world missionary movement. War, particularly among Christian nations, put that dream out of reach. Because of his German background, he was appalled at the prospective carnage. At home, higher taxes, inflation, and uncommon discord over the war made American society more conflict-ridden than it had appeared for many years. Simultaneously, however, Wanamaker had strong feelings of patriotism and a love of things military.

On August 1, 1914 many of Wanamaker's employees along with Rodman and his second wife, Violetta, were in Europe. Two weeks later Rodman telegraphed from London, "No toys here. Cannot get replies from Walls apparently in Harve with McClellan. D Ralson Cressman awaiting steamer. Have telegraphed but unable know if they can leave. Doing our best with Beercroft. Better use your judgement about further orders." Because of the conditions in Europe, including opportunities the war might create, Rodman decided to stay in England through late September, returning in early October. Other family members were in Europe as well. Minnie Warburton, Wanamaker's daughter, was at Carlsbad trying to figure out the best way to get home.[25]

Wanamaker's buyers were still operating in France. To provide them with money, he bought pounds sterling from the House of Morgan, putting the money in Rodman's account. His buyers stayed in Paris even though the city was on the verge of siege. He also sent his linen buyer with $150,000 to Glasgow to make purchases there. Wanamaker figured that if Russia remained in the war and could not raise flax, the linen purchased would be very valuable.[26]

As Wanamaker had done so often by skilled merchandising and unique showmanship, he benefitted from the chaos in Europe. One of his buyers preparing to leave France bought about 200 designer dresses at bargain prices. In an adventure, she took the dresses and her other belongings in a car to Le Havre to reach one of the last liners to leave that city. In a page-long advertisement in the New York papers, Wanamaker announced, "SEVENTY-ONE PARIS GOWNS AND WRAPS To be Exhibited in the Wanamaker Auditorium Tomorrow and Friday of this week, at 11 and 2." The advertisement recounted the buyer's adventures in rescuing the dresses from France.[27]

The war left economic conditions very clouded. The New York Stock Exchange closed for several months to prevent a crash. As large amounts of gold were transferred to England, money became even more scarce than it had been before the conflict. Interest rates shot up to 9 and 10 percent, which kept Wanamaker from borrowing money. Since few customers were buying, he had a cash problem, but he was not in as much trouble as some of his competitors.[28]

Despite all of Wanamaker's efforts to move his merchandise, the normally slow August selling period was the worst he had ever seen. One of the first casualties of the recession was Lord & Taylor, which fell into bankruptcy. Associated Dry Goods, the first real chain of department stores, bought it out. Then Claflin, a pioneering retail chain, failed. After Claflin's bankruptcy, lenders refused to lend money to retailers at any price, leaving Wanamaker unable to borrow $316,000 he needed to pay a tax bill. By the end of September, Wanamaker wrote, "We are poor but hopeful & doing our best, everybody wants money as the ways to get help are closed all round to almost all but collateral borrowers or such as make certified statements."[29]

Unemployment increased and by 1915 inflation had set in. As was his usual policy, Wanamaker tried to keep all his workers employed even though business slipped. Wanamaker also allowed his credit customers leniency in meeting their bills. In one case, he allowed a contractor who owed him $80,000 due on October 1, 1914, to pay $20,000 down and the rest in April. With money hard to come by, Wanamaker took precautions with his personal and store expenditures. He wanted to avoid the serious situation of the last panic. His annual expense in New York for the *New York Evening Post* for 1914 was about $300,000, which he cut sharply for the next year. By June 1915, the economy was still weak, forcing Wanamaker to dismiss some of his employees after shifting others around the store.[30]

In the fall of 1915, the financial situation turned around as business picked up and interest rates fell to 5 percent. Led by munitions making, manufacturing turned around. Textiles revived as domestic manufacturers replaced foreign goods. With the returning prosperity, Wanamaker became philosophical about the situation, reflecting, "It is painful to think that any prosperity at this time is a result of the grievous war." Despite returning prosperity, full employment did not return until 1916.[31]

In 1914, Wanamaker maintained neutrality, painting himself as a child of the various warring parties because his father had a German name and his mother was French. He wrote that, as a private citizen, it was his duty to support the efforts of the president in keeping the country neutral. Given the volatility of public opinion and Wanamaker's tendency to make candid public statements, he sometimes got into trouble. In July 1915, he proposed that the United States arbitrate the war even if it meant lending the warring nations money to end the conflict, an idea that angered many people who rejected any thought of lending money to Germany for any purpose.[32]

As a retailer who needed the friendship of the public, he began to move with the growing anti-German sentiment in the country. Before the selling season in 1915, he ordered his buyers to refrain from purchasing German goods and not to display any such goods they might already possess. American-made goods or goods from the Allies replaced items formerly imported from Germany. Since nearly all toys came from Germany, that department was hurt. During the next few years, toys made in the United States gradually replaced these toys. Wanamaker regarded this as the beginning of a new industry in the United States.[33]

To appeal to sympathy with England during the war, Wanamaker opened the London Shop in 1915. All of the clothing and various other paraphernalia sold in the store came from England. Wanamaker appealed to his customers that, in purchasing outerwear, their "British cousins endors[ed] these topcoats, sir. . . ." One particularly appealing group of clothing for both men and women copied the dress style of British officers.[34]

Wanamaker maintained neutrality on the war until spring, 1915, when the sinking of the *Lusitania* began to push him toward a more belligerent attitude toward Germany. Three of his employees, going to Europe on business, were on the ship and lost their lives. Wanamaker sent a response to the *Philadelphia Evening Journal* on May 10, writing, "Whoever are responsible for the conduct of the war must have lost their heads."[35]

As the crisis worsened, Wanamaker assumed his accustomed role as the civic voice of Philadelphia. For Wanamaker's business this was particularly important, because he had a Teutonic-sounding name at a time when Philadelphia, like the rest of the country, was turning anti-German. Wanamaker chaired a meeting backing Wilson's stern message to the Kaiser after the *Lusitania* sinking. He became chairman of the Philadelphia chapter of the National Security League and mobilized his employees, creating the Red, White and Blue Cross Association. He even created a women's battalion, but was careful to emphasize that he did not want to harm their womanliness: "I am quite willing that the drilling of the women for Military Exercises, shall take a form that will be more conductive to gracefulness and to the spirit of women, the majority of whom would never choose to take a military step."[36]

The European War also changed the Wanamakers' personal lives, as trips to German spas were no longer possible and travel to other parts of the continent might be dangerous. In 1915, Rodman's daughter Marie Louise and her husband went back to France. Mary Wanamaker was quite concerned, but accepted her granddaughter's need to be in her French home. But John and Mary themselves would never see Europe again, substituting American vacations. In 1916 Wanamaker spent a large part of the winter in an effort to regain his strength aboard Rodman's boat *Nirvana* off the east coast of Florida, about 25 miles south of Miami. Wanamaker so loved sailing, with its relaxing atmosphere and a chance to fish, that he vowed not to take up residency in a hotel after that trip. Like many of his winter journeys Mary was not with him, but he played host to former Secretary of State William Jennings Bryan. During the summer, Wanamaker spent time sailing the southern part of the Hudson River, again without Mary who disliked the sea, although in August she spent time on the ship as it sailed around New England from Newport. She spent most of the summer in the White Mountains.[37]

With 1916 a presidential election year, Wanamaker reluctantly attended the Republican convention in Chicago, after being urged to go by Boies Penrose to help reunite the party after the disastrous 1912 split. At the meeting he was dismayed by the maneuvering of the Roosevelt delegation at the convention, "trying to scuttle the Republican ship and they may do mischief as they did in 1912." Wanamaker supported Supreme Court Justice Charles Evans Hughes, the eventual nominee, but unlike four years earlier, there was no mention of Wanamaker's name for vice president.[38]

During the campaign Wanamaker was part of a 50-member advisory committee to the Republican National Committee along with Roosevelt and Taft. Wanamaker stirred up controversy by paying for a twelve-page advertisement written by him, attacking Wilson's tariff policy. "It seems so plain and simple to me, and yet so many of our conscientious, well-meaning citizens do not seem to understand, that without a proper protective tariff the bottom of the nation's prosperity drops out, and our people are sent to the bread-line." In retaliation Democrats charged that Wanamaker was getting even for the $100,000 he had paid in fines for bringing goods illegally into the country. Although most New York and Philadelphia newspapers refused to publish the attack because of the large contracts they had with the merchant, it did appear in the *New York American*.[39]

Wilson's election to a second term in November 1916 was followed in January 1917 by the German threat to resume unrestricted submarine warfare, which resulted in a severing of diplomatic relations. Wanamaker heard about this decision aboard his boat *Osiris* on the way to Florida, where he spent several months trying to regain his health. Because of the impending war, Wanamaker often expressed regrets to his son about not being in Philadelphia to aid him in making important decisions. Writing satirically on February 2, Wanamaker noted, "This noble craft of its kind has not sighted any battle cruises nor U-Submarines." Wanamaker soaked up the sun, writing, "My strength comes back slowly but I can feel it coming day by day." The ship was docked off Ft. Meyers about one mile from where Edison had his home. There Wanamaker stayed at the Hotel Royal Palm, an old but very fancy residence. While Wanamaker was aboard his boat, Mary, his two daughters, and several other relatives were in St. Augustine. With the threat of war in March, Mary went home by train.[40]

After hearing that the United States had broken off diplomatic relations with Germany, Wanamaker feared another threat to his business. He warned Rodman that money would become dear again. He recalled all of his women buyers from Europe before hostilities broke out, but before they left, he had them buy all the silk possible to prevent Gimbel's and Stern's from outbidding him.[41]

As late as February 1917, Wanamaker still hoped for peace. "It would be the height of madness for Germany to force war upon America," he wrote to Rodman. Expressing astonishment that the public now wanted war while previously approving of Wilson's effort to stay out of the conflict, he wrote, "It seems as though the American people had suddenly lost their senses. Of course to say this out loud would put us . . . under a ban." Wanamaker represented the view of many Americans whose businesses were threatened by the war. He doubted that more war would end the conflict that had already raged for so many years. "Horrors haunt me in the thought of the U.S. heedlessly rushing into . . . bloodiness," he wrote. He expressed these views in an editorial, but worried that critics would construe it as an attack on the president before he addressed Congress.[42]

With so much bad news during February, Wanamaker was happy that it passed without a great loss of sales. Wanamaker remained optimistic that even if war came, people would still have to buy goods, but he was concerned that he would lose salespeople if everyone put on a uniform. Although Wanamaker expected the problem to be limited, he wrote, "I doubt very much that a necessity will ever arise for America to maintain a standing army."[43]

While in Florida, Wanamaker prepared for the worst, suggesting the stores cut back on staff to save a million dollars while reducing all credit obligations by selling real estate. He was also concerned about the effect a shortage of sugar would have on the restaurants. He felt it might be better to close them, rather than serve inferior meals.[44]

When the United States entered the war in April, 1917, Wanamaker promptly ended all opposition and turned the stores in both New York and Philadelphia into war service centers and symbols of patriotism. As in earlier crises, Wanamaker's became a center of civic functions in Philadelphia and a barometer for the popular mood in the city. Reflecting the rise of patriotism, Wanamaker devoted much of his advertising to patriotic themes. Describing his store windows, Wanamaker wrote, "One window is dressed with President Wilson and his War Cabinet Officers . . . another is dressed for France, in which the statue of Jeanne d'arc is wrapped with the tricolor." Like many other Philadelphians, he was particularly devoted to the flag. At the dedication of the Booth Memorial Building, Wanamaker said, "Liberty to unfurl the American flag from every roof, home, and church, school house, hall, store, and workshop is the right fashion of Philadelphia. This city more than any other should be an example to the United States." As the war progressed, Wanamaker became increasingly bellicose. In an introduction to a book by Dr. George Pentacost, the pastor of Bethany Church, Wanamaker called the conflict a "war for Righteousness . . . God is looking at what we are doing."[45]

As a member of the Board of Education for which he had been chosen in 1913, Wanamaker followed popular opinion by supporting the elimination of German from the curriculum. In a long attack on Germans and German civilization, he argued that Germans used their language to foster their rule and the idea of German superiority. "The use of the German language was intended to keep the Germans living in the United States as aliens and as agents of Germany," Wanamaker said, even though he was a former president of the Pennsylvania German Society.[46]

At times, Wanamaker could still view the excesses of anti-German feelings with a grain of humor. One customer wrote him an angry letter because he had used the term Kris Kringle in a Christmas advertisement. Wanamaker replied, "I never knew that Germany had a patent on Kris Kringle or the name or I surely would not have used the term."[47]

When war broke out, Wanamaker advertised that the store would do its duty by sending its employees into the service and continuing to sell good merchandise at the lowest price possible. It would not engage in any war profiteering. "It is not a question of how the war will affect business but of how my business may best serve my country at such a time," he said in one ad. Despite this homily, Wanamaker had engaged in profiteering in silk and linen bought in the opening days of the war.[48]

During the conflict, Wanamaker emphasized patriotism, support of the president, and good works to end the war. An Armistice Day advertisement read, "The Best Benefactor That Manhood Ever Had Among the Nations of the World is the United States of America." While supporting the war effort, Wanamaker claimed maximum publicity for the business. In April 1917, General Joffre, the French commander, visited Philadelphia on a fund-raising mission and was assisted by Wanamaker. In July 1917, Wanamaker put a patriotic banner over all his advertising.[49]

In keeping with wartime austerity, Wanamaker tried to cut his personal expenditures. "Whatever I can do for Liberty Bonds and for the Red Cross and the YMCA, I want to do; and while I am asking other people to economize I could not feel comfortable if I were not doing likewise," he wrote. The Wanamaker family supported many wartime charities. John gave $20,000 to local hospitals in financial straits, while Mary and one of their daughters supported a Bethany project to distribute aid packages to the troops. Mary also made a large contribution to the work of Billy Moody, who ran a YMCA Camp for servicemen at Northfield, Massachusetts. Moody was delighted with the contribution, praising her for her continued support and recalling his long ties to the Wanamakers going back to childhood, "the affection of childhood has remained undiminished. . . ."[50]

Despite the effort to keep up the appearance of participating in everyone's miseries during the war, the Wanamakers continued to live a rich lifestyle. During 1916 and 1917, Mary spent $18,019 on clothes. Although there were no more trips to Europe, the war did not curtail summer or winter travel. In early 1918, Wanamaker spent the winter in Florida aboard his new yacht, the *Hibiscus*, docked at Daytona. Mary also spent the winter in Florida at a hotel, writing, "I am so thankful that we are privileged to move out of the coldness into these summer climes."[51]

At the beginning of the war, Wanamaker kept up his optimism in the future prosperity of the United States, believing the war would give a tremendous boost to the retail and industrial sectors. Purchases by the federal government kept the factories running, but also created merchandise shortages. Citing the retail experience in England and Australia as reasons to expect a wartime boom, Wanamaker did not foresee the absence of young men in the service as a cause for alarm by retailers. He urged one of his piano suppliers to keep up his business, writing, "there is nothing even in the close of the war likely to interfere with American prosperity, as she will have the best preparation to supply the world with its many needs."[52]

The war created many problems, however, including taxes, new government regulations, inflation, scarcity of goods, and a lack of workers. As the conflict progressed, Wanamaker believed a gang of ignorant individuals led by Wilson was mishandling the economy. The 5 percent tax on the wholesale inventory of musical instruments particularly incensed him. Wanamaker got the two senators from Pennsylvania, Philander Knox and Boies Penrose, to oppose the tax. He was also enraged by coal shortages during the war, but he went along with government suggestions that retailers close their stores for an extra day. Wanamaker shut the stores on Mondays, beginning on January 20, 1918. In conformity with government regulations, Wanamaker's 15,000 employees worked from 9 a.m. to 6 p.m. during the rest of the week and 9 a.m. to 2 p.m. on Saturdays. During the summer, the stores continued to close on Saturdays during July and August but began the longer Saturday hours during December.[53]

During the war, 1,490 individuals from Wanamaker's two stores went into the service; of these, seventeen from the Philadelphia store and about the same number from the New York store died. Although

Wanamaker often aided the families of his employees in the service, he did not continue their salaries. Thus, he reversed a policy followed in 1916 when he paid employees serving in Mexico with Pershing's forces. Nevertheless, he had great pride in the accomplishments of his employees who served in the war. "The sense of the human family of the Store is very dear to me, that we are very much more than a Store, keeping up the interest we have in each other and the pride we have in the great service that the boys have done in the war," he wrote.[54]

Wanamaker became a major supporter of the Liberty Loan drives. He gave his employees the option of making regular salary dedications to buy the bonds. During the Third Liberty Loan, his 15,000 employees contributed $5 million to the campaign. Wanamaker bought $20 million worth of the bonds himself. The whole effort brought Wanamaker a great deal of publicity and good will, particularly during Secretary of the Navy Josephus Daniels' visit to the Philadelphia store.[55]

The Brotherhood house at Bethany, which he owned, was turned over to soldiers and sailors on leave, providing recreational facilities and some housing. During the first year of American involvement in the conflict, 8,000 servicemen made use of the house. Wanamaker picked up most of the expenses for this operation. Bethany Church, also, became one of the major rendezvous points for men in the military in the southwestern part of the city, and it often provided evening suppers for them.[56]

Price increases hit all segments of the population during the war. Soaring prices and a lowered quality of goods made operating the stores very difficult. Wanamaker complained that he could not make a profit because he could not charge much more than was required to break even.[57]

Despite his complaints, 1917 was a busy year for the Philadelphia store, which served an average of 53,000 customers per day. During the Christmas season, trucks delivered as many as 55,560 packages in one day. Despite claims of scarcity of goods, Wanamaker carried more than 7,000 different items in home furnishings. In his usual way, Wanamaker urged his salespeople to overcome the despair hanging over Christmas because of the war: "Try to keep the sunshine all around you, that the people may catch some of it and carry it home, and that the children there and the old people may have a better Christmas, because they have got some of the spirit of it from yourself."[58]

Inflation caused Wanamaker to look for scapegoats. He blamed the government for keeping money very scarce, a policy that hurt both the manufacturing and the retailing sector. He also attacked manufacturers, who he felt were benefitting from wartime conditions to raise prices on shoddy goods, a charge that angered one of his longtime woolens manufacturers.[59]

Because of the inflation, salaries in the store did not keep up with the higher cost of living. Although employees received raises in 1917 and 1918, wages remained behind the price increases, which led many of Wanamaker's employees to leave for defense industries. Trying to calm the anxieties of his workers, Wanamaker wrote, "we have in mind our good people and are trying to take care of them, though these are very difficult times." But the discrepancy between Wanamaker's pay scale and the reality of wartime prices left many persons in the organization discontented.[60]

To retain employees who could make twice as much in war industries, Wanamaker introduced a bonus system. At the end of 1918, Wanamaker paid bonuses totaling almost $100,000 to his employees in Philadelphia. On January 1, 1919, Wanamaker introduced a quarterly bonus for all employees with more than one year of service, but simultaneously they lost their 10 percent discount on purchases. In May 1919, he ended the bonus system, but he restored the discount on merchandise and raised it to 20 percent. In 1920, Wanamaker distributed 15,000 shares of stock to employees.[61]

He could, however, be very hard in dealing with employees who felt they were underpaid. Shortly after the war ended, one female employee complained she was underpaid and in a "cage" in her job and should be making $25 per week. Wanamaker wrote her "It hurts me to think that people feel 'underpaid' and think they haven't 'fair play' in this house, where I am spending my life." He went on to castigate her that she was educated in the store and does simple clerical work, indicating she should be grateful to have a job. He gave her a week off with pay to see if she could find a position paying $25 per week.[62]

While Wanamaker constantly complained about the high costs of doing business, the Wanamaker enterprises remained quite profitable during the war years. For the five years 1914 through 1918, Wanamaker made a total profit of $8,726,791, or an average of $1,745,358 annually. His worst year was 1918, when his profits were $649,593. By contrast, during the years 1909 through 1914, the Wanamaker Corporation made $5,997,804.[63]

Turning 80 in 1918, Wanamaker began to feel the effects of his age, suffering a series of illnesses that kept him incapacitated for long periods. In October 1917, he slipped and fell, hurting his shoulder, which caused him great pain and left him indisposed for several weeks. A few months later, he came down with a cold, which left his throat in very bad condition. His doctors ordered him to bed. However, he was not able to shake his illness, spending parts of May, June, and July in bed. He then went for a cure to a spa in Bedford Springs, Pennsylvania, arriving in late July and staying for six weeks. His bouts with illness carried over into 1919, when he was ill for most of the fall. Although his correspondence did not diminish, he began to curtail his trips to New York. In 1919, almost six months elapsed between visits. His first visit to the city in the latter part of the year was to accept the presidency of the World Sunday School Union.[64]

When the war ended on November 11, 1918, Wanamaker held a great civic celebration in Philadelphia, inviting several dignitaries, including the Secretary of the Navy. More than 20,000 people came to the Great Court, more than attended President Taft's dedication of the building in 1911. The celebration in 1918 was only the beginning of a round of civic celebrations at both Wanamaker stores as he used the Armistice to focus public attention on his business. During May 1919, he held a public reunion for the 28th Division at the Philadelphia store. One woman who attended the festivals wrote, "Such a wonder time we had in your store. . . . I feel that we should express our appreciation. You know you give us pleasure, but I wonder, if you really know how we all do enjoy it. It was a wonderful sight. I never saw such a sight. You have given us so many other pleasant times too." On September 14, 1919, Rodman Wanamaker turned the New York store out to greet General John J. Pershing, the commander of the American forces in Europe. Although John Wanamaker did not attend because of his health, other upper-level management people came from Philadelphia. In October, Rodman greeted the King and Queen of Belgium and participated in a grand civic celebration for them that included a banquet. In the latter part of 1919, John Wanamaker held a birthday anniversary for Theodore Roosevelt, the first one after the former president's death, to help raise funds for a Roosevelt memorial. Wanamaker felt that Roosevelt should be accorded the honor due a former president. For Wanamaker, the store was a part of the civic life of the city, entertaining visiting delegations from all parts of the world. Wanamaker wrote, we are "doing our very best to hold up the Philadelphia flag and backing it with good will."[65]

As part of the process of getting the store back to its pre-war position as the center of Philadelphia's civic culture, Wanamaker held the largest musical event in the store's history. In 1919, Charles M. Courboin played the organ while Leopold Stokowski conducted the Philadelphia Orchestra before 15,000 persons in the Grand Court of the store. The Philadelphia Orchestra event launched a series of regular evening organ concerts that played to more than 80,000 persons that year.

After the war the economy continued to suffer severe dislocations. The wartime inflation continued unabated. Wanamaker charged that high prices were the result of profiteering by speculators who bought up large amounts of merchandise in get-rich schemes. The end of the war produced many shortages. The destruction of flax fields in Russia produced an acute decline in the linen trade. Wanamaker was reluctant to substitute cotton for linen in fine handkerchiefs and other products.[66]

Hard times also led to increased crime in the city, forcing Wanamaker and other merchants on Chestnut Street to put up street lights that the city could not afford. Because of the crime problem, economic conditions, and labor unrest, Wanamaker felt 1919 was among the most trying years he had faced in business. He blamed the Wilson administration for mishandling the Liberty Loans, which led to high interest rates and the decline of the economy. Wanamaker also turned bitter about Wilson's foreign policy, turning against the Versailles Treaty, which he initially had supported. While vacationing at Bedford Springs, he went to a church where the minister came out in favor of the Versailles Treaty. "If I had been in the Church among strangers, I would have walked out of the church during the delivery of the sermon," he wrote to Rodman.[67]

Despite the economic problems, Wanamaker tried to restore the store to its position before the war. In the summer of 1919, he sent Nancy McClellan to Paris to look over the Salon collections to brighten up the store. Business also picked up. More than two million people visited the Philadelphia store in December 1919, overcrowding the facilities and the elevators and causing security problems.[68]

During the war years, Mary Wanamaker had been in frail health, spending the winter months in Palm Beach. In 1919, while returning from the resort, Mary was in a train accident and was rescued through a window. When she arrived in Washington, she stayed in a hospital but never recovered completely. During late 1919 and into 1920 she did not leave her house, except to attend the wedding of her grandson Barclay Harding Warburton in December 1919. About the time of the wedding, Mary wrote what amounted to a farewell note to Rodman, who had been the crutch she leaned upon during John's long absences. "This is my beloved boy—who has the multitude around him and he is not conscious why! every day a joy and comfort to his Mother—Why such a blessing has been given her God above knows. Wherever he is she is sure of his constant prayers and earnest love."[69]

Mary became worse on December 28, 1919. She remained for several months at the Ambassador Hotel in Atlantic City, before going back to Philadelphia. In March, Wanamaker held out some hope for her, but she had already been bedridden for four months. By the late spring, her physical condition declined still further and in August 1920, she died. Wanamaker was greatly shaken by the death of his wife of sixty years. Upon Mary's death, Wanamaker wrote to his sister that he spent the entire week at Lindenhurst rather listlessly. He was unable to get back to work. "I have walked over the lawn and down through the woods and over in dear mother's old fashioned garden.... But oh for the vanished hand that was always reaching out to us with something to give for our good. What a wonderful life she lived and how all of us will miss her." A few weeks later he wrote, "As I came away, I said 'Good Morning' to the old chair that Mrs. Wanamaker used to use so much and I said 'Good Morning' to her as usual." Wanamaker wrote in late October, "I am very much broken down by the long sorrow that has over-shadowed us, not for weeks but for many months."[70]

A few weeks before Mary Wanamaker died, the Rev. Pentacost of

Bethany died, which also greatly affected the merchant. Wanamaker had intended to go with him to the world Sunday school conference and spend up to six months in an evangelistic visit to Asia. His wife's illness and death prevented the trip. Because he was left so weak by the experience, he was even unable to attend the Pennsylvania Sunday School State Convention, although he was honorary president and chairman of the board.[71]

Depressed over Mary's death and his own physical disabilities, in the fall of 1920 Wanamaker stopped going to New York City and even left for Florida before the December shopping month to avoid any chance of catching a winter cold. When in Philadelphia, he spent only three or four hours per day in the store.[72]

Wanamaker's absence freed Rodman to make changes on his own that John might not have approved. For example, Rodman purchased the *New York Press* and folded into it the *Book News,* the pioneering book journal that had begun as an advertising effort for Wanamaker's bookstores. The *Book News* had become one of the premier literary magazines in the United States, not only carrying reviews by prominent writers, but excerpts from their forthcoming works as well. The dismantling of the journal devastated Wanamaker. "It was a source of sorrow to me when I missed it and found out it had slipped away," he wrote. "We had a good subscription for it and thousands of people were sorry to lose it." Wanamaker secured a job with *The Public Ledger* for Mrs. Robert Carson, the editor of *Book News,* who had started as a girl with Wanamaker and had published several books.[73]

Inflation continued to be the most serious problem for the stores and the chief source of complaints from customers. Wanamaker answered charges of price-gouging by defending retailers and blaming high manufacturing costs as the chief culprit. During the war when costs increased every two months, he held down prices by combining the higher-priced goods with earlier purchases, charging the difference between the two. As costs came down in 1920, Wanamaker gave the customer the benefit of lower prices.[74]

The high prices in 1920 provided Wanamaker with his last great piece of showmanship. On May 1, 1920, Wanamaker reduced all prices in the stores by 20 percent. He gave no advance notice to either the Federal Reserve or to most of his own employees; only ten people in the two stores knew about the sale. The promotion, which covered all his goods, created a general sensation in the newspapers and among government officials, who praised the move as a major strike against inflation. Although rival retailers followed his lead, Wanamaker gained major publicity from the move. The price reductions were an astonishing success, clearing most of his shelves.[75]

Wanamaker's sales came at the peak of the inflation. Prices by November 1920 had fallen. Wanamaker tried to pass these lower rates along to his customers and held sales before the Christmas season. But Wanamaker bought conservatively, refusing to buy deeply discounted, but lower-quality goods. Buyers went into the marketplace and encouraged his traditional sources of merchandise to lower their prices.[76]

Because he was in Florida, Wanamaker delegated a number of tasks he usually performed himself to keep the store under control during the hectic Christmas season. Rodman's son, John Wanamaker, who had served as a major in the army during the war, was his grandfather's eyes and ears making daily inspections of the store, taking responsibility for making sure everything ran safely. Other lieutenants handled the appearance of the store and the general responsiveness of salespersons to their customers. Thomas Horney, who took on many of Wanamaker's Bethany responsibilities, checked the waiting rooms, the wash rooms, and the employee rooms, while William McCaughan, his secretary, wandered around the store, giving Wanamaker daily reports.[77]

Although inflation created problems in merchandising and in keeping employees and the public happy, it did not have a negative influence on profits. From 1919 through 1923, the Wanamaker Corporation made a net profit of $12,154,616, or an average of $2,430,923 per year, a steady increase from the war years. During the next half decade during the Roaring 1920s, the legacy left by John Wanamaker for his heirs proved even more profitable, as from 1924 through 1928 the enterprises made $19,684,662 for a five-year average profit of $3,932,692. These figures are net profits for each year.[78]

In April 1921 when Wanamaker returned from Florida, he celebrated his 60th anniversary in business with a grand sale and ceremony at the store. He was also given the keys to the city at Independence Hall by Mayor J. Hampton Moore, who was a close friend and former employee. Various celebrities from around the country sent telegrams of congratulations which were read at the affair.[79]

From June until late September 1921, with Rodman in Europe, John resumed his old routine of spending one day in Philadelphia and the next in New York. The vigor of his activities in the store sometimes made people forget how old and in ill health he was. On May 16, 1921, for example, Wanamaker at age 83 did a tour of the Philadelphia store's seventh through eleventh floors, which were primarily devoted to stock and factories. He then wrote a four-page memorandum, asking many detailed questions about the operations of the store.[80]

In 1922 Wanamaker opened a radio station in the Philadelphia store to publicize his business and to provide customers with an incentive to buy radios. Thus, Wanamaker's joined other retailers such as Bamberger's in Newark and Kauffman's in Pittsburgh in making early use of this new media to gain publicity. At first the station's programming consisted of concerts emanating from the store given by the various musical groups there and by the organ.[81]

Wanamaker resumed a heavy charity schedule and at times he seemed as if he were constantly in motion. As president of the World Sunday School Association, he invited Britain's wartime leader David Lloyd George to speak before Sunday school groups in Washington and Philadelphia. He was still active in the Pennsylvania State Sunday School Association, going to the annual convention in Pittsburgh and giving $10,000 toward the erection of a state building.[82]

In November 1921, Wanamaker gave a reception for Viscount Shibusawa of Japan who was attending the Naval Disarmament Conference in Washington. The Viscount had been friendly with Wanamaker for several years and was one of the hosts for the World Sunday School Conference in Tokyo. This was the first reception given by him since Mary's death. Shibusawa, according to Wanamaker, was the second most prominent individual in Japan. To Wanamaker this was part of an opportunity to spread Christianity to that land.[83]

Although at Bethany Wanamaker transferred church leadership to younger men, he remained Bethany's symbolic leader. When well, he gave regular sermons at the Bible Union, attended board meetings, and tried to dominate activities at the church. He continued to carry a large part of the financial burden.[84]

Toward the end of 1921, Wanamaker's health began to fail. Developing another cold, he delayed his departure for Florida. Leaving in mid-January and staying until April 25, he spent most of the time aboard a small boat with his doctor and a servant. His letters to his sister Elizabeth Fry were upbeat and humorous. Rodman was also optimistic, writing his sister, "When you and I were kids we hardly ever thought there would be almost thirty members of our household in Florida at one time, which includes Father and his little boat."[85]

When John returned to Philadelphia from Florida, he picked up another cold in May. By June 1, Wanamaker was still not well, suffering from a second cold on top of the one he got coming home from Florida. Wanamaker had to forgo attending the graduation exercises at the Wanamaker Commercial Institute, which had been established 40 years earlier at Bethany and was open to persons of any religion—Catholic and Jew, as well as Protestant. Despite his problems, he did attend some banquets and continued to be active in Sunday school work. Wanamaker also participated in planning the 1926 celebration of the 150th anniversary of American independence.[86]

By early summer, the business, which had been running badly, began to pick up. Prices were still a problem, with fresh goods selling for a price 10 percent higher than the previous year. However, Wanamaker felt that sales and competition were bringing prices down.[87]

By August 1922, he resumed a full set of activities. He was on the School Board and the Sesquicentennial project, and he still managed to handle his World Sunday School responsibilities. But to retain his energy, he restricted his activities at Bethany, which caused him to feel a sense of loss. "I can't tell you how much I am losing, in not having my Sundays at Bethany," Wanamaker wrote to Bethany's minister, Rev. A. Gordon Maclennan. "I hope that I will be able to return very soon, if not to take my old part to at least be a listener."[88]

Rodman was in Paris during the summer on his usual buying trip and vacation; in his absence, Wanamaker devoted some of his time to the operations of the New York store. When Rodman came home on September 6, Wanamaker went to New York to meet with him. On October 2, he was well enough to entertain a meeting of Presbyterians at Lindenhurst. However, by October 13, Wanamaker was laid up with a cold similar to the one that had stricken him earlier in the year. His secretary dispatched a series of letters informing individuals that Wanamaker was unable to attend engagements because of his illness.[89]

Wanamaker wrote his final letter, dated November 9, to Commander Evangeline Booth. In it, he urged her not to go ahead with her plans to leave the command of the Salvation Army in America until she spoke with him after his illness. "It was a sacred command bestowed upon you by the father of the Army. You cannot leave what your father deeded to you," he wrote. "I am much better and hope to see you soon."[90]

Staying at his home in Philadelphia's Center City, Wanamaker was visited regularly by three physicians. Because the illness was similar to the respiratory problems he had suffered for many years, the doctors were hopeful about his survival. In fact, they stopped issuing regular bulletins about his health. On December 11, 1922, Wanamaker was in good spirits and had not had his persistent cough for several days. He slept soundly through the night, but was awakened by a coughing fit at 4:45 in the morning. Unable to stop coughing, he suffered a heart attack and fell unconscious soon afterward. At 8 a.m. on December 12, at 84 years of age, John Wanamaker died.[91]

Wanamaker's funeral on December 14 at Bethany Church drew a crowd of 15,000 people, most of whom stood in the snow outside the church, which could only hold about 2,500 mourners. Inside the building were many of the major business, political, and religious personalities from the Philadelphia metropolitan area. The service and memorials became a civic celebration recounting the past half century of Philadelphia's development. In a sense, the funeral was a tribute both to the merchant and to the city, a theme that figured prominently in the eulogies given by Mayor Henry Moore and former Governor Edwin Stuart, both of whom worked in the store as children, and Senator George Wharton Pepper, a neighbor in the city and political ally. In a symbolic gesture of unity, 175 honorary pallbearers represented various religious and ethnic groups within Philadelphia, a revitalization ceremony that would be unusual on the local level today and would occur only at the time of the death of a president or former president of the United States. The City Council suspended operations, public schools had a half-day holiday, the Philadelphia stock exchange closed, and all the department stores in the city closed during the funeral. In his speech, Senator Pepper summarized the relationship of Philadelphia to Wanamaker, praising him for his longtime efforts to promote the city. "Mr. Wanamaker has enriched Philadelphia materially and spiritually," Pepper said. "His wonderful store stands as a monument to his power to imagine great results and then make them a reality. His commercial life is an example of an unwavering service to his community." Wanamaker was buried in the cemetery of the Episcopal Church of St. James the Less, off Fairmount Park, where both Mary and Tom were interred. During the funeral and burial, members of John Wanamaker's many musical organizations performed. Mary Vogt, the organist at the store, played at Bethany; the Bethany choir sang at the cemetery, while Captain T.C. Jones of the Wanamaker Institute played taps.[92]

Wanamaker left more than $40 million to his heirs. Almost all of the stock in the store had been transferred to Rodman about two years earlier, giving him about $35 million of the estate. Through this maneuver, John Wanamaker ensured that his two stores would enjoy continuity. To each of his two daughters, Wanamaker left $1 million and non-voting preferred stock in the corporation that ran the store. Money for this bequest came from $3 million in insurance that he carried on his life. Smaller grants were made to his grandchildren and to several charities. He left sums of money to the Williamson School in Media, Pennsylvania, with which he had been associated since the death of his friend Joseph Williamson. Money was also left to help with the schooling of indigent children, to support Bethany, and to maintain several other charities in which Wanamaker had a long-term interest, including the Friendly Inn.[93]

Rodman, who had developed into a showman exceeded only by his father, was 55 at the time of Wanamaker's death. Rodman controlled the stores' operations until his death after a short illness in 1928. After that, the Philadelphia store remained under the control of the Rodman Wanamaker Estate, which benefitted his three children and his grandchildren. Many persons who had been associated with John and Rodman Wanamaker, such as William Nevin and Joseph Appel, continued to play important roles in the store. Rodman's son, John Wanamaker, Jr., held a senior position and his son John Wanamaker III rose to become president of the business.[94]

The Wanamaker family did not sustain the founder's empire, however. In 1956, with New York's major retailing area established thirty blocks to the north, the New York store was closed. Soon afterward, the Stewart Building burned down. In 1979, the Wanamaker Trust sold the Philadelphia store to the Carter Hawley Hale chain. The store retained its name, but passed out of family hands. By the time the store was sold it had become run down and the Wanamaker chain, in the words of one retailing expert, was troubled by "poor management, poor merchandising and a lack of a marketing strategy."[95]

Beginning in 1987, control over Wanamaker's main store and its suburban mall stores rested with the Washington department store chain Woodward & Lothrop, owned by A. Alfred Taubman, a Detroit real estate executive. The 1911 building in Philadelphia still dominated the central business district, but Woodward & Lothrop turned the upper floors into an office building, leaving a smaller store occupying the lower four floors with no restaurant, no toy department, and few of the services that Philadelphians remembered.

Like many of its contemporaries, including Macy's, Woodward & Lothrop in the early 1990s went into bankruptcy. In June 1995, Wanamaker's was sold to the May's chain, and Wanamaker's became a Hecht's department store. In 1996, May's bought Strawbridge & Clothier in a fitting piece of irony. Most of the former Wanamaker's were renamed Strawbridge's, but the center city store became a Lord & Taylor's. Thus, the fate of Wanamaker's was similar to many other department stores in the late twentieth century. Eroding central cities, competition from discount houses, and bad financial management left the stores vulnerable.[96]

But the difference was the anguish expressed by Philadelphians at the closing of Wanamaker's. On August 28, 1995, the day of the closing, the *Philadelphia Inquirer* published a special section, "John Wanamaker, Philadelphia Says Goodbye." Devoted to the special place which the store held at the center of Philadelphia's public life, "Philadelphia Says Goodbye" contained reflections by metropolitan residents on the impact the store had on their lives. Thomas Hine, an architectural critic, perhaps best summed up the reasons that the disappearance of Wanamaker's hurt Philadelphia's psyche. "It's not a building or a store, but a place," he wrote. "Its Grand Court complete with the bronze eagle John Wanamaker purchased to be its focus ranks with Rittenhouse Square as one of Philadelphia's most important public places." Hine and others who reflected on Wanamaker's mentioned the significance to their lives of the Crystal Tea Room with its 1,400 seats, the grand organ recitals, the Christmas light shows, and the toy store. Almost seventy-five years after John Wanamaker's death, the building at Juniper and Chestnut continued to symbolize both the spirit of John Wanamaker and the spirit of the city itself. For the residents of the city, who felt it was the heart of Philadelphia, the tears over Wanamaker's were also tears for Philadelphia.

With Wanamaker's name removed from his building, his chief remembrance remains the statue built next to City Hall soon after his death. The monument, a standing sculpture of the merchant in mid-life, reflects what Wanamaker meant to Philadelphia. It simply reads: "JOHN WANAMAKER CITIZEN."

Bibliographic Essay

*T*he major source of Wanamaker materials is the Historical Society of Pennsylvania. After his death, the managers of the store kept Wanamaker's office, including most of his papers, together as a small museum. Although the public could visit the office located in the Philadelphia store, his papers were largely unavailable to scholars. After the store was sold in 1979 by the Wanamaker estate, the historian William Leach was given permission to use the manuscripts. With the conversion of the eight upper floors of the Philadelphia store into an office building, the contents of the office as well as the extensive archives of the Wanamaker Corporation were transferred to the Historical Society of Pennsylvania. Since the Historical Society received the papers, some work has been done to catalog them by William Allen Zulker, an amateur archivist, who has also published *John Wanamaker, King of Merchants* (Wayne, Pa. 1993). The biography contains interesting facts about the merchant's life, forty-nine photographs selected from the tens of thousands of pictures in the collection, and footnotes and a bibliography which are useful to a researcher using the collection.

The core of the collection is Wanamaker's letterbooks, which contain copies of letters sent by him from 1876 until 1922. From 1885 until his death, Wanamaker sent about 300 letters per month to customers, creditors, suppliers, and political and religious associates. These letters provide a continuous portrait of Wanamaker and his enterprises. The letters are supplemented by his correspondence with his family after 1888. This collection contains letters to Rodman, Mary, Thomas, and John Wanamaker, letters between them, and some letters from colleagues.

The Wanamaker Papers also include Wanamaker's private account books, personal papers of his sons, and records of various other economic activities. Sales figures as well as store expenses were maintained in other volumes, some of which are available in the Wanamaker collection. The Wanamaker Papers also include some personal diaries, speeches, clipping books, advertising copy, and thousands of pieces of personal memorabilia. The materials also include tens of thousands of photographs. These pictures cover every aspect of the department store's activities from 1876 until Wanamaker's death. For the years after his death, an even larger archive contains a collection of visual materials documenting the store until the mid-1980s.

Another valuable source within the papers are the note card files of Herbert Adams Gibbons. Found among the several dozen file cabinets are clippings from newspapers, scraps of paper from the Wanamaker papers, and interesting correspondence with store officials. Gibbons maintained the note files until his death, so they include valuable materials on the Wanamaker family and on the store from 1926 through the 1940s.

The *Golden Book of the Wanamaker Stores* (1911) was published in two volumes to celebrate the fiftieth anniversary of the opening of Wanamaker and Brown and the dedication of the new Philadelphia building. Interspersed with pictures of various Wanamaker enterprises is a selection of his speeches, advertising pieces, and a narrative history of Wanamaker's. It is the entrepreneur's most comprehensive effort to justify his retailing methods. Volume One contains the history of Wanamaker's; Volume Two was published after Taft's visit to Philadelphia and contains a transcript of the ceremonies and various reactions to them.

The Urban Archives at Temple University contain the clipping files of the *Philadelphia Bulletin*, deposited there after that newspaper went out of business in 1981. In the files are hundreds of stories on John Wanamaker, his family, and the store. These clippings as well as the photojournalism collection are a valuable addition to the Wanamaker collection itself.

The *Dry Goods Economist* was the major trade journal for department stores. Its issues discuss everything from shoplifting, to displays, to financial management. Because of the prominence of the Wanamaker stores, the *DGE* gave them a reasonable amount of coverage. But more importantly, it focused on general trends within the industry, giving the researcher a general index against which to judge individual stores and the industry as a whole. Furthermore, *DGE's layout is quite impressive, making it one of the most beautiful magazines in the early twentieth century.*

Unlike industrial and financial leaders of the late nineteenth century and early twentieth century such as John D. Rockefeller, Andrew Carnegie, and Jay Gould, whose reputations were stained by journalists and historians disturbed by the evils of industrialism, the leading merchants of the era such as John Wanamaker, Marshall Field, and Edward Filene were largely untouched. Wanamaker enjoyed a good press in the closing days of his career, helping to erase his memories of earlier attacks on him by journalists and writers upset by the monopolistic tendencies of the department store and by his political campaigns. He was subjected to bad publicity near the end of his life for the low wages paid in the store. But at his death, the praise he received in the Philadelphia newspapers probably exceeded any figure of his generation in that city. When he died in 1922, prosperity had returned, and the boom in the 1920s promoted the reputation of many businessmen.

During the decade after his death, three books appeared on Wanamaker. At the time of Wanamaker's death, Herbert Adams Gibbons, a professor at Princeton, was under contract to write the official biography of Wanamaker. He interviewed the merchant and walked around the store with him and had access to all his correspondence and to his private diary. Gibbons' labors, which included meticulous research outside Wanamaker's private files, resulted in a two-volume work with footnotes and an extensive bibliography. This biography, *John Wanamaker* (New York, 1926), reprinted in 1971 by Kennikat Press (Port Washington, New York), remains the most authoritative source on Wanamaker. By the standards of early twentieth-century authorized biographies, Gibbons' writing is interesting and full of insights into early retailing. But as would be expected, it glosses over Wanamaker's flaws as a businessman and presents Wanamaker as he wanted to be presented. Gibbons never mentions the stores' low wages and accepts Wanamaker's contention that he created a "new type of store" which was not a department store. Except for Rodman and Thomas Wanamaker, and a few references to Robert C. Ogden, Gibbons does not mention other individuals who worked with Wanamaker.

Shortly after Wanamaker's death, Russell Conwell, the minister at the Baptist Temple in Philadelphia, the founder of Temple University, and one of the leading evangelical preachers of the era, published *The Romantic Rise of a Great American* (New York, 1924). It had little claim to scholarship and used Wanamaker's life as a moralistic lesson. It does contain stories based upon conversations with the merchant and does tie Wanamaker's life to the broader religious movements of the era. The volume is probably more useful for the insights it gives into Conwell than for what it explains about Wanamaker. Conwell's book perpetuates the Horatio Alger quality of Wanamaker's life. The stories in it are reproduced in a children's book by Olive Burt, *John Wanamaker, Boy Merchant* (Indianapolis, 1952).

Joseph Appel, who worked as an advertising executive for Wanamaker, wrote *The Business Biography of John Wanamaker, Founder and Builder* (New York, 1930), the last full-length biography of the Philadelphian. Using the same records as Gibbons, Appel has some very good insights into Wanamaker's advertising methods and the organization of the store at the turn of the century. Started with Rodman Wanamaker's approval, the book was written after Rodman's death. The book contains a long tribute to him, discussing his role as a merchandiser. As a long associate of the Wanamakers, Appel is less scholarly than Gibbons and more personal.

Another source is Philip Whitwell Wilson, *An Unofficial Statesman—Robert C. Ogden* (Garden City, New York, 1924). Based on the Ogden Papers in the Library of Congress, the book is a laudatory account of the life of Wanamaker's partner. But it does discuss the early operation of the Wanamaker store, the purchase and operation of the New York store, and Ogden's philanthropy, including his leadership at the Hampton Institute and the contribution Wanamaker made to African-American charities. Lengthy quotes from Ogden's speeches and writings survey Ogden's advertisement campaigns for the New York store. Like Gibbons and Appel, Wilson defends the department store as a logical outgrowth of late nineteenth-century economic developments.

Recently, historians looking at cultural developments at the turn of the century have argued that department stores had a corrupting influence on the morals of American society. The most concerted attack on Wanamaker has come from William Leach, *Land of Desire: Merchants, Power, and the Rise of a New American Culture* (New York, 1993). Leach was the first modern historian to make use of the Wanamaker Archives, while they were still in the department store. Leach summarized his view of Wanamaker: "But when it came to his own life and his own place in the world—his own public image—Wanamaker turned to religious activity out of some need to sanctify his business. Money was always in his thoughts. The concept of 'abundance' which he invoked again and again in his private notebooks, had as much to do in his mind with money as with grace and holiness" (p. 212). Leach holds Wanamaker partially responsible for turning America away from Puritan values in which people were motivated by a desire to construct community. Instead, society became controlled by business, with the individual turned into a consuming machine, with little purpose in life except to buy the latest fashion. *Land of Desire*, the title of which is a direct Wanamaker quote, stresses the negative aspects of consumerism—an interpretation of the department store that is different from this book. The book is brilliantly written and is an important starting point for anyone interested in the department store.

Leach's approach is based on Antonio Gramsci's idea of cultural hegemony, also the starting point for several other books on the department store. Elaine S. Abelson in *When Ladies Go A-Thieving, Middle-Class Shoplifters in the Victorian Department Store* (New York, 1989) discusses the psychological impact the new consumer culture had on women, driving them to the distraction of taking merchandise from the stores. Like Leach, Abelson takes a negative position on the department store movement. Although she only discusses Wanamaker directly in connection with his crime detection work, her book takes to task Wanamaker and other manipulators of consumer tastes.

Susan Porter Benson in *Counter Cultures: Saleswomen, Managers, and Customers in American Department Stores, 1890-1940* (Urbana, 1986) writes, "The department store as a social and economic institution was enduringly contradictory, at once a vibrant center of the delights of consumption and an arena of persisting class and gender conflict, a business that was highly profitable yet torn between its roles as vendor of merchandise and purveyor of culture." In her conclusion, Benson views consumer culture from a different perspective, looking at the varied problems faced by the department store owner, his employees (most of whom were women), and his customers. Her evaluation of these new giant retail outlets is consequently less negative than Leach.

Benson's book, which makes a contribution to both the history of gender and to business history, reinforces the conclusions of Neil Harris in his essay on museums, fairs and department stores in *Cultural Excursions* (Chicago, 1990). Harris argues that department store founders, particularly Marshall Field and John Wanamaker, created structures that more profoundly influenced taste and promoted the development of the arts and crafts than museums, which were largely warehouses for the relics of Western civilization until their reconstruction after World War II. At that time, they copied many advertising methods formerly used by the department stores.

Jackson Lears has written several books on the rise of the consumer culture at the end of the nineteenth century. His *Fables of Abundance, a Cultural History of Advertising in America* (1994) is a study of the rise of modern advertising in America and its relationship to the way it shaped American society. Central to his thesis is the relationship that advertising had to historical efforts to use magic to transform peoples' lives. Although Lears makes only a few references to Wanamaker, this study analyzes the cultural milieu in which the modern department store flourished.

For a study of Wanamaker's predecessor in retailing, see Stephen N. Elias, *Alexander T. Stewart, the Forgotten Merchant Prince* (Westport, Conn., 1992). Elias traces the merchant's career and gives important material on the rise of the department store.

An important source for an understanding of Wanamaker's connection to religious movements is Marion L. Bell's *Crusade in the City: Revivalism in Nineteenth-Century Philadelphia* (Lewisburg, 1977). Bell discusses the various movements in Philadelphia from the 1820s until the 1870s. Her chapters on the 1850s revival and on Moody contain insights into Wanamaker and his relationship to the other members of a circle of Protestant laymen who dominated religious and business life. Her conclusions about the transformation of Philadelphia evangelicals from reformers to conservatives are particularly interesting.

Notes

Chapter 1

1. John Wanamaker (hereafter referred to as J.W.) to Rev. C.M. Boswell, December 21, 1917, Letterbooks; Wanamaker Diary, Jan. 6, 1860; John C. Thompson and George Van Deurs to J.W., Jan. 1900, Gibbons Files, Wanamaker Papers, Historical Society of Pennsylvania.

2. Leigh Eric Schmidt, *Consumer Rites, The Buying and Selling of American Holidays* (Princeton, 1995), 1-37.

3. Wendt, Lloyd and Herman Kogan, *Give the Lady What She Wants!* (Chicago, 1952); Susan Porter Benson, "Palaces of Consumption and Machines for Selling: The American Department Store, 1880-1940," *Radical History Review* 21 (Fall, 1979), 199-221.

4. Herbert Adams Gibbons, John Wanamaker (New York, 1926, reprinted in Kennikat Press Scholarly Reprints. Port Washington, N.Y., 1971), I, 7.

5. John William Ferry, *A History of the Department Store* (New York, 1960); Neil Harris, *Cultural Excursions, Marketing Appetites and Cultural Tastes in Modern America* (Chicago, 1990), 56-96.

6. *Golden Book of the Wanamaker Stores* (n.p., 1911), I, 27.

7. Gibbons, *John Wanamaker*, I, 1-6.

8. Joseph H. Appel, *The Business Biography of John Wanamaker, Founder and Builder* (New York, 1930), 19-21; John Wanamaker to John S. and Margaret Furey, January 8, 1850, Family Correspondence.

9. John Wanamaker to Rodman Wanamaker, May 28, 1897, Personal Correspondence, Wanamaker Papers, HSP; Gibbons, *John Wanamaker*, I, 21.

10. Gibbons, *John Wanamaker*, 21.

11. James O'Flaherty, "Big Men in the Retail Game: John Wanamaker," *Chips from the Blarney Stone*, January, 1912, in "Family," Herbert Gibbons Files, Wanamaker Papers, Historical Society of Pennsylvania; Russell Conwell, *The Romantic Rise of A Great American* (New York, 1924), 6-7; Appel, *Business Biography*, 7.

12. O'Flaherty, *Chips*; Note dated May 10, 1920, "Family," Gibbons Files, Wanamaker Papers.

13. William H. Wanamaker to J.W., Sept. 29, 1901, and Louise W. Frey to J.W., Jan. 25, 1872, Personal Correspondence.

14. Thompson Brown, "From Messenger Boy to Merchant Prince," *Our Day*, September, 1897, 412-13; Philadelphia *Evening Ledger*, July 11, 1938; J.W. Passports, in Wanamaker Papers.

15. *Success*, August 1900, "Personal," Gibbons Files, Wanamaker Papers.

16. "Certificate of Exemption for a Drafted Person on Account of Disability," Wanamaker Papers, HSP.

17. Letter dated July 4, 1903, from Cape May, "Speeches," Gibbons Files, Wanamaker Papers; J. W. to Rodman Wanamaker, April 17, 1903, Personal Correspondence.

18. Dr. Francis E. Clark, *Christian Endeavor World*, May 29, 1919; "Diary", Jan. 6, 1860, Wanamaker Papers.

19. *The Globe and Commercial Advertiser*, December 14, 1922; Appel, *Business Biography*, xv.

20. Herbert Gibbons to John McClure, February 25, 1927, Personal Biography Files, Gibbons Notes, Wanamaker Papers, HSP; *The Globe and Commercial Advertiser*, December 14, 1922.

21. "Personality," Gibbons Files, Wanamaker Papers.

22. "Speeches," Gibbons Files, Wanamaker Papers.

23. *Evening Ledger*, July 11,1838.

24. William Bullitt, *It's Not Done* (New York, 1926), 9 and 16.

25. J.W. to Rodman Wanamaker, July 31, 1915, Personal Correspondence.

26. Joseph Appel, *The Business Biography of John Wanamaker*, 13-24.

27. J.W. to A.T. Thompson, July 17, 1916, Letterbooks; *Sunday School World*, October 1896; J.W. to John Neff, Sept. 6, 1865, Miscellaneous Letters, Wanamaker Papers; Joseph Appel, *The Business Biography*, 22.

28. Elizabeth M. Geffen, "Industrial Development and Social Crisis," in Russell F. Weigley, ed., *Philadelphia, A 300 Year History* (New York, 1980), 307-363.

29. Gibbons, *John Wanamaker*, 13-15.

30. Joseph Appel, *The Business Biography*, xvii.

31. Gibbons, *John Wanamaker*, I, 22-29.

32. *Men's Wear*, Feb. 10, 1950; Conwell, *Romantic Rise*, 25.

33. Joseph Appel, *The Business Biography*, 30-31.

34. Gibbons, *John Wanamaker*, 57-62.

35. J.W. to Harold Lowden, June 5, 1908, and James William Marshall, July 9, 1918, Letterbooks.

36. J.W. to Rev. H.P. Sloan, September 11, 1914, Letterbooks.

37. Gibbons, *John Wanamaker*, 31-33.

38. John Chambers to Samuel Aaron, March 26, 1824, "Family Correspondence," Wanamaker Papers; Anonymous (probably John Wanamaker), "Thanksgiving Sermon, By The Rev. John Chambers, November 24, 1859. With a Brief History of the First Independent Church, of Philadelphia. By One of Its Members." (Philadelphia, 1859).

39. *Ibid.*, 18.

40. J. W. to S.A. Keem, Dec. 14, 1906, and Rev. Charles E. Wheeler, Nov. 24, 1894, Letterbooks.

41. James Robinson to John Wanamaker, Dec. 4, 1905, Personal Correspondence, Wanamaker Papers.

42. J.W. to William J. Milligan, Sept. 24, 1913, Letterbooks; "Thanksgiving Sermon By the Rev. John Chambers," 52.

43. J.W. to A.M. Shute, November 29, 1917, Letterbooks.

44. January 1, 1860, John Wanamaker Diary, Wanamaker Papers, HSP; Gibbons, *John Wanamaker*, 39-45; Conwell, *Romantic Rise*, 26.

45. Newspaper clipping in Personal Correspondence (1889), Wanamaker Papers.

46. J.W. to Mary Wanamaker, July 11, 1902, and J.W. to Rodman Wanamaker, March 12, 1903, Personal Correspondence.

47. Philadelphia *Ledger*, April 14, 1908; *New York World*, March 9, 1928; J.W. to Rodman Wanamaker, June 14, 1895 and Mary Wanamaker, January 21, 1895, Personal Correspondence.

48. "Religion," Gibbons File, Wanamaker Papers; Appel, *Business Biography*, xv.

49. Schmidt, *Consumer Rites*, 19 ff.

50. Joseph H. Appel, *The Business Biography*, XVI.

51. Francis S. Clark to J.W., April 1906, Personal Correspondence.

Chapter 2

1. John William Ferry, *A History of the Department Store* (New York, 1960) and Daniel Boorstin, *The Americans, the Democratic Experience* (New York, 1973), 101-109. Lloyd Wendt, *Give the Lady What She Wants* (New York, 1952), 65-75.

2. Leon Harris, *Merchant Princes, An Intimate History of Jewish Families Who Built Great Department Stores* (New York, revised edition, 1994); Perry, *A History*, 145.

3. Neil Harris, *Cultural Excursions, Marketing Appetites and Cultural Tastes in Modern America* (Chicago, 1990), Chapter 3.

4. *A Peep into Catharine Street, or the Mysteries of Shopping. By a Late Retailer* (New York, 1846), 1.

5. *Ibid.*, 2.

6. Stephen N. Elias, *Alexander T. Stewart, The Forgotten Merchant Prince* (Westport, Conn., 1992); *New York Sun*, April 11, 1876.

7. *New York Times*, April 11, 1876.

8. Edward Hungerford, *The Romance of a Great Store* (New York, 1922), 13-14.

9. J.W. to Rodman Wanamaker, n d., Letterbooks; Michael Miller, *The Bon Marché* (Princeton, N.J., 1982).

10. *McElroy's Philadelphia Directory for 1857* (Philadelphia, 1857).

11. *McElroy's Philadelphia City Directory for 1861* (Philadelphia, 1861), 109; *Menswear*, Feb. 8, 1951.

12. *Gospill's Philadelphia Business Directory, 1869* (Philadelphia, 1869).

13. "Cash Book for Wanamaker's and Brown's," Wanamaker Papers.

14. Files in the Wanamaker Papers, HSP dated Dec. 26, 1864 and Feb. 28, 1895.

15. *Dry Goods Economist*, March 25, 1911.

16. Wanamaker and Brown, Pa. 140, 210, R.G. Dun Collection, Baker Library, Harvard University.

17. Wanamaker and Brown, Pa. 140, 66 and 112, R.G. Dun Collection.

18. Gibbons, *John Wanamaker*, 106.

19. Frank G. Carpenter, "A Talk With John Wanamaker," a Syndicated Sunday Article, October 1897, in "Advertising," Gibbons Files.

20. *McElroy's Philadelphia Directory* (Philadelphia, 1865). Conwell, *Romantic Rise*, 101.

21. "Advertising," Gibbons Files, Wanamaker Papers.

22. Gibbons, *John Wanamaker*, 88.

23. Philadelphia *Evening Star*, November 12, 1874.

24. "Advertising," Gibbons Files.

25. *Poor Richard's Almanac*, January, 1876, in Wanamaker Papers.

26. J.W. to H.A. Wise, July 26, 1876, Letterbooks.

27. J.W. to Charles Brown Jr, September 30, 1914, Letterbooks.

28. Wanamaker and Brown, Pa. 140, 66 and 112, R.G. Dun Collection, Baker Library, Harvard University.

29. "Advertising," Gibbons Files.

30. Robert Ellis Thompson, *Life of George H. Stuart* (Philadelphia, 1890), 128-130.

31. Gibbons, *John Wanamaker*, 50.

32. J.W. to Mr. Marshall, Dec. 2, 1886, Letterbooks and Wanamaker Letterbook for 1883-1884, 507.

33. *Down Town Record*, September, 21, 1894.

34. J.W. to Smith, Nov. 5, 1880, to Pastor, Oct. 22, 1885, and Dr. Smith, April 13, 1885, Letterbooks.

35. "Religion," Gibbons File, Wanamaker Papers.

36. Pa. 140, 210, R.G. Dun Collection, Baker Library, Harvard University. .

37. Wanamaker and Comapany, Pa. 146, 165, R.G. Dun Collection.

38. J.W. to Messrs McLaughlin Bros., Jan. 16, 1878, Letterbooks and Wanamaker and Company, Pa. 146, 165.

39. *Ibid.*

40. *Ibid.*, 164.

41. *Methods of Business of the Largest Establishment in THE WORLD for the Manufacture and Sale of MEN'S WEAR* (Philadelphia, 1876); *Philadelphia Evening Star*, November 12, 1874; Wanamker and Compamy, Pa. 146, 164.

42. *Golden Book of the Wanamaker Store*, 150-158.

43. *Sunday Mercury*, March 13, 1883; *The Day*, August 31, 1877.

44. J.W. to My Old Friend, Nov. 2, 1877, Letterbooks.

45. *Life of Stuart*, 276; Jean Miller Schmidt, "Souls or the Social Order, The Two Party System in American Protestantism," in Jerald C. Bauer and Martin E. Marty, *Chicago Studies in the History of American Religion*, (Brooklyn, N.Y., 1991), 41-45.

46. J.W. to Moody, July 16, 1885; F. Norm Babcock to J.W. , Jan. 16, 1914, Letterbooks; *Life of Stuart*, 271-287.

47. Marion L. Bell, *Crusade in the City, Revivalism in Nineteenth-Century Philadelphia* (Lewisburg, 1972); George H. Stuart, *Life of Stuart* (Philadelphia, 1890), 272ff; W.F.P. Noble, *A Century of Gospel Work* (Philadelphia, 1876).

48. Bell, *Crusade in the City*, 233-234.

49. J.W. to Dwight Moody, Oct. 5 and Oct. 17, 1899; J. W. to William Moody, Feb. 5, 1900, Letterbooks.

50. Gibbons, *John Wanamaker*, 153-260; *Lippincott's Magazine*, December, 1876; *Public Ledger*, Sept. 17, 1922.

51. J.W. to J. Hampton Moore, June 7, 1921, Letterbooks.

52. Dorothy Gondos Beers, "The Centennial City, 1865-1876," in Weigley, *Philadelphia*, 45-47; *Lippincott's Magazine*, December, 1876.

53. Neil Harris, *Cultural Excursions, Marketing Appetites and Cultural Tastes in Modern America* (Chicago, 1990), 31-40.

54. J.W. to William B.H. Down, May 4, 1921, Letterbooks; *Philadelphia Ledger and Transcript*, May 20, 1885.

55. Wanamaker and Co., Pa., 146, 165; "Covenant Pennsylvania Railroad Company to John Wanamaker," June 8, 1876; Jos. Lesley statement for Pennsylvania Railroad, Nov. 11, 1875; "Brief of Title to Premises on West Side of Thirteenth St.... Conveyed by the Estate of Thomas Kelly to The Pennsylvania Railroad, Nov. 1, 1852," Wanamaker Papers; Sam Perkins to J. W., December 19, 1881 and John Swartz to J.W., June 4, 1877, Letterbooks.

56. J.W. to Mr. J.A. Reynolds, Jan. 17, 1887, Letterbooks.

57. *Methods of Business of the Largest Establishment in* THE WORLD *for the Manufacture and Sale of* MEN'S WEAR (Philadelphia, 1876).

58. Scrapbook on the death of Alexander Stewart in Wanamaker Papers, HSP.

59. *Dry Goods Economist,* March 25, 1911

Chapter 3

1. Gibbons, *John Wanamaker,* I, 180.

2. *Golden Book of the Wanamaker Stores,* II, 97.

3. J.W. to E. C. Knight, April 10, 1886, Letterbooks.

4. *Philadelphia Ledger and Transcript,* May 20, 1885; Lloyd Wendt and Herman Kogan, *Give the Lady What She Wants* (Chicago, 1952), 163.

5. John Wanamaker, Founder's Day Address, 1906 in Wanamaker Papers.

6. Joseph Appel, *The Business Biography,* 82-83; Lloyd Wendt and Herman Kogan, *Give the Lady What She Wants* (New York, 1952), 58; Mary Ryan, *Women in Public: Between Banners and Ballots, 1825-1880* (Baltimore, 1990).

7. *Philadelphia Inquirer,* March 9, 1877; *Philadelphia Store News,* Vol. 1, No. 1 (September 1883), in Wanamaker Papers.

8. L. Straus to J.W., April 12, 1883, Letterbooks; "Anniversary Herald," April 15, 1909.

9. *Philadelphia Store News,* Vol. 1, No. 1 (September 1883).

10. J.W. to Mr. J.A. Reynolds, Jan. 17, 1887 and Charles Taylor, April 21, 1883, Letterbooks.

11. Pa. 156, p. 419, R.G. Dun Collection; *Golden Book,* I, 70-71.

12. *Golden Book of the Wanamaker Stores,* II, 177.

13. Schmidt, *Consumer Rites,* 159 ff.

14. *Philadelphia Store News,* 1, (September 1883); "Catalogue of Goods at the Wanamaker Grand Depot" (1878), in the Wanamaker Papers.

15. *Outlook,* Dec. 27, 1922; Conwell, *Romantic Rise,* 81-82.

16. J.W. to McKean, Jan. 7, 1886, Letterbooks; Philip Whitewell Wilson, *An Unofficial Statesman, Robert C. Ogden* (Garden City, N.Y., 1924), 86-87.

17. "Address to the American Academy Annual Meeting in 1900," in Wanamaker Papers.

18. *Golden Book of the Wanamaker Stores,* I, 119 and II, 212; Wilson, *Unofficial Statesman,* 82-88.

19. *Golden Book of the Wanamaker Stores*, I, 86.

20. *The Day*, August 31, 1877; Gibbons, *John Wanamaker*, 177.

21. *Golden Book of the Wanamaker Stores*, I, 39.

22. Pa., 146, 1(a), R.G. Dun Collection, Baker Library.

23. *The Day*, August 9, 1877; Pa., 146, 1(a), R.G. Dun Collection, Baker Library.

24. Pa., 146, 1(a), (Aug. 9, 1877) and (Aug. 13, 1877), R.G. Dun Collection, Baker Library.

25. J.W. to Messrs McLoughlin Bros., August 9, 13, 1877 and Jan. 16, 1878 and William A Hard, August 29, 1877, Letterbooks.

26. J.W. to unknown party, Feb. 15, 1878, Kinsey Manfrey & Co., October 19, 1977, William Hard, August 31, 1877, Messrs Perry Wenball Day & Co. September 4, 1877, W.M. Bunk, Jan. 4, 1878, and illegible, Feb. 20, 1878, Letterbooks.

27. J.W. to Mr. Barry, Jan. 15, 1888, and H.A. Witherspoon, January 14, 1878, Letterbooks; Pa. 156, 119, R.G. Dun Collection, Baker Library.

28. Pa. 156, 119, R.G. Dun Collection, Baker Library; J.W. to Messrs Hard & Co., June 13, 1878, Joseph Brook, Feb. 25, 1878, and Jon. DeBoot, March 8, 1878, Letterbooks.

29. J.W. to H. B. Claftin Co., May 21, 1878, C.S. Jeffray, April 27, 1878, and Messes Hard & Co., June 13, 1878, Letterbooks.

30. J.W. to Messrs Hard & Co., June 13, 1878 and The Trustees of the Girard Estate, June 27, 1878, Letterbooks; Pa. 156, 120, R.G. Dun, Baker Library, Harvard University.

31. Pa. 156, 129, Dun Records, Baker Library.

32. J.W. to Messrs McLoughlin Bros., Jan. 16, 1878, Letterbooks.

33. J.W. to W.H. Whitty, April 10, 1880, Dr. J.S. Eshleman, Oct. 9, 1884, Unknown correspondent, Jan. 21, 1882, Judge Thayer, April 24, 1884, and Mary Lycett, Oct. 15, 1884, Letterbooks.

34. John H. Appel, *The Business Biography*, xv-xvi.

35. J.W. to D.B. Oaul, Nov. 15, 1881, E.A. Sargeant, Jan 7, 1882, Dr. William Pepper, Jan. 4, 1882, and note dated Feb. 20, 1886, Letterbooks.

36. "Grand Depot," Gibbons Files, Wanamaker Papers.

37. J.W. to George S. Garrett, October 4, 1879, C.G. Buell, Dec. 13, 1881, Brush Electric Co. , May 11, 1888, Letterbooks.

38. J.W. to Thomas Dolan, March 18, 1886, Letterbooks.

39. J.W. to R. Howard Taylon, March 11, 1887, Letterbooks J.W. to Moody, July 16, 1885, Wanamaker Letterbooks; *Down Town Record*, September, 21, 1894.

40. Philadelphia *Times*, May 4, 1887.

41. E. Digby Baltzell, *Philadelphia Gentlemen* (Glencoe, Ill., 1958).

42. John Wanamaker to unknown correspondent, Dec. 27, 1881, Letterbooks; Walter Davenport, *Power and Glory: The Life of Boies Penrose* (New York, 1931).

43. J.W. to Caleb Cope, June 20, 1887, Mrs. Jacob Miller, Dec. 30, 1882, Letterbooks.

44. J.W. to Charles A. Tracy & Co., Oct. 24, 1884, Letterbooks; Conwell, *Romantic Rise*, 104.

45. J.W. to George W. Childs, William M. Singerly, A.K. McClure, W.W. Harding, Robert S. Davis, Dennis F. Dealy, and Dr. E. Moricky, June 20, 1887, Letterbooks.

46. George W. Childs to J.W., August 3, 1885, Personal Correspondence, Wanamaker Papers.

47. J.W. to Mrs. Kocherfyer, July 11, 1883 and J.W. to Miss J. Ohl, Letterbooks.

48. An advertisement placed in New York newspapers, July 28, 1915, "Advertising," Gibbons Files, Wanamaker Papers; Appel, *Business Biography*, 383 ff.

49. "Editorials and Other Writings," Gibbons Files.

50. J.W. to Mr. Butler, July 13, 1883, June 12, 1885, and Howard Gibbs, January 20, 1888, Letterbooks.

51. J.W. to Butler, June 12, 1885, Letterbooks.

52. J.W. to Dr. M. Cook, Oct. 6, 1884, and E.M. Baxter & Co., April 2, 1886, Letterbooks.

53. J.W. to William Mason, May 18, 1886, Letterbooks.

54. J.W. to Geo. Forester, Feb. 16, 1887, Letterbooks; "Ben Perley Poore, *et. al.* Vs. John Wanamaker *et. al.* USCC in Equity 42, Oct. Sess. 1886," National Archives, Mid-Atlantic Branch.

55. Thomas Bryson, "Walter George Smith and General Grant's Memoirs," *Pennsylvania Magazine of History and Biography* 94 (1970), 233-244; Frederick Anderson, *et. al.*, eds., *Mark Twain's Notebooks and Journals*, Berkeley California, 1979), 3, 250.

56. Susan Porter Benson, *Counter Cultures, Saleswomen, Managers, and Customers in American Department Stores, 1890-1940.* (Urbana, Illinois, 1986), Chapter 4; Gibbons, *John Wanamaker*, II, 259ff.

57. J.W. to Duncan S. Miller, Nov. 26, 1883, Letterbooks.

58. J.W. to W.L. Corrin, Nov. 21, 1887, and Willard M. White, Jan. 2, 1883, Letterbooks; Russell H. Conwell, *Romantic Rise*, 86-87.

59. J. W. to Geyer's Stationer, May 19, 1887, Letterbooks.

60. *Philadelphia Inquirer*, April 9, 1887; *Evening Bulletin*, July 1, 1887.

61. "CREED For the Salesmen and Women of the Wanamaker Store, New York." November, 18, 1912, Wanamaker Papers.

62. Philadelphia *Press*, April 7, 1887.

63. Philadelphia *Press*, January 1888.

64. J.W. to Miss Maud Potter, Dec. 18, 1886, Mrs. Louise Koecker, June 4, 1885, and Wilson Evans, December 21, 1876, Letterbooks.

65. J.W. to M.D. Duncan, *et. al.*, May 19, 1886, Butler, May 21, 1886, Daniel T. Oreme, April 2, 1887, and Brainard, n.d., but July 1, 1887, Letterbooks.

66. Wilson, *An Unofficial Statesman*, 50 ff.

67. J.W. to Sam Wanamaker, April 10, 1885, J.W. letter, June 25, 1885, Letterbooks.

68. Wilson, *An Unofficial Statesman*, 75 ff.

69. J.W. to Butler, Jan. 28, 1887, Letterbooks.

Chapter 4

1. William Allen Zulker, *King of Merchants* (Wayne, Pa., 1993), 114-123; "Politics," Gibbons Files, Wanamaker Papers.

2. Theo S. Cuyler to Unknown, April 11, 1898, Personal Correspondence; William Thorne in the *Globe*, June 1901, Gibbons Files, "Politics," Wanamaker Papers.

3. Speech during the Congressional Campaign of 1894 in "Editorials and Other Writings," Gibbons Files, Wanamaker Papers; *Pennsylvania Herald*, November, 1898.

4. John Wanamaker to William R. Nicholson, Jr., May 9, 1922, Letterbooks.

5. J. W. to Rev. G.W. Patterson, Nov. 27, 1905, Letterbooks; Seventh Ward Address, September 13 1898, "Politics," Gibbons Files, Wanamaker Papers.

6. Speech in the Congressional Election of 1894, "Editorials," Gibbons Files.

7. J.W. to William Ludlow, Oct. 13, 1884, Letterbooks.

8. Conwell, *The Romantic Rise of a Great American,* 122-123.

9. J.W. to Hon. John Estabrook, Nov. 2, 1883, Letterbooks.

10. *Philadelphia Bulletin,* June 10, 1882; Philadelphia *Inquirer,* June 21, 1882.

11. John Wanamaker to William Bullitt, April 7, 1883, Letterbooks.

12. J.W. to Don Cameron, Nov. 24, 1887 and D. Scull, Esq., Jan. 25, 1887, Letterbooks.

13. J.W. to The Honorable Select and Common Councils of Philadelphia, Dec. 16. 1886 and Finance Committee, 1886, Letterbooks.

14. "Political Activities," Gibbons Files, Wanamaker Papers.

15. J.W. to Don Cameron, Nov. 24, 1887, Letterbooks.

16. James A. Kehl, *Boss Rule in the Gilded Age, Matt Quay of Pennsylvania* (Pittsburgh, Pa., 1981).

17. *Chattanooga News,* March 2, 1912, Gibbons Files, "Politics," Wanamaker Papers; Philadelphia *Public Ledger,* March 24, 1926; Kehl, *Boss Rule,* 16 ff.

18. "Publicity of Election Expenditures" (n.p.,1905); *North American Review,* Dec. 24, 1922; Kehl, *Boss Rule,* 102-112.

19. A.M. McClure, *Old time notes of Pennsylvania,* Vol. 2, p. 572; J.W. to Rev. J.L. Goodknight, Jan. 18, 1893, Letterbooks.

20. J.W. to Rodman Wanamaker, July 9, 1891, Personal Correspondence.

21. J.W. to Rodman Wanamaker, Sept. 26, 1990, Personal Correspondence.

22. *Harper's Weekly,* March 14, 1889.

23. Robert C. Ogden to J.W., n.d., Personal Correspondence.

24. J.W. to Rodman Wanamaker, July 7, 1890 and Oct. 24, 1890, Personal Correspondence; *The New York World,* January 12, 1890. *The Philadelphia Record,* June 9, 1891; *Nation,* June 11 and July 2 and 16, 1891

25. J.W. to Rodman Wanamaker, n.d. Personal Correspondence.

26. McClure, *Old Time Notes of Pennsylvania,* 573-4; *New York Times Magazine,* June 28, 1925.

27. J.W. to Samuel Bunting, Jan 4, 1893, Letterbooks.

28. *Philadelphia Bulletin,* Jan. 1, 1913.

29. Memorandum by John Wanamaker in "Politics," Gibbons Files.

30. J.W. to John Field, Dec. 13, 1887, and J.W. to Messrs. Howard Lockwood & Co., Dec. 28, 1892, Letterbooks.

31. From John Wanamaker stenographic notes of a conversation with S.S. McClure, in "Politics," Gibbons Files; *Philadelphia Bulletin*, Jan.1, 1913.

32. *Southwest Postal News*, Oct. 12, 1910.

33. *Annual Report of the Postmaster General of the United States for the Fiscal Year Ending June 30, 1891* (Washington, D.C., 1891), 48; Gibbons, *John Wanamaker*, 285-288.

34. *North American*, October 28, 1907.

35. J.W. to William Kaese, December 13, 1892, Letterbooks.

36. J.W. to Fourth Assistant Postmaster General, Dec. 28, 1892, Letterbooks.

37. J.W. to J.F. Southworth, Nov. 30, 1894, Jan. 11, 1893 to an unknown correspondent, and Alfred Darling Cushing, Jan. 10, 1895, Letterbooks.

38. J.W. to C.N. Bliss, July 8, 9, and 13, 1896 and Mrs. Julia Watts, Nov. 16, 1894, Letterbooks.

39. J.W. to George Rossaler, Nov. 17, 1894 and S. Marshall Williams, Nov. 19, 1894, Letterbooks.

40. J.W. to Edward J. M., Jan. 27, 1895 and to Senator, Jan. 27, 1895, Letterbooks.

41. J.W. to Irwin Birdman, Sept. 19, 1896 and Rev. M.L. Smith, Jan. 23, 1897, Letterbooks.

42. J.W. to Rodman Wanamaker, July 3, 1896, Personal Correspondence; J.W. to Rev. B. F. White, Jan. 19, 1897, Letterbooks.

43. For a discussion of the reform in Philadelphia see Howard F. Gillette, Jr., "Corrupt and Contented: Philadelphia's Political Machine, 1865-1887" (Ph.D. diss.: Yale University, 1970) and John D. Stewart II, "Philadelphia Politics in the Gilded Age" (Ph.D. diss.: St. John University, 1973).

44. J.W. to Irwn Birdman, Sept. 19, 1996, Letterbooks; Kehl, *Boss Rule*, 206-211.

45. "For the U.S. Senate Hon. John Wanamaker" (n.p., n.d.) in Personal Correspondence.

46. "WHAT THE ELECTION OF WANAMAKER WOULD MEAN" (n.p., n.d.); Philadelphia *Taggart's Sunday Times*, November 29, 1896.

47. Clark T. Baldwin to Hon. C.C. Kauffman, Jan. 29, 1896 and J.W. to Rodman Wanamaker, Dec. 4, 1896, Personal Correspondence.

48. J.W. to Tom Whittaker, Jan. 11, 1897, Thomas Chapman, January 13, 1897 and Rev. Thomas Brown, Jan. 14, 1897, Letterbooks; J.W. to Rodman Wanamaker, Dec. 4 and 8, 1996, Personal Correspondence; Kehl, *Boss Rule*, 211.

49. J.W. to Albion Tourghe, Jan. 11, 1897, Charles Hedges, Jan. 11, 1897, and E.L. Rhodes, Feb. 5, 1897, Letterbooks.

50. *Philadelphia Bulletin,* May 24, 1897; J.W. to James Livesay, July 12, 1897, Letterbooks.

51. J.W. to Frank Leach, Sept. 9, 1897 and Prof. Edward McGill, Feb. 9, 1898, Letterbooks.

52. E.A. Hancock to J.W., Feb. 4, 1898, Personal Correspondence; J.W. to Rev. S. Agnew Crawford, March 24, 1898 and B.F. Jacobs, March 15, 1898, Letterbooks.

53. A.K. McClure to John Wanamaker, March 12, 1898, Personal Correspondence.

54. *Public Ledger,* April 16, 1898; *The Speeches of Hon. John Wanamaker on Quayism and Boss Domination in Pennsylvania Politics* (Philadelphia, n.d.).

55. J.W. to William Wilson, June 11, 1896, Letterbooks.

56. J.W. to Dr. C.E. Taylor, Oct. 11, 1898, J. Kauffman, Oct. 18, 1898, A.J. Nickerson, Oct. 10, 1898, and Roscoe McCormick, Oct. 24, 1898, Letterbooks; *Philadelphia Bulletin,* Sept. 19, 1903.

57. J.W. to Roscoe McCormick, Oct. 24, 1898, Letterbooks.

58. J.W. to Governor Daniel Hastings, April 23, 1898, Letterbooks.

59. Mary Wanamaker to J.W., May 20, 1898, Personal Correspondence.

60. J.W. to William Nevin, April 15, 1899, Letterbooks.

61. J.W. to T.D. Marshall, Nov. 11, 1898 and M.B. Howard, Nov. 25, 1898, Letterbooks.

62. J.W. to Post, Jan. 5, 1899, J.A. Dowing, Jan. 12, 1899, and Harris Boader, Feb. 4, 1899, Letterbooks; Kehl, *Boss Rule*, 214 ff.

63. J.W. to Kauffman, April 22 and May 6, 1898, Letterbooks.

64. J.W. to William Sellers, Nov. 27, 1899 and Benjamin Harrison, Dec. 19, 1899, Letterbooks.

65. *Philadelphia North American,* December 18, 1922.

66. J.W. to E.W. Halford, Oct. 27, 1900, Letterbooks.

67. J.W. to Joseph B. Throop, May 2, 1901, Letterbooks.

68. J.W. to Rev. William Pickop, Oct. 18, 1901, Letterbooks; *Philadelphia Bulletin*, Sept. 19, 1903.

69. John Wanamaker to Rodman Wanamaker letters for December 1901, Personal Correspondence.

70. J.W. to M.G. Schwenk, Sept. 19, 1902, Letterbooks.

71. Newspaper clipping, n.d., in Personal Correspondence.

Chapter 5

1. J.W. to Thomas Wanamaker, Feb. 14, 1903, Mary Wanamaker to Rodman Wanamaker, n.d., file under October 1905, Personal Correspondence.

2. Charles Wagner, *My Impressions of America*, translated by Mary Louise Hindes (N.Y., 1906).

3. Bill from John Wanamaker Department Store to Mrs. Wanamaker, Feb. 6, 1905, Personal Correspondence; J.W. to James Bushrod, Feb. 4, 1895, Letterbooks.

4. J.W. to Rodman Wanamaker, June 11, 1907, and Mary Wanamaker to Rodman Wanamaker, Sept. 19, 1901, Personal Correspondence.

5. J.W. to Mrs. J.T. Wallace, Jan. 10, 1895, Letterbooks; and J.W. letter Feb. 27, 1907, in "Merchandising," Gibbons Files.

6. Newspaper clipping in Personal Correspondence (1889).

7. Mrs. Buchanan to Mary Wanamaker, August 2, 1887 and Mary Wanamaker to Thomas Wanamaker, n.d., Personal Correspondence.

8. J.W. to Rodman Wanamaker, July 29, 1898, Personal Correspondence.

9. J. H. Heaton to J.W., July 23, 1904, Gibbons Files, "Family;" Mary Wanamaker to Rodman Wanamaker, 1888, 18th of ?, Personal Correspondence; Appel, *Business Biography*, xi-xiv.

10. J.W. to Rodman Wanamaker, Sept. 25, 1891 and Jan. 2, 1891, Personal Correspondence; "The John Wanamaker Commercial Institute Bulletin," March 17, 1928.

11. J.W. to Rodman Wanamaker, June 14, 1895; J.W. to Mary Wanamaker, January 21, 1896; Barclay Warburton to J.W., Jan. 22, 1896; Mary Wanamaker to Rodman Wanamaker, July 3, (1903), Personal Correspondence.

12. J.W. to Benjamin Demming, Dec. 26, 1894, and J.W. to Hon. W.J. Sewell, Feb. 23, 1898, Letterbooks.

13. J.W. to Judson Hill, April 5, 1895 and Robert McElroy, Jan. 14, 1896, Letterbooks; *Philadelphia Bulletin*, Nov. 3, 1902; "Wanamaker Biography," in the *Bulletin* Collection, Urban Archives, Temple University.

14. J.W. to Rev. William Patterson, March 11, 1903, Hugh Cook, March 11, 1903, and Edward Meade, Nov. 9, 1900, Letterbooks.

15. J.W. to Rodman Wanamaker, Aug. 23, 1893, Sept. 1, 1893, and Dec. 8, 1893, Personal Correspondence.

16. J.W. to C.W. McMurson, Dec. 25, 1894, and Judge Dean, Oct. 11, 1897, Letterbooks.

17. Thomas Homey to J.W., Dec. 17, 1895, Personal Correspondence; J.W. to Robert C. Ogden, March 2, 1897, Letterbooks.

18. J.W. to Rodman Wanamaker, Jan. 7, 1897, and Dec. 2, 1897, Personal Correspondence.

19. J.W. to Robert Coyle, Sept. 7, 1897, and William Reynolds, Feb. 1, 1897, Letterbooks.

20. J.W. to Henry L. Meyers, Aug. 22, 1896, Letterbooks.

21. Stephen N. Elias, *Alexander T. Stewart, The Forgotten Merchant Prince* (Westport, CT, 1992), Chapter 9; John De Brot to J.W. April 15, 1882, "New York Store," Gibbons Files.

22. Appel, *Business Biography*, 121 ff.; "Scrapbook on Alexander Stewart," Wanamaker Papers.

23. J.W. to Rodman Wanamaker, Aug. 28, 1896, Personal Correspondence.

24. Mary Wanamaker to Rodman Wanamaker, Sept. 21, (1896?) and n.d., probably November 1896, Personal Correspondence.

25. J.W. to Rodman Wanamaker, Oct. 23, 1896 and Oct. 31, 1896; Mary Wanamaker to Rodman Wanamaker, Nov. 18, 1896, Personal Correspondence; Wilson, *An Unofficial Statesman*, 75-88.

26. *Art in Advertising*. Vol XI (November 1898), 296.

27. J.W. to Rodman Wanamaker, Nov. 20, 1896, and Dec. 18, 1896, Personal Correspondence.

28. New York Sales for 1897, and Robert F. Ogden to J.W., Dec. 24, 1896, Personal Correspondence; J.W. to Samuel McKeever, Feb. 5, 1897, and Robert Ogden, August 11, 1897, Letterbooks.

29. J.W. to Robert C. Ogden, Dec. 21, 1898, Letterbooks.

30. J.W. to Robert Ogden, Aug. 6, 1897, Paul Hashbringer, Sept. 15, 1897 and Mrs. Ann Morris, Jan. 22, 1896, Letterbooks.

31. J.W. to Rudolph Fitzpatrick, Jan. 10, 1895 and John Branson, Feb. 10, 1897, Letterbooks.

32. J.W. to B.T. Moors, Feb. 10, 1897, Letterbooks.

33. Philip Nord, *Paris Shopkeepers* (Princeton, 1986); Ledgerbooks for 1900 and 1901 in Wanamaker Papers; *Exposition Journal,* 1899, in "Philadelphia Store, 1861-1922," Gibbons Files, Wanamaker Papers.

34. *Golden Book of the Wanamaker Store,* I, 248.

35. "History of Retail Merchandising," Gibbons Files.

36. *Chester Times,* Dec. 6, 1894; *Exposition Journal,* 1899, "Philadelphia Store," Gibbons Files.

37. Memo in Personal Correspondence n.d., Wanamaker Papers; Conwell, *Romantic Rise,* 76-78.

38. For catalogs of many of these events see "Philadelphia Store," Gibbons Files; *Golden Book of the Wanamaker Stores,* I, 240-41.

39. Jackson Lears, *Fables of Abundance* (New York, 1994).

40. Memo in Personal Correspondence, n.d.

41. J.W. to E.A. Endkins, Aug. 28, 1896, Letterbooks.

42. J.W. to Robert Ogden, July 9 and 12, Aug. 2, 1987, August 16, 1897; Monarch Cycle Company, Oct. 25, 1897, July 29, 1898; Waltham Manufacturing Company, Dec. 30, 1898, Letterbooks.

43. J.W. to A.G. Seiberling, April 14, 1899, Letterbooks.

44. *Golden Book of the Wanamaker Stores,* I, 276.

45. *Golden Book of the Wanamaker Stores,* I, 240-241.

46. W.N. Benson to Rodman Wanamaker, Nov. 29, 1895, and J.W. to Rodman Wanamaker, April 16, 1897, Personal Correspondence; "Anniversary Herald," April 1, 1908.

47. "Catalogue of High-Class Modern Paintings on Exhibition at Wanamaker's 1894," Wanamaker Papers; Wagner, *Impression of America,* 12; Zulker, *John Wanamaker,* 50-52.

48. *Golden Book,* I, 248.

49. Appel, *Business Biography,* 412-413.

50. *Golden Book,* I, 258.

51. For a discussion of the symbolic meaning of the piano to middle class homes see *The New York Times,* "Arts and Leisure," May 28, 1995.

52. J.W. to Keading, Dec. 18, 1894, Letterbooks; "Editorials and Other Writings," Gibbons Files; Appel, *Business Biography*, 383-399.

53. *Golden Book of the Wanamaker Stores*, I, 1107.

54. Appel, *Business Biography*, 386.

55. J.W. to Singerely, Aug. 11, 1897, Letterbooks.

56. Herbert Gibbons to John McClure, Feb. 25, 1927, "Advertising," Gibbons Files.

57. J.W. to J.Benford Samuel, Dec. 3, 1897 and J.W. to unknown correspondent, Dec. 2, 1897, Letterbooks.

58. J.W. to J.O.R. Corliss, Jan. 7, 1901; J.W. to Robert C. Ogden, March 13, 1899, Letterbooks.

59. J.W. to T. Powderly, Aug. 6, 1896; J.W. to Mrs. J.P.P. Brown, Feb. 15, 1897; J.W. to A.S. Richardson, n.d., Letterbooks.

60. J.W. to J.F. Baker, Dec. 13, 1899, Letterbooks.

61. J.W. to John William, Oct. 30, 1900, Letterbooks.

62. J.W. to Miss Henderson, March 7, 1895, Letterbooks.

63. Russell H. Conwell, *Romantic Rise*, 86-87.

64. Susan Porter Benson, *Counter Cultures: Saleswomen, Managers, and Customers in American Department Stores, 1890-1940.* (Urbana, Illinois, 1986), Chapter 4.

65. J.W. to David Hollingsworth, Jan. 19, 1897, Letterbooks.

66. *Golden Book of the Wanamaker Stores*, I, 33.

67. J.W. to Hon. Henry C. McCormick, Dec. 16, 1897, Letterbooks.

68. Herbert Gibbons to John McClure, Feb. 25, 1927, the Gibbons Files, "Advertising," *Dry Goods Economist*, March 25, 1911.

69. "Address of Honorable John Wanamaker, Dedicating the Halls and Classrooms of THE AMERICAN UNIVERSITY OF TRADE AND APPLIED COMMERCE, in the Wanamaker Store, Philadelphia, April 8, 1916, This Being the 55th Anniversary of the Founding of the Business," Wanamaker Papers.

70. "Employees Wanamaker Stores," Gibbons files,

71. J.W. to Frank McFadden, Dec. 12, 1899, Letterbooks.

72. J.W. to J.C. VanPelt, Dec. 29, 1898, Letterbooks.

73. Charles W. Shelmire to J.W. April 19, 1909, "Employees," Gibbons Files.

74. *Women's Home Companion*, January, 1905; J.W. to Miss R.A. Bradley, Nov. 5, 1894, Letterbooks.

75. Appel, *Business Biography*, 346.

76. See Personal Correspondence for 1897 and J.W. to Rodman Wanamaker, July 1, 1898, Personal Correspondence.

77. J.W. to Rodman Wanamaker, July 15, 1898; Mary Wanamaker to Rodman Wanamaker, Dec. 17, (1898?), Personal Correspondence.

78. "Directory of Lit Brothers," n.d., Personal Correspondence.

79. Memo in Personal Correspondence, n.d., Wanamaker Papers, HSP.

80. J.W. to Robert C. Ogden, Oct. 29, 1898; J.W. to Rodman Wanamaker, Sept. 10, 1897, Letterbooks.

Chapter 6

1. J.W. to R.W., June 11, 1907, Personal Correspondence.

2. J.W. to Hugh Cork, April 16, 1904 and other correspondence in the Wanamaker letterbook for Sept. and October, 1904.

3. J.W. to James McCormick, Oct. 14, 1906, to Rev. Frank Johnson, Oct. 24, 1905, to Reuben. A. Torrey, Sept. 16, 1905, Letterbooks.

4. J. W. to David McConaughy, Jan. 5, 1905 and Hugh Cook, March 11, 1903, Letterbooks.

5. J.W. to W.F. Daum, Oct. 6, 1903, Letterbooks.

6. J.W. to Rev. Charles Dickey, Oct. 17, 1907 and Robert Jarvis, Sept. 25, 1911, Letterbooks.

7. J.W. to Joseph Grieves, May 3, 1900, Letterbooks; Mrs. Edward Pancoast to John Wanamaker, Dec. 30, 1904, original in "Bethany," Gibbons Files.

8. "Advertising," Gibbons Files.

9. J.W. to Rev. William Patterson, April 14, 1908 and Rev. Charles Dickey, Oct. 17, 1907, Letterbooks.

10. J.W. to Frank Clement, Nov. 24, 1903, Mr. Apgar, April 26, 1904, and Rev. Charles Dickey, Jan. 10, 1907, Letterbooks.

11. J. W. to Francis Gallager, Jan. 18, 1905, and Honorable William J. Milligan, April 21, 1908, Letterbooks.

12. J.W. to Rodman Wanamaker, n.d., Personal Correspondence.

13. Tom Wanamaker to J.W., Aug. 19, 1902, Personal Correspondence.

14. J.W. to Mrs. Edith Gaines, June 25, 1902 and Robert Ogden, July 18, 1902, Letterbooks.

15. J.W. to Gordon S. Corrigan, June 25, 1902, Letterbooks.

16. The "Private Ledger, for the Years 1899-1909," in J.W. Papers; J.W. to Rodman Wanamaker, May 1, 1908, Personal Correspondence.

17. *A Little Hand-book of Philadelphia Together with Certain Annals of the Wanamaker System* (Philadelphia, 1899); Private Ledger, 1899, 54-55, Wanamaker Papers; J.W. to Rodman Wanamaker, June 30, 1908, Personal Correspondence.

18. "Private Ledger," 1899, 136 and 202-260, Wanamaker Papers; J.W. to Rodman Wanamaker, Feb. 16, 1907, Personal Correspondence.

19. Tom Wanamaker to J.W., Jan. 26 and 27, 1900, and J.W. to Rodman Wanamaker, March 9, 1903, Jan. 23, 1907, Personal Correspondence.

20. "History of the Department Store," Gibbons Files, Wanamaker Papers.

21. *Golden Book of the Wanamaker Stores*, I, 205 and 212; J.W. to Rodman Wanamaker, April 12, 1907, Personal Correspondence.

22. J.W. to Rodman Wanamaker, n.d., Personal Correspondence.

23. J.W. to Frank Allen and George Mutter, Oct. 31, 1903 and J.H. Woodford, Sept. 10, 1903, Letterbooks.

24. J.W. to Thomas Wanamaker, Aug. 27, 1903, Letterbooks; Gibbons, *John Wanamaker*, 83-98; Appel, *Business Biography*, 154-159.

25. W.J. McC. to John Wanamaker, July 24, 1902; J.W. to Rodman Wanamaker, Nov. 17, 1910 and Dec. 16, 1910, Personal Correspondence.

26. *A Little Hand-book of Philadelphia Together with Certain Annals of the Wanamaker System* (Philadelphia, 1899); Edward Paxson to John Wanamaker, April 11, 1900, copy in the Gibbons Files under "Philadelphia Store, 1861-1922," Wanamaker Papers.

27. J.W. to William Nevin, March 23, 1912, Letterbooks.

28. *Real Estate Record*, March 18, 1903.

29. J.W. to William Haddock, Oct. 3, 1905, Letterbooks; John Wanamaker, "Part of the History of the Wanamaker Business which is of Special Interest to each of Those Who Belong to the Store Family."(Philadelphia: Times Printing House, 1904).

30. Wanamaker to Haddock, Oct. 3, 1905, and July 9, 1908, Letterbooks; J.W. to Rodman Wanamaker, July 12, 1908, Personal Correspondence.

31. J.W. to D.H. Burnham & Co., April 9, 1904, Letterbooks.

32. J.W. to John M. Cornell, March 22, 1904, Letterbooks.

33. John Wanamaker to John Griffiths & Son, Oct. 2, 1903 and to Morris Jessup, Nov. 11, 1905, Letterbooks; Gibbons, *John Wanamaker*, 98 ff.

34. *New York Evening Post*, December 22, 1902; *Boston Transcript*, December 23, 1902; "New York Store," Gibbons Files.

35. J.W. to Robert C. Ogden, March 2, 1905, Letterbooks.

36. J.W. to Thomas Liliid, Dec. 20, 1904 and Robert Ogden, Feb. 22, 1905, Letterbooks.

37. Mary Wanamaker to Rodman Wanamaker, June 5, (no year, 1906 file), and Thomas Wanamaker to J.W., Dec. 17 and 20, 1906, Personal Correspondence.

38. J.W. to Rodman Wanamaker, Feb. 16, 1907, Personal Correspondence.

39. J.W. to Rodman Wanamaker, Dec. 30, 1908 and Aug. 16, 1909, Personal Papers and to Rev. Joseph K. Dixon, Jan. 3, 1907 and The Vice President, Feb. 23, 1911, Letterbooks; Notice in the Gibbons file, "The North American Indian and New York;" Susan Applegate Krouse, "Photographing the Vanishing Race," *Visual Anthropology* 3, 213-233.

40. J.W. to Rodman Wanamaker, Aug. 4, 1908, Nov. 5, 1908, and Nov. 11, 1909, Personal Correspondence.

41. Gibbons, *John Wanamaker*, 110-111; Appel, *Business Biography*, 126 ff.; Personal Correspondence from Jan. to April, 1907.

42. J.W. to Robert C. Ogden, July 6, 1905, Letterbooks.

43. J.W. to Robert Ogden, July 13, 1905 and July 6, 1905, Letterbooks.

44. J.W. to Ogden, Sept. 29, 1905, Letterbooks; J. W. to Miss McClelland, Oct. 31, 1912; "New York Store," Gibbons Files.

45. *Golden Book*, I, 293 ff.

46. Article from the *New York American* from 1908 in "New York Store," Gibbons Files.

47. Tom Wanamaker to John Wanamaker, Aug. 16, n.d., in undated materials, Personal Correspondence.

48. J. W. to T.D. Marshall, Oct. 30, 1906, Rickey, Brown, and Donald, Oct. 27, 1906, and the American Bridge Company, Oct. 16, 1906, Letterbooks.

49. J.W. to Richey, Browne, and Donald, Dec. 13, 1906 and L.L. Rue, Vice President, The Philadelphia National Bank, Dec. 27, 1906 Letterbooks.

50. Thomas Wanamaker to John Wanamaker, Aug. 16, n.d., in undated materials and Charles B. Dunn to Rodman Wanamaker, July 9, 1907, Personal Correspondence; J.W. to John Claflin, Oct. 28, 1907, Letterbooks.

51. J.W. to Rodman Wanamaker, May 1, 1908, June 4, 1908 and July 1, 1908, Personal Correspondence; John Neff Oburn, March 31, 1908, Letterbooks.

52. Memo of Buyers Meeting, n.d. and Thomas Wanamaker to J.W., Aug. 16, n.d., Personal Correspondence.

53. J.W. to W.H. Burnham to J.W., Feb. 11, 1907, Personal Correspondence.

54. J.W. to Mary Wanamaker, May 18, 1908, folded into Private Ledger, 1899, Wanamaker Papers.

55. Mary Wanamaker to Rodman Wanamaker, August 7, (1907) and to J.W., August 10, n.d., in undated files, Personal Correspondence.

56. Mary Wanamaker to Rod Wanamaker, Dec. 25, 1907, Personal Correspondence.

57. Mary Wanamaker to Rodman Wanamaker, Jan. 20, (1908) and Jan. 25, 1908, Personal Correspondence.

58. Wanamaker Diary, March 6, 1908 and letter from John Wanamaker on March 20, 1908, Personal Correspondence.

59. J.W. to E.E. Gary, March 5, 1908 and William Nevin, March 23, 1912, Letterbooks.

60. *New York Press*, Sept. 10, 1908; J.W. to John Claflin, Oct. 28, 1907, Letterbooks.

61. J.W. to C.B. Moulton & Co., Nov. 2, 1907, Samuel Ward, Nov. 15, 1907, L.F. Domerich & Co., Nov. 21, 1907, and R.D. Boutsch, Nov. 22, 1907, Letterbooks.

62. J.W. to Bradford Morrill, April 6, 1908 and Joseph D. Williams, Nov. 4, 1907, Letterbooks.

63. J.W. to Rodman Wanamaker, March 25, 1911 and Feb. 4, 1909; Memoradum in handwriting of J.W., n.d. but in 1909 files, Personal Correspondence.

64. J.W. to Rodman Wanamaker, Feb. 9, 1909, Personal Correspondence.

65. J.W. to Rodman Wanamaker, Feb. 9, 1909, Personal Correspondence.

66. J.W. to Rodman Wanamaker, Feb. 10, 1909, Personal Correspondence.

67. J.W. to Rodman Wanamaker, Nov. 10, 1910, March 14, 1911, Dec. 13 and 14, 1910, Personal Correspondence.

68. Found in several memos undated in Box 30, Wanamaker Papers.

69. J.W. to Rev. Alfred Kelley, Jan. 17, 1911; Letterbooks; Memo dated Nov. 10, 1914 and J.W. to Rodman Wanamaker, Aug. 23, 1913, Personal Correspondence, For salaries a few years after Wanamaker's death, see "John Wanamaker's New York Employees Receiving $5,000 a Year," Miscellaneous Papers.

70. J.W. to William H.B. Hayward, Jan. 7, 1913 and Elizabeth D. Wray, Dec. 17, 1912, Letterbooks.

71. J.W. to General Fire Extinguisher Co., May 12, 1908 and Charles S. Dunn, May 31, 1908, Letterbooks. *Philadelphia Record*, Sept. 10, 1912.

72. J.W. to Rodman Wanamaker, April 26, 1910 and July 21, 1908, Personal Correspondence; J.W. to G.H. Cilley, Jan. 14, 1916, Letterbooks.

73. J.W. to Rodman Wanamaker, Feb. 2, 1916, Personal Correspondence.

74. J.W. to Rodman Wanamaker, Oct. 14, 1908, and Oct. 9, 1908; Memorandum, no date, in October to December, 1908, Personal Correspondence.

75. J.W. to Rodman Wanamaker, Dec. 30, 1910 and Dec. 20, 1910, Personal Correspondence; Gibbons Files, "Philadelphia Store, 1861-1921."

76. J.W. to Rodman Wanamaker, May 29, 1911; J.W. Memorandum, Nov. 14, 1910, Personal correspondence.

77. J. W. to Rodman Wanamaker, Nov. 3, 1910, Personal Correspondence.

78. *The Architectural Record*, June 1911.

79. *Golden Books of the Wanamaker Stores*, I, 277-288.

80. Dennis F. Crolly to John Wanamaker, March 21, 1922, "Philadelphia Store, 1861-1922," Gibbons Files.

81. *Golden Book*, II, 177-180; Schmidt, *Consumer Rites*, 162-167; J.W. to B.W. Friman, Feb. 25, 1907, Letterbooks.

82. *Golden Book*, II, 174-177.

83. "French and Flemish Tapestries of Bygone Centuries, On Exhibition in The John Wanamaker Store, Philadelphia, Paris, New York."(n.p., n.d.); "Vesuvius In Grand Eruption on Exhibition at Wanamaker's" (n.p.: Times Printing House, n.d.); *Everybody's*, September 1907. *Philadelphia North American*, October 10, 1922.

84. *Golden Book*, I, 258.

85. "Address of Honorable John Wanamaker, Dedicating the Halls and Classrooms of THE AMERICAN UNIVERSITY OF TRADE AND APPLIED COMMERCE, in the Wanamaker Store, Philadelphia, April 8, 1916, This Being the 55th Anniversary of the Founding of the Business."

86. J.W. to Hon. Rudolph Forster, Dec. 26, 1911, and D.H. Burnham, Jan. 5, 1912, Letterbooks; *Golden Book of the Wanamaker Stores*, Volume II contains a transcript of the ceremonies.

Chapter 7

1. *Golden Book of the Wanamaker Stores*, II, p. 18

2. J.W. to P.P. Lynn, Aug. 21, 1913. and Mrs. Arthur Phillips, Jan. 18, 1918, Letterbooks.

3. J.W. to F.W. Spicer, June 18, 1915 and Michael Ryan, March 18, 1915, Letterbooks.

4. J.W. to Gorge Pentacost, Aug. 17, 1915, Gilbert Stansell, Oct. 29, 1913, and Walter Crock, Dec. 27, 1917, Letterbooks.

5. J.W. to Charles Stelze, Feb. 27, 1915, and Billy Sunday, March 31, 1915, Letterbooks.

6. J.W. to Rev. Charles Nisbet, Oct. 1, 1915, Letterbooks.

7. J.W. to John S. Greenwell, Oct. 25, 1915; T.A. Hayes, April 12, 1916; Evangeline Booth, April 13, 1916; Hon. John M. Patterson, May 27, 1919; William Simpson, May 11, 1917, Letterbooks.

8. J.W. to Rodman Wanamaker, Nov. 2, 1911, Personal Correspondence, and Will O. Gibbons, Nov. 11, 1905, Letterbooks.

9. J.W. to Mary Wanamaker, Feb. 19, 1911, Personal Correspondence.

10. J.W. to Rodman Wanamaker, April 12 and 16, 1912 and July 8, 1914, Personal Correspondence.

11. A note signed June 15, 1912 on board the *Kaiser Wilhelm II*. "Political Activities," in Gibbons Files; *Omaha News*, June 19, 1912 in "Scrapbooks-1912," Wanamaker Papers.

12. *Salt Lake City Telegram*, June 25, 1912; *Los Angeles Tribune*, June 20, 1912 in "Scrapbooks-1912."

13. John Wanamaker to Nancy Wanamaker June 1912, "Political Activities," Gibbons Files.

14. Cassius E. Gillette to J.W. Oct. 22, 1912, "Political Activities," Gibbons Files.

15. *New York Herald*, Oct. 7, 1912; John Wanamaker to Rodman Wanamaker, Oct. 2, 1912, Letterbooks.

16. *New York Herald*, Oct. 31, 1912; *Rochester Times*, Nov. 4, 1912.

17. J. W. to J.B. Martindale, Nov. 19, 1912, Letterbooks; *New York Times*, April 10, 1913; Gibbons, *John Wanamaker*, II, 258.

18. J. W. to Ryerson Jennings, Dec. 20, 1912, Letterbooks.

19. J.W. to William Loeb, Jr., Nov. 29, 1911 and Jan. 4, 1913, Letterbooks, and Franklin MacVeagh to J.W., Feb. 13, 1913, Personal Correspondence; *Philadelphia Evening Bulletin*, May 6, 1913. John Wanamaker to Unknown, May 11, 1913; Gibbons Files, "Philadelphia Store, 1861-1922."

20. J.W. to Clarence Spayd, May 15, 1913, T.D. Marshall, May 20, 1913, and Henry Wise, June 4, 1913, Letterbooks.

21. J.W. to Rodman Wanamaker, July 13, 1913, Personal Correspondence.

22. J.W. to Rodman Wanamaker, July 23, 1913, and Aug. 5, 1913, Personal Correspondence.

23. J.W. to Rodman Wanamaker, June 10, 1914, and to Charles Simonet, June 13, 1913, Personal Correspondence.

24. J.W. to Hon. William B. Smith, Aug. 31, 1914; Letterbooks; "Patriotic Activities," Gibbons Files.

25. Rodman Wanamaker to J.W., Aug. 14, 1914 and Sept. 15, Personal Correspondence.

26. J.W. to Rodman Wanamaker, Aug. 28 and 31, 1914, Personal Correspondence.

27. *New York Times*, Aug. 26, 1914

28. J.W. to Rodman Wanamaker, Aug. 10, 1914, Letterbooks.

29. J.W. to Rodman Wanamaker, March 14, June 30, and Sept. 28, 1914, Personal Correspondence.

30. J.W. to Mrs. T.H. Baker, Feb. 11, 1915, Catherine Bush, Jan. 26, 1914, John Appel, Jr., Aug. 14, 1914, L.R. Stoddard, Oct. 2, 1914, P.F. Madigan, Oct. 12, 1914, Jan. 14, 1915, and Alexander Paul, June 19, 1915, Letterbooks.

31. J. W. to Richard Austin, Oct. 9, 1915, Edward Randolph Wood, July 1, 1915, and Mrs. Annie McFall, Oct. 16, 1915 Letterbooks.

32. J.W. to Mr. Preio, Sept. 16, 1914 and M.R. Martin, July 26, 1917, Letterbooks.

33. J.W. to William M. Canaby, Aug. 20, 1915 and George Ethridge, Dec. 10, 1918, Letterbooks.

34. "Advertisements for the London Shop," Box 101, Wanamaker Papers.

35. Gibbons, *John Wanamaker*, II, 379-380.

36. J.W. to Rodman Wanamaker, June 24, 1915, Personal Correspondence.

37. Garnel to Mary Wanamaker, n.d., filed in 1915, Personal Correspondence; William McCaughan to Rodman Wanamaker, Feb. 18, 1916, J.W. to Mary Wanamaker, (1915), Personal Correspondence.

38. J.W. to Unknown Correspondent, June 7, 1916, Personal Correspondence.

39. *New York Evening Telegraph*, October 23, 1916 and *New York American*, Nov. 5, 1916.

40. J.W. to Rodman Wanamaker, Feb. 2 and 7, 1917 and March 11, 1917, Personal Correspondence.

41. J.W. to Rodman Wanamaker, Feb. 4, 1917, Personal Correspondence.

42. J.W. to Rodman Wanamaker, Feb. 7 and 19, 1917, and March 29, 1917, Personal Correspondence.

43. J.W. to Rodman Wanamaker, March 1, 1917, Personal Correspondence.

44. J.W. to Rodman Wanamaker, March 6, 1917, Personal Correspondence.

45. "I Wonder What is Going on in Our Store? Look Inside for the Good-News Items from the Wanamaker Store." (Philadelphia, 1918).

46. Speech in "Patriotic Activities," Gibson Files, Wanamaker Papers.

47. J.W. to Mrs. Frances Cooper, Dec. 21, 1917, Letterbooks.

48. Gibbons, *John Wanamaker*, II, 408.

49. J.W. to Rodman Wanamaker, April 30, 1917 and July 20, 1917, Personal Correspondence.

50. J.W. to Rodman Wanamaker, Dec. 11, 1917 and Billy Moody to Mary Wanamaker, Feb. 22 (1918), Personal Correspondence; J.W. to John F. Coninger, May 25, 1918, Letterbooks.

51. J.W. to Mary Wanamaker, Jan. 20 and 22, 1918; and J.W. to Rodman Wanamaker, Sept. 7, 1917, Personal Correspondence.

52. J.W. to J.T.W. Davis, June 4, 1917, and to George Miller, May 23, 1917, Letterbooks.

53. J.W. to Rodman Wanamaker, Feb. 11, 1918, Personal Correspondence; Boies Penrose, May 9, 1917, Letterbooks.

54. J.W. to Mrs. M. Nicholas, May 26, 1917, and Miss Christine Regan, Nov. 20, 1919, Letterbooks.

55. J.W. to J.D. Williams, May 20, 1917, O.C. Davis, Nov. 18, 1921, and Josephus Daniels, May 4, 1918, Letterbooks.

56. J.W. to P.B. Folwell, May 29, 1918, Letterbooks.

57. J.W. to Jerome R. Keesuck, May 31, 1918, Letterbooks.

58. "Employees-Christmas Letter (1917)," "Employees," Gibbons Files.

59. J.W. to Joseph D. Sawyer, Sept. 25, 1918 and Albert Gifford, June 4, 1918, Letterbooks.

60. J. W. to Mrs. M. McCloskey, Sept. 25, 1918, Letterbooks.

61. J.W. to Rev. C.M. Boswell, Dec. 21, 1917, Letterbooks.

62. J. W. to Miss Mary Donnelly, June 14, 1919, Letterbooks.

63. Net Earnings Memo in Box 30 C, Wanamaker Papers.

64. J.W. to Anna Mautz, Nov. 29, 1917, Mollie Wannemacher, Aug. 12, 1918 and Evangeline Booth, Nov. 4, 1919, Letterbooks.

65. J.W. to Josephus Daniels, Dec. 12, 1918, Anna K. R. Knight to J.W., n.d. (May 15, 1919), George Wharton Pepper, Oct. 22, 1919, Clarke P. Pond, Sept. 4, 1919, Letterbooks; J.W. to Rodman Wanamaker, Oct. 2, 1919, Personal Correspondence.

66. J. W. to Ferdinand French, Jan. 14, 1920 and Charles Calwell, Aug. 28, 1921, Letterbooks.

67. J.W. to W.H. Eisenhower, Nov. 8, 1919, Henry I. Yohn, Nov. 7, 1919, and L.L. Rue, Jan. 1, 1920, Letterbooks; J.W. to Rodman Wanamaker, Aug. 1919, Personal Correspondence.

68. J.W. to Rodman Wanamaker, June 7, 1919, Personal Correspondence; J.W. to Thomas Eldridge, Dec. 29, 1919, Letterbooks.

69. Mary Wanamaker to Rodman Wanamaker, 1919?, Personal Correspondence.

70. J.W. to Libbie Wanamaker, Aug. 28, 1920, Personal Correspondence; J.W. to Miss Olive Matthews, Oct. 5, 1920 and Annie Knowles, Oct. 15, 1920, Letterbooks.

71. J.W. to Percy Clay, Oct. 14, 1920, Letterbooks.

72. J.W. to Evangeline Booth, Dec. 4, 1920, Letterbooks.

73. J.W. to John J. Spurgeson, Oct. 19, 1920, Letterbooks.

74. J. W. to Blanche Welson, Nov. 3, 1920 and H.G. Barton, Dec. 2, 1920, Letterbooks.

75. J.W. to Henry G. Forest, Nov. 4, 1920, Letterbooks.

76. J.W. to Frank McClain, Nov. 13, 1920, Letterbooks.

77. J.W. to John Wanamaker, Jr., Dec. 1, 1920; Dripps, Dec. 1, 1920; Thomas Horney, Dec. 1, 1920, Letterbooks.

78. Net Earnings Memo in Box 30 C, Wanamaker Papers.

79. Gibbons, *John Wanamaker*, II, 446-7.

80. J.W. to Evangeline Booth, Sept. 20, 1921, Letterbooks.

81. J.W. to Charles Thorman, May 31, 1922, Letterbooks.

82. J.W. to David Lloyd George, Oct. 6, 1921 and William Decker, Oct. 5, 1921, Letterbooks.

83. J. W. to George Wharton Pepper, Nov. 28, 1921, Letterbooks.

84. J.W. to John D. Rockefeller, Dec. 30, 1921, Letterbooks.

85. Rodman Wanamaker to Mrs. Barclay Warburton, Jan. 25, 1921, Personal Correspondence.

86. J. W. to Brigadier R. Griffith, May 23, 1922, George Embick, June 2, 1922, Harry Paisley, June 1, 1922, and J. Hampton Moore, June 2, 1922, Letterbooks.

87. J. W. to R.G. Dun Co., June 28, 1922, Letterbooks.

88. J.W. to Rev. A. Gordon Maclennan, Aug. 21, 1822, Letterbooks.

89. J. W. to P.P. Lynn, Aug. 28, 1922 and Rev. William Fulton, Sept. 21, 1922, Letterbooks.

90. J.W. to Commander Evangeline Booth, Nov. 9, 1822, Letterbooks.

91. *Philadelphia Evening Bulletin*, Dec. 12, 1922.

92. *Ibid.*, Dec. 14, 1922.

93. *Ibid.*, May 25, 27, June 14, 15, 1926, June 18, Nov. 28, 1928.

94. Appel, *Business Biography*, 439ff.; *The Philadelphia Inquirer*, Section D, Aug. 28, 1995.

95. *The Philadelphia Inquirer*, Aug. 28, 1995.

96. *Ibid.*, July 14, 1996 and Jan. 18, 1997.

Index